Damien Lewis is a number one bestselling author whose books have been translated into over forty languages worldwide. For decades he worked as a war and conflict reporter for the world's major broadcasters, reporting from across Africa, South America and the Middle and Far East and winning numerous awards. His books include the World War Two classics *Churchill's Secret Warriors*, *SAS Ghost Patrol* and *Hunting the Nazi Bomb*. A dozen of his books have been made or are being made into movies or television drama series. He has raised tens of thousands of pounds for charitable concerns connected with his writings.

ALSO BY DAMIEN LEWIS

Damien Lewis

SAS

NAZI HUNTERS

**THE ULTRA-SECRET SAS UNIT AND THE
HUNT FOR HITLER'S WAR CRIMINALS**

Quercus

First published in Great Britain in 2015 by Quercus as *The Nazi Hunters*.
This paperback edition published in 2019 by

Quercus Editions Ltd
Carmelite House
50 Victoria Embankment
London EC4Y 0DZ

An Hachette UK company

A CIP catalogue record for this book is available
from the British Library

PB ISBN 978 1 78747 789 6
Ebook ISBN 978 1 78429 390 1

10 9 8 7 6 5 4 3 2 1

PICTURE CREDITS (Plates numbered in order of appearance)
© Imperial War Museum: 1, 2, 5, 14, 19
Mirrorpix: 3
National Archives/T. Roberts 4, 7, 8, 15, 16, 17, 18, 20, 21, 24
© Bundesarchiv 6
© National Portrait Gallery/Bassano Ltd. 9
© National Portrait Gallery/John Gay 10
www.specialforcesroh.com/John Robertson 11
www.forum.keypublishers.com 12, 13
Getty Images 20, 21
Source unknown 25
Supplied by author 26

Text designed and typeset by Hewer Text Ltd, Edinburgh

Printed and bound in Great Britain by Clays Ltd, Elcograf S.p.A.

For Moussey.
For those who never returned.

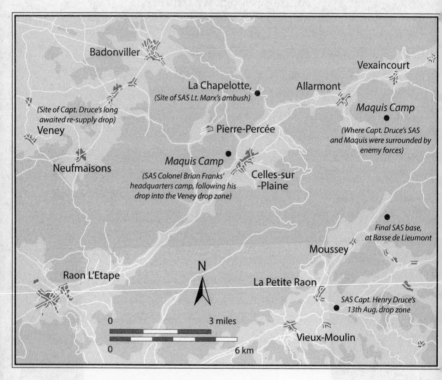

SAS Operation Loyton - Mission Area

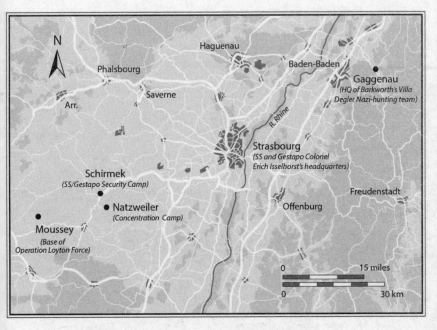

SAS Nazi Hunters - Immediate Area of Operations

Acknowledgements

In researching this book I was able to speak to a number of people in the UK, the USA, France and elsewhere, and to rely upon the recollections and assistance of many. My very special thanks and gratitude are extended to them all, and my apologies to those I have inadvertently forgotten to mention. I am especially grateful to those former SAS members from the Second World War who shared with me their recollections, and to those former French Resistance members from the Vosges who did the same. In no particular order I wish to thank the following: Jack Mann (UK); Chris Boulton (UK); Michael Jarrett (UK); Philip Eyers (France); Tony McKenny (Australia); David Henry (Australia); Tean Roberts (UK); Simon Fowler (UK); Maxene Lemaire (France); Sim Smiley (USA); Paul Sherratt and Anne Sherratt (UK); David Lewis (France); Eric Chauffele (France); Madeleine Fays (France).

My gratitude as always to my literary agent, Annabel Merullo, and film agent, Luke Speed, for helping make this book such a success, and to all at my esteemed publishers, Quercus, for same, including Charlotte Fry, Ben Brock and Fiona Murphy. I'd also like to thank Josh Ireland.

My editor, Richard Milner, deserves very special mention for deciding to commission this book based upon a back-of-the-envelope sketch about what the story entailed. Such spirited and brave decision-making is all too rare in the world of publishing today, and is, I hope, rewarded by the pages that follow.

A special mention must also go to Peter Message, an extremely gifted schoolboy and budding Second World War historian who read and commented with aplomb on this book at early manuscript stage.

One other individual who cannot be named – a former SAS soldier of some repute – deserves my very special gratitude for bringing this story to my attention in the first place and for convincing me that it really did need to be told. Thank you.

I am also indebted to those authors who have previously written about some of the topics dealt with in the pages of this book. In alphabetical order they are: Keith E. Bonn (*When the Odds Were Even*); Colin Burbidge (*Preserving the Flame*); Roger Ford (*Fire from the Forest* and *Steel from the Sky*); John Hislop (*Anything but a Soldier*); Tim Jones (*SAS: The First Secret Wars*); Anthony Kemp (*The Secret Hunters*); Paul McCue (*SAS Operation Bullbasket*); Gavin Mortimer (*The SAS in World War Two*); Christopher Sykes (*Four Studies in Loyalty*).

And of course, thanks as always to Eva, David, Damien Jnr and Sianna, for not resenting Dad spending so much of his time locked away . . . again . . . writing . . . again.

Damien Lewis, Dorset, 2015.

Author's Note

There are sadly few, if any, survivors of the Second World War Special Forces operations depicted in these pages, or from the French Resistance (the Maquis), or of the Nazi hunters who operated immediately after the war. Throughout the period of the research for and the writing of this book I have endeavoured to contact as many of these individuals as possible, in addition to the surviving family members of those who have passed away. If there are further witnesses to the stories told here who are inclined to come forward, please do get in touch with me, as I may be able to include further recollections on the operations portrayed in this book in future editions.

The time spent by Allied servicemen and women as Special Operations Executive (SOE) agents, Special Forces operators, and working with the Resistance was often deeply traumatic, and many chose to take their stories to their graves – especially those who ended up captives of the enemy. Memories tend to differ, and apparently none more so than those concerning operations behind enemy lines. The few written accounts that do exist of such missions also tend to diverge in their detail and timescale, and locations and chronologies are often contradictory. That being said, I have done my best to provide a comprehensible sense of time and place in the story as written.

Where various accounts of a mission appear to be particularly confused, the methodology I have used to reconstruct where, when and how events took place is the 'most likely' scenario. If two or more testimonies or sources point to a particular time or place or sequence of events, I have opted to use that account as most likely. Where necessary I have recreated small sections of dialogue to aid the story's flow.

The above notwithstanding, any mistakes herein are entirely of my own making, and I would be happy to correct them in future editions. Likewise, while I have endeavoured to locate the copyright holders of the photos, sketches and other images used in this book, this has not always been straightforward or easy. Again, I would be happy to correct any errors or omissions in future editions.

Preface

The suggestion for this book came from out of the blue.

I happened to meet up with a Special Air Service (SAS) soldier who had risen to some degree of rank and influence at 'the Regiment', as it is known. That soldier – I'll call him 'Steve'; he asked for his real name not to be used, as is the wont of SAS operators – and I had become friends over the writing of several books.

I had just published *Churchill's Secret Warriors*, the story of the wild Danish Viking warrior Anders Lassen – the only member of the British SAS ever to win the Victoria Cross – and his band of Special Forces desperadoes, those who had taken Churchill's 1940 edict to 'set Europe aflame' and made it a reality, spreading chaos and terror behind the German lines and breaking just about every rule of war.

I gave Steve a copy of *Churchill's Secret Warriors*, and mentioned that I was hopeful that a film might be made based upon the book.

Steve glanced around the restaurant – we'd met at BAFTA, the British Academy of Film and Television Arts, for it seemed like a fitting venue for our breakfast chat – and, typically, he cracked a joke.

'So, do you get to mix with the rich and famous? Do you get

to meet – who's that woman who plays Lara Croft, in *Tomb Raider*? – yeah, Angelina Jolie?'

Steve remarked that *Churchill's Secret Warriors* should make a fantastic basis for a film. Only two veterans of the Regiment are honoured by having their statues at the SAS's Hereford base. One is David Stirling, the founder of the SAS. The other is Anders Lassen. Steve reckoned a film telling of Lassen and his band of brothers' exploits was long overdue. The story deserved as wide an exposure as possible.

For a moment he studied the cover of *Churchill's Secret Warriors*, turning it over in his massive, gnarled hands. At six-foot-three and wide as a barn door, he wasn't your average BAFTA visitor, and I could see him getting the odd, surreptitious look from those enjoying their eggs Benedict and espresso.

He glanced at me – level gaze, face all serious for a second. 'You know, there's another SAS tale from the Second World War that needs to be told. Never has been. There's a danger it never will be.'

'Go on,' I prompted. 'I'm listening.'

'You ever heard of Op Loyton? Most haven't. But to those of us who have it's known as the SAS's Arnhem. In late '44 an SAS force parachuted into the Vosges Mountains to arm and raise the French Resistance and spread havoc behind enemy lines. Unfortunately, they landed amongst an entire German Panzer division. Bad timing, bad intelligence. Ran out of food, ammo, explosives, weaponry, not to mention anywhere to run. Hence: the SAS's Arnhem.

'Eventually, they found sanctuary of sorts in a French village called Moussey. When the Germans realized they couldn't kill or capture all the SAS, they rounded up the Moussey villagers and carted them off to the concentration camps. But you know the most amazing thing? Not a villager talked. No Moussey villager ever revealed the location of the SAS base or gave them away.

'For weeks the German military combed the surrounding forests and mountains, and over time they captured dozens of our guys. Handed them over to the Gestapo and SS, at which point they disappeared in the *Nacht und Nebel* – the night and the fog. And that's when the story really starts to get interesting . . .'

Steve went on to explain how at the end of the war over thirty Operation Loyton men were listed as missing in action. The then commander of 2 SAS, Colonel Brian Franks, refused to let matters rest there. He promised the families that he would find out what had happened to the missing: he also felt the Regiment owed it to the villagers of Moussey – from where so many had been taken, never to return – to do likewise.

Moussey sits within a densely forested, high-walled valley, one which became known as 'the vale of tears', and with good reason. Across its length, approaching one thousand villagers had been carted off by the Gestapo to suffer what was at the time an unknown fate. As far as Colonel Franks was concerned, the SAS owed it to all the missing to trace their whereabouts, to track down their oppressors and to see justice done.

The trouble was, the SAS was about to be disbanded. After the war Winston Churchill had been voted out of power, the minds of a war-weary British public turning towards peace, and the days of what had often been accused of being a private army of maverick rule-breakers looked numbered. By October 1945 the SAS Regiment had lost the battle for survival. It was formally disbanded, or so the official version of history says.

But the reality was somewhat different. In truth, even as the SAS veterans were returned to their units for demobilization, a small cadre of hand-picked officers and men was sent into Germany to trace the Op Loyton and Moussey missing and to hunt down their killers. These men – who wore the SAS beret and the winged-dagger cap badge – were formed into covert manhunting units, becoming known as 'the Secret Hunters'.

In short, the Secret Hunters refused to accept that the war was over, waging their own private battle to track down some of the most brutal of the Nazi war criminals.

The operations of the Secret Hunters were totally deniable and off-the-books. So covert were their activities that few within the SAS even knew of their existence. They were run from an office in London's Eaton Square, with direct radio communications to and from the field, and with the full backing of Winston Churchill, whose power and influence post-war was still manifest, despite his defeat in the 1945 general election.

Their operations were orchestrated by a Russian prince who had fought with the Special Forces during the war, and who had a deeply personal reason for wanting to see the Nazi killers brought to justice. Under Prince Yuri 'Yurka' Galitzine's sleight of hand a budget was wheedled out of the War Office for a unit that never officially existed.

Under his and Colonel Franks' guidance, the Secret Hunters tracked the Nazi war criminals from Italy to Norway, and from western France across Germany and into the Russian zones. They employed every means necessary and proved wildly successful in hunting down the killers, but in doing so they antagonized the hidebound British military and the wider Allied establishment mightily.

The manhunting operations of the Secret Hunters also served to fulfil another vital purpose, as far as the Regiment was concerned. Operating well into 1948, they managed to keep the Regiment alive long enough for Colonel Franks to found 21 SAS Artists Rifles – the Territorial Army unit which would eventually form the basis of the SAS proper, when it was reconstituted in the 1950s.

As Steve pointed out, the Regiment still commemorates the Moussey deportations to the concentration camps, and the hundreds who never returned..The SAS dead are buried alongside Moussey's own victims in the village churchyard – a place of homage for those who have vowed never to forget the sacrifice so given. Steve figured this was a piece of vital, living history and a book well worth the writing, not to mention a story whose telling was long overdue.

I'd heard something about the SAS Nazi hunters before. One or two other Special Forces friends of mine had mentioned their activities. I'd long been fascinated by the story, but the trouble was: how would one go about telling it? Their activities had been so shrouded in secrecy that little documentation was likely to exist, and I doubted if there were any survivors from their small number.

But a couple of weeks later a very special parcel arrived in the post. It consisted of the largest and heaviest 'book' I have ever had the pleasure to peruse: a special edition of the official SAS war diary from the Second World War. The war diary made a brief and typically understated mention of the activities of the SAS Nazi hunters. Despite its brevity, it did constitute the first official acknowledgement I had ever seen that the unit had indeed existed.

The Secret Hunters were commanded by SAS veteran Major Eric 'Bill' Barkworth, a man of iron principle, unbreakable spirit and a maverick single-mindedness almost without compare. Barkworth would prove himself to be a fantastically gifted investigator, detective, interrogator . . . and a manhunter extraordinaire.

The SAS war diary records: 'In May 1945 [Colonel] Franks received a report that the bodies of British soldiers had been found in Gaggenau, in Germany, and sent his Intelligence Officer, Major E.A. Barkworth, to investigate. The Barkworth unit set up base . . . and began their hunt. In October 1945, the SAS was disbanded. Franks came to an unofficial arrangement with one individual from the War Office and the unit continued. It operated totally openly, as if it was official. The unit ended its hunt in 1948, three years after the SAS was disbanded.'

Just a few, carefully chosen words, accompanied by four photographs of the SAS at Moussey, paying their respects at the village war memorial – but official recognition nonetheless that the SAS Nazi hunters had existed.

Even this was extraordinary, considering the accepted version of history has it that the SAS was disbanded in 1945 and only reformed again in the fifties to carry out anti-insurgent operations in Asia. For example, Philip Warner's 1971 official history of the SAS mentions the 1945 disbandment of the SAS, and observes that 'that was that', until their official 1950s reformation. Acclaimed as 'the first complete official history of the SAS Regiment', this has become the accepted version of what happened.

Such a venture as the SAS Nazi hunters, involving a few dozen carefully chosen men – and even they being instructed never to talk about their work, and to keep written records to an absolute minimum – would, I suspected, be notoriously difficult to research. Fragmentary evidence would have to be painstakingly pieced together – rather as the Secret Hunters themselves had had to painstakingly build their case files on the most wanted of the Nazi war criminals.

So began a research odyssey that took me into some of the darkest of places, revealing the horrors visited upon captured Special Forces operators and commandos by a group of senior Nazis who must have known by then that the war was lost. But it was also a story of the incredible bravery and heroism demonstrated by British and Allied Special Forces operators, not to mention the French Resistance and the ordinary villagers who fought alongside them. There was even the occasional 'good German' who risked his life to try to do what was right.

In time the story took me to north-eastern France, to Moussey itself, and to a dark and brooding concentration camp that sits deep within the highland forests some 9 miles to the east of the village. It took me to the National Archives in Kew, and to the few surviving files concerning the activities of the SAS Nazi hunters, most of which are stamped with a 'destroy by' date, but which have miraculously managed to survive the predations of those who might wish to censor history.

It took me to the private papers, filed at the Imperial War Museum, of Prince Yurka Galitzine and others – those amongst the Secret Hunters who never believed that their work should remain untold and unrecorded – who had opted (against orders, and against those governmental 'gagging' contracts that they had signed) to lodge their papers somewhere they might eventually be rediscovered. Those individuals took considerable risks in refusing to let the truth be hidden, and for that they deserve our admiration and our gratitude.

From the archives of the Imperial War Museum – to whom I'm grateful for enabling such materials to be kept safe for posterity – the trail took me to a few of those survivors of SAS operations in World War Two who are thankfully still with us. And finally, I came to the most unexpected, not to mention shocking, of revelations, ones concealed within a group of CIA files held at the American National Archives, in Washington DC. In September 2007 the CIA was forced, under the 1999 Nazi War Crimes Disclosure Act, to release some 50,000 pages of records documenting relations between the Agency and prominent Nazis in the years following the Second World War.

By the end of the war, Hitler's Germany was no longer the principal enemy of the 'free world'; Stalin's Russia had taken on that mantle. Barely had the last shots been fired when the Allies began rounding up senior Nazis with experience of fighting against or spying on the Russians, in order to shelter and recruit them. They were brought into various covert intelligence outfits – the foremost of which was the Gehlen Organization, run at first by US Army Intelligence, but effectively from 1948 onwards by the CIA.

Those recently declassified CIA files revealed that, in several instances involving senior Nazis with intimate knowledge of operating against the Russians, the justice so resolutely sought by the SAS Nazi hunters may in truth have been denied them.

This, therefore, is a story that delves into secret worlds within secret worlds, peeling away layer upon layer of intrigue and subterfuge. To reach a core of inalienable truth has remained challenging, but at the very least the opportunity of telling the story of Operation Loyton, the Moussey deportations and massacres, and the activities of the Secret Hunters that followed has been a huge and much-cherished privilege.

Some may ask whether it is important that the memory of such horrors and the hunt for the perpetrators is kept alive, some seventy years after the events unfolded? Is it not raking over old coals? I don't believe so. It is vitally important that we remember the heroism and the sacrifice, and the terrible war crimes and crimes against humanity, so that those dark transgressions may never be repeated.

I am sure there is more to tell about this hidden and compelling chapter of history, and I look forward to whatever revelations may result from the publishing of this book.

But first, let me take you to a lone British warplane flying into occupied France in the late summer of 1944.

Chapter One

The Armstrong Whitworth Whitley bomber thundered through the inky darkness, her twin propellers clawing at the unseasonable skies. It was 12 August 1944, approaching midnight over northern France, and by rights the continental summer should have rendered the weather warm and balmy, the skies calm and clear.

But the flying conditions that war-torn August had proved challenging, especially for an RAF aircrew tasked with dropping a stick of parachutists into a remote, densely forested chain of mountains 500 miles behind the German lines. Several times now the present mission had been called off at the last moment, and for the men squatting on the cold floor of the aircraft's fuselage it was a relief finally to be going into action. But that didn't make the atmosphere any less tense or electric, not when they were faced with a mission such as this.

The deafening roar of the aircraft's twin Rolls-Royce Merlin engines made conversation all but impossible, and the SAS soldiers were lost in their thoughts. As so often seemed the case, the men of the Regiment had been tasked with a formidable mission, but were saddled with the most outdated equipment the War Office had to offer. One glance down the

Whitley's dark and echoing hold revealed how unsuitable she was for a stick of parachutists to jump from.

Designed in the mid 1930s, the Whitley had been obsolete even before the start of the war, and in 1942 she had been withdrawn from front-line operations. A medium-weight bomber, by this point the aircraft was mostly used for towing gliders into action, and she had certainly never been intended as a parachutist's jump platform. Owing to a design quirk she flew with a marked nose-down attitude, which meant the floor of the cramped, slab-sided fuselage sloped at a dizzying angle towards the cockpit. Worse still, the SAS men would be jumping into the night via a coffin-shaped hole in the floor, and it was the process of leaping through the open grave of the Whitley's gaping bomb bay that would make for such a perilous exit.

The men of the SAS had nicknamed it 'ringing the bell'. At the approach to their intended drop zone they would line up on one side of the opening, sitting with their legs dangling over the shadowed abyss. Upon the jump light switching to green-for-go, they would propel themselves forward into the howling darkness. But the bomb doors had been designed for releasing 7,000 pounds of relatively compact munitions, as opposed to a dozen-odd human beings. In jumping through the narrow gap the men risked smacking their heads with an almighty clang: thus, *ringing the bell*.

Any parachutist who did ring the bell would find himself badly concussed, or even unconscious and plummeting to earth like a stone; hardly an ideal state in which to steer oneself onto a drop zone marked by only a handful of bonfires lit by the

French Resistance. Or at least, *hopefully* lit by the French Resistance. The Gestapo and SS had been known to light signal fires and lie in wait, particularly when they had secured intelligence about the timing and location of an impending Allied airdrop.

The lone aircraft thundered onwards, the moonless night her cloak and her protector.

Armed with only a single machine gun in the nose, and four in the tail gunner's turret, the Whitworth was highly vulnerable from directly below or above, and with a maximum speed of a little over 200 mph she was hardly likely to outrun the Luftwaffe's nimble night fighters. The first the SAS men would know of such an attack was when the bursts of cannon fire lanced through the thin skin of the hold, tracer rounds ripping into the fuel tanks housed in the wings, and punching a dragon's breath of fiery death through the disintegrating fuselage.

The Whitworth's aircrew hoped to flit through the darkness undetected. The parachutists were about to drop into the Reich's last bastion of defence – the rugged Vosges Mountains, which straddle the Franco-German border. It was there that Hitler had ordered the *Wehrmacht* to make a do-or-die last stand, to prevent at all costs the Allies from achieving the unthinkable and driving east into the Fatherland. Accordingly, the stakes on this mission – code-named Operation Loyton – could hardly have been higher.

The Whitley's bomb aimer crouched in the front turret, directly below the nose gunner. Above him, the pilot and co-pilot/navigator sat side by side in the cockpit. Tonight, of

3

course, the bomb aimer had no steely death to drop from the skies – or at least, not a conventional bomb load. Instead, his task – along with the navigator – was to detect a tiny, matchbox-like clearing in the midst of the densely forested mountains, onto which they would unleash those men whose fighting repute had made them the foremost of Hitler's – and the Reich's – adversaries.

If the SAS could be safely delivered, their mission was to raise and arm a French Resistance army of thousands, and to attack the enemy's communication and supply lines, spreading terror and chaos in their rear. This, it was hoped, would convince the front-line troops of the *Wehrmacht* that their defences were crumbling, and that US General George Patton's 3rd and 7th Armies were punching through their lines. If they could be persuaded to abandon their positions along the Vosges' rugged 'west wall' – a series of heavily fortified trenches and formidable gun emplacements set amongst the natural defences of the foothills – the way into Germany would be wide open.

For Captain Henry Carey Druce, the commander of this mission, the phrase 'sardine can' came to mind as he surveyed the Whitley's cramped hold. He was squeezed shoulder to shoulder with the men of his stick, and burdened down with so much weaponry and kit that he was barely able to move. The five-man RAF crew would be exchanging a constant stream of chat over the intercom as they counted off the landmarks leading into the drop zone, but Druce was cut off from all of that, rendered deaf and almost blind in the darkened hold.

It was a hugely unsettling feeling.

In fact, for reasons way beyond Druce's control the entire genesis of the present mission had been decidedly disconcerting; indeed, even his very recruitment into the SAS had been something of an accident.

Until recently, Druce had been serving with the SOE, a unit born of the iron will of Winston Churchill, and formed wholly in the shadows. In the summer of 1940 Britain's iconic wartime leader had called for the creation of a clandestine force tasked with setting the lands of enemy-occupied Europe ablaze.

The SOE had been formed under the aegis of the Ministry for Economic Warfare, making it totally separate from the military. It became known as the 'fourth armed service' and operated under a series of cover names – including the innocuous-sounding 'Inter-Services Research Bureau' and, perhaps most suitably, 'The Racket'. Officially, the SOE didn't exist, which made it perfect for carrying out the kinds of missions that broke the rules of war, and which the British government could deny if all went wrong.

Druce felt the contents of his stomach lurch into his throat as the Whitley hit a particularly nasty pocket of turbulence. It wasn't the first time that he'd flown into hostile territory. On one of his previous operations for the SOE, Druce had been dropped into enemy-occupied Europe to retrieve escaped prisoners of war. But he was betrayed and taken captive. Held in a Gestapo prison, he'd found himself before a Gestapo officer, facing interrogation.

'Remember, you are my prisoner,' the Gestapo man had warned Druce. 'And so, you must tell me everything.'

'Actually, it is I who should be taking you and your fellows captive,' Druce had calmly replied. 'Your military is all but defeated, so you'd best surrender to me.'

In the momentary confusion caused by the remark, Druce had seized his chance and leapt out of a nearby window. He'd escaped the Gestapo's clutches and, being a fluent French speaker, he had made his way through occupied France to England, disguised as a local. In the process he'd travelled on foot through the very region that he was poised to parachute into now, the Vosges Mountains, but his pending return had come about purely by a stroke of fortune.

Sometime after his epic escape from the enemy, Druce had found himself on a train heading for one of Britain's wartime parachute training schools. Colonel Brian Franks, the Commander of 2 SAS – the SAS Regiment at that time consisting of 1 and 2 SAS Brigades, plus a number of 'foreign' brigades operating alongside them – happened to be sharing the same railway carriage. The two men fell into conversation and Franks asked Druce the obvious question: what he was up to right then?

Druce had shrugged, good-naturedly. 'I'm really at a loose end. No one seems to want to employ me.'

'Well, you'd better come and join us,' Franks had told him.

Thus Druce had been recruited into the SAS. He'd joined A Squadron, 2 SAS, which at the time consisted of some sixty-odd men. As 2 SAS was made up of four squadrons, there were far too many operators for Captain Druce to get to know them all, but he quickly became familiar with the dozen men of his stick. The trouble was, they included few of those presently sharing the Armstrong Whitworth Whitley aircraft with him.

Until that very afternoon the dozen men aboard this warplane had been commanded by another SAS officer, a veteran of operations in North Africa. But just a few hours ago that man had gone to see Colonel Franks and revealed that the almost unthinkable had transpired.

'I really feel I can't go on,' he'd confessed. 'I can't lead the mission. I just have lost my nerve.'

He wasn't the first to fall victim to the acute stress caused by repeated sorties behind enemy lines. Even the most unlikely candidate could find himself at risk of what the men had come to call 'crapping out' – not being able to take it any more. It was something that they all dreaded, for if a man's nerve cracked during a mission he became a serious liability to his fellow operators.

In Druce's opinion, that officer had proved himself one of the bravest men around. It was hellishly difficult to turn around at the eleventh hour and admit that you couldn't go through with a mission. Even so, when Colonel Franks had telephoned him out of the blue and asked him to take over, he had been somewhat aghast. He'd had a bare few minutes in which to grab his kit, prepare his weapons and race to catch a train to the airfield from which the mission was being mounted. There had been no time to familiarize himself with his new command.

He'd asked Colonel Franks for one thing: he wanted his own sergeant, the redoubtable Scot, David 'Jock' Hay, to accompany him, so he did at least know one man in 'his' stick. But as to the rest of the men, Druce could barely put a name to a face.

Of course, it must have been doubly disconcerting for them, as they had done all their pre-mission training and preparations with their regular stick commander. No reason had been given for the man's sudden withdrawal. It had been judged best to keep his 'crapping out' quiet. But Druce was known only as a recent recruit to the Regiment, and that made him an unknown quantity – a wild card.

It was all the more unsettling because Captain Henry Druce was actually to be known as Captain 'Drake' for the duration of the coming mission. Having been held prisoner by the enemy before, his real identity would be known to the Gestapo, which might increase the risk of him being captured now.

Druce – *Drake* – had reached RAF Fairford in Gloucestershire with barely an hour to go before L-hour (the allotted time for lift-off). Fairford had been nicknamed 'The Cage', and with good reason. It was a closed-off, high-security facility ringed by searchlights and watchtowers, from which no one slated with a mission was ever allowed to exit. Even going to the loo seemed to require three armed escorts!

Upon arrival at The Cage, Druce was rushed into the ops room to join the others getting the 'griff': the final mission briefing. Two of the Regiment's stalwarts, Major Eric 'Bill' Barkworth and his right-hand man in 2 SAS's Intelligence Section, Sergeant Fred 'Dusty' Rhodes, proceeded to outline what was coming.

With the Allies having broken out of their D-Day beachhead, the German retreat was underway. Allied commanders believed that their version of the Blitzkrieg would prove inexorable, as superior Allied air power and ground forces rolled a demoralized enemy back into Germany. There was even talk of the war being over by Christmas. The natural barrier of the Vosges Mountains would form the *Wehrmacht*'s final defensive line, and Op Loyton was a mission designed to make 'merry hell' for the enemy in those densely forested hills.

Having passed through the area in the not-too-distant past, Druce pointed out that the terrain would prove ideal for guerrilla warfare. But Barkworth – one of the 'old and bold' within the Regiment, and an ice-cool operator par excellence – made it clear what was expected of him. His task wasn't to go about blowing things up, or at least *not yet*. He was to link up with the French Resistance and establish a secure base and drop zone, so that he could call in the main body of Operation Loyton.

Colonel Franks was in attendance in The Cage, and he made it clear that he intended to put two entire squadrons – approximately 120 men – onto the ground in the Vosges. It was Druce's mission to shepherd in that larger force. Only once that was done could he start blowing everything to kingdom come.

To underline the importance of Operation Loyton, Franks declared that he was keen to deploy; such a senior SAS commander would rarely, if ever, risk heading so far behind enemy lines. One other person was chafing at the bit: Sergeant Dusty Rhodes, Barkworth's right-hand man. Rhodes – a tough and phlegmatic Yorkshireman – was itching for some action, but his present role largely precluded it. As 2 SAS's Intelligence Cell, he and Barkworth were privy to every mission presently underway, so if either were captured and forced to talk, the consequences could prove disastrous.

Barkworth and Rhodes had little option but to remain in the rear with the gear, as the saying goes. Yet, as they delivered their eleventh-hour briefing to Druce, little did they suspect that the coming operation would catapult these two uniquely talented men into the assignment of a lifetime – one of unimaginably high stakes, horror and intrigue. But all of that lay many months in the future.

For now, Colonel Franks seemed to have chosen his replacement mission commander admirably. Captain Druce was of medium height, but a real barnstormer of a man. He would demonstrate a tireless stamina when moving through the plunging valleys of the Vosges, but more to the point, considering what was coming, he was blessed with a rare fearlessness – bordering on the reckless. Druce would prove to be a maverick and a high-spirited trickster par excellence.

Just twenty-three years old, Druce had been schooled first at Cheam, in Surrey, where he was in the same class as the Duke of Edinburgh. From there he went to Sherborne School in Dorset, followed by the Royal Military College, Sandhurst. He'd initially volunteered for the Glider Pilot Regiment, but discovered a more natural home for his talents lay within the SOE. Fluent in French, Dutch and Flemish, and blessed with an insatiable thirst for adventure, Druce was also a natural fit for the SAS.

Druce would earn renown within the SAS as being the 'top hat warrior'. Sporting a black silk top hat and corduroy trousers on operations, he would demonstrate a vital quality amongst those tasked with behind-enemy-lines operations: total unflappability. In one incident he accosted a fleeing German motorcycle trooper, discovering a cured ham secreted within his saddlebag. As the soldier refused to give up his motorbike with suitable alacrity, Druce proceeded to whack him around the face with the ham, unseating him, at which point he passed the meat around his ravenous men.

One of the original Operation Loyton maps – one that Druce doubtless pored over as the Whitley aircraft droned onwards towards its uncertain date with destiny – has been preserved for posterity in the official Operation Loyton war diary. The map is marked with a tiny black circle, with beside it written 'Captain Druce Party 13 Aug DZ'.

The DZ (drop zone) is sandwiched between La Petite Raon and Vieux-Moulin, two tiny French hamlets lying less than 3 miles south-west of a village called Moussey. Otherwise unremarkable, Moussey would come to have a real significance for the SAS. But as Druce studied that map, he must have wondered where in the surrounding forests and mountains – including the aptly named Les Bois Sauvages (the Wild Woods) – the Maquis might have made their base.

Not so many months before making this flight, Druce had trodden the rugged hills of the Vosges disguised as a Frenchman as he escaped from the enemy. He knew the kind of territory they were dropping into here. He sensed an opportunity to wage shoot 'n' scoot guerrilla warfare – the SAS's speciality – using the remote highland forest as the sanctuary in which they would evade an enraged enemy, before regrouping, rearming and resting, ahead of the next hit-and-run attack.

Druce relished the prospect. There was little obvious bravado about him, but somehow his men would come to feel as if they were never truly in trouble when under his command, no matter how bad their situation might seem.

And, as the warplane rumbled onwards towards that distant drop zone, things were about to get very troubled indeed.

Chapter Two

At around two o'clock in the morning the Whitley's dispatcher roused the parachutists. They'd taken off five hours earlier and most had ended up dozing through the noisy, claustrophobic flight. The aircraft had been routed away from obvious bombing targets and had avoided the enemy night fighters and ground fire, leaving the men free to sleep largely undisturbed.

'Twenty minutes to the DZ!' the dispatcher yelled above the engine noise. 'Twenty minutes to the jump!'

As the Whitley began to lose altitude – the men would make the jump from 1,000 feet – the dispatcher passed around a bottle of rum, in case anyone fancied a last-minute shot of Dutch courage. That done, he gave the signal to 'stand up – hook up'. Twelve shadowy figures rose to their feet, strapping their parachutist's tough, canvas kitbag to their right leg, and forming up in line in jump sequence.

Each man clipped the soldier in front's parachute cord – his 'static line' – to a rope that ran the length of the fuselage. As they leapt from the aircraft the static line would remain attached, flipping free the jumper's Model X parapack and releasing the rigging lines and parachute. Nervous excitement drove away the last vestiges of sleep.

As each man checked the line of the jumper in front, not a few hands were seen to be shaking. With some, doubtless, this was the stomach-knotting surge of fear, but with most, Druce included, it was the effect of the adrenalin that was pumping through their veins.

There was a high-pitched whine of hydraulics as the bomb doors inched apart, their opening accompanied by an inrush of fresh air. It proved surprisingly cold. The Whitley could lose only so much altitude, for the Vosges rise to over 4,600 feet in height and, even in summer, conditions on the higher reaches were known to be bitter.

The dispatcher strode down the line of men, making a final check. To his consternation he found that somehow Druce's static line had been threaded through his parachute harness. Had he jumped then, he would have been left dangling beneath the fuselage, with no way either to parachute to earth or to ease his way back inside the aircraft.

Every member of Druce's stick wore a pair of rubber-soled boots – perfect for silent operations – plus a special paratrooper's Denison smock, with a strap that fastened between the legs to prevent it from billowing out during the descent. Dome-shaped helmets with chinstraps had replaced the old-style, wide-rimmed British Army 'tin hat'. And in each of their sets of webbing was stuffed the distinctive SAS beret, with the iconic winged-dagger cap badge affixed.

Since the summer of 1944 the SAS had been supposedly 'banned' from wearing their distinctive sandy-coloured beret. With the Regiment's return from North African and Mediterranean operations, it had been subsumed into regular British Airborne Forces. Many argued this was all part of an effort by the military establishment to exert some form of control over the freewheeling, largely self-directed force – one that had faced repeated accusations of being a 'private army'.

Whatever the truth of the matter, the men of the SAS had been ordered to adopt the bright-red Parachute Regiment beret. Unarguably distinctive and warlike, it was fine for front-line combat troops, but with its high visibility it was hardly suited to a covert force inserting far behind enemy lines. Many vowed to adopt the red beret only once their sandy ones had worn out – and they were proving remarkably hard-wearing. Others had opted for a peaked khaki mountain cap, which would prove a useful head covering for operations in the Vosges.

Other recent kit changes had proved somewhat more popular. The SAS's old faithful, the .45-calibre Thompson sub-machine guns – the so-called 'tommy gun' favoured by 1930s gangsters and 1940s elite operators alike – was still around, but mostly it had been replaced by the lighter-weight 9mm Sten gun, nicknamed the 'baked bean can'.

The trusty Lewes incendiary bomb had been superseded by the 'Gammon bomb'. The Gammon consisted of a weight of plastic explosive (PE) housed in a canvas bag, connected to a fuse than would detonate upon impact and no matter the angle at which the makeshift grenade struck its target. The most common size employed a kilogram of PE, and whoever threw it had to keep his mouth open, to avoid blowing out his eardrums. The great advantage of the Gammon over the Lewes was that it could disable heavy vehicles, crucial when going up against the might of German armour.

The talismanic Fairbairn-Sykes fighting knife – with its 7-inch blade, heavy handle to give a firm grip in the wet, cross-guard to prevent hands slipping, plus two razor-sharp edges and a sharp, stiletto profile – was still standard SAS issue as the tool for silent killing. But as the war had progressed, most had learned just how hard it was to knife a man to death. Normally, it required two soldiers to do it properly – one to hold the victim, and the other to drive in the blade – and it was invariably a messy, somewhat hit-and-miss affair.

Recently, a 'Fighting Knife Mark II' had been developed. Known affectionately as the 'Smatchet', it resembled a cross between a hatchet and a machete. A miniature version of the original Fairbairn-Sykes knife was also available. With a flat thumb and forefinger grip, and a 3-inch blade, it was designed to be hidden in the lapel of a jacket. There was also a robust flick knife on offer for the real aficionados.

But, if close-up killing was required, experience had proved that it was generally easier to shoot an adversary in the head with a pistol. To that end, the excellent Browning 9mm 'Hi-Power' GP35 had replaced the heavy and cumbersome Colt .45. Likewise, the .303 Lee–Enfield rifle had been supplanted by the superlative American .30 calibre Winchester M1-A1 carbine, which was half the weight of the British rifle. Though not as accurate at long range, it had a semi-automatic rate of fire, and its ammunition weighed half that of the British .303 round, meaning far more could be carried.

The folding-stock version of the M1 carbine was perfect for paratroopers. The M1 – designed by two junior machinists at the Winchester Repeating Arms Company during their spare time – was to become one of the most widely used weapons amongst Allied forces in the Second World War. Captured German weaponry was also much in demand, especially the Schmeisser sub-machine gun. Once such a weapon had been seized, SAS operators tended to be loath to give it up.

Personal kit was stowed in a canvas Bergen – a military rucksack – with an external steel frame. The heavier British 'Compo' rations had been replaced by twenty-four-hour ration packs containing tinned sardines, cheese, meat dripping, oatmeal biscuits, soup cubes, tea, sweets and chocolates. A new and super-efficient lightweight stove had been developed, one that burned solid-fuel Hexamine blocks, similar to firelighters.

Each parachutist's Bergen-load of gear was stuffed inside his canvas 'leg bag', which was strapped to his right leg for the jump. The leg bag was held in place by clips, and would be released and lowered once the parachutist had jumped, to be left hanging some 15 feet below him. That way, the bag would land first, taking the impact of its own weight.

Or at least, that was the theory. In practice the leg bag had proved cumbersome to deploy, and was more often dangerous rather than helpful to the parachutist. It had a habit of snagging during exit, or failing to release and lower properly, with disastrous consequences for the jumper.

Writing in the Operation Loyton war diary, Colonel Franks commented on the leg bag as being 'utterly useless. This has been proved and pointed out time and again. Present leg bags MUST NEVER be taken on operations again.'

Unfortunately, the Op Loyton advance party was saddled with the leg bags. One of those figures strapping on this 'utterly useless' contraption was Captain John Hislop, in effect Druce's second in command. As he prepared for the jump, he reminded himself of the somewhat cumbersome code words to be exchanged with the Resistance – more commonly known as the Maquis.

'*Nous sommes les guerriers de Malicoco*' (we are the warriors of Malicoco), the SAS soldiers were to declare, though no one had the slightest idea where 'Malicoco' might be.

'*Bamboula vous attend*' (Bamboula awaits you) was the expected reply, though who on earth 'Bamboula' might be was anyone's guess.

As Hislop was well aware, some of the less erudite of the men had struggled to master the unwieldy exchange. Mostly, they were fighters, not linguists – their new commander, Captain Druce, being the obvious exception. Hislop wasn't overly happy about their last-minute change of command, and he wondered what kind of man Druce might prove to be on the ground.

'At the time we had no idea why this change was made, and found it disconcerting,' Hislop remarked. As Druce had only joined the SAS recently no one knew him well, or was particularly aware of his capabilities.

Hislop wasn't entirely an SAS man, and he was, if anything, even more of a colourful character than Druce. With his remarkably boyish face, swept-back dark hair and laughing slits of eyes, Hislop was the archetypal dashing Englishman, and he revelled in such an image. His was a slight, polo player's physique, compared to Druce's rugby player's robustness but, on the coming mission, both would prove themselves to have the hearts of lions.

He and Druce had met only once before, at 2 SAS's then headquarters, which was situated at the end of Prestwick golf course, in Ayrshire, Scotland. Of course, Hislop had heard stories about Druce's epic escape from the enemy, one that had taken him on foot across half of occupied Europe in 'phenomenally short time'. It had ended with Druce reaching London and checking himself into Piccadilly's Berkeley Hotel, as if he'd just been out for a short stroll in Green Park.

As the powerful figure of Druce braced himself beside the Whitley's uncertain exit, he was trying his damnedest to memorize all the names of his men. Goodfellow, Dill, Lodge, Crossfield, Hall, Stanley . . . he repeated the names like a mantra. Hislop, by contrast, was imagining himself astride a speeding horse on a racecourse; he'd found it was the best way to steel himself for such a leap into the unknown.

Hislop had refused the tot of rum that had been passed around the aircraft – on the basis that most jockeys ride best sober, and parachuting couldn't be greatly different. Born in Quetta, India, in 1911, at thirty-three years of age Hislop was very much the 'old man' of the stick. His father, Major Arthur Hislop, served in India with the 35th Scinde Horse, but his son's interests had proved to lie more with the racing fraternity. Over the ten years of his racing career, John Hislop had proved himself one of the finest amateur jockeys of all time.

At the outbreak of war he had, by his own admission, tried to wangle himself a position that would enable him to carry on with the main business of the day: race riding. Citing a 'regrettable lack of military aptitude', Hislop's commander at the 21st Anti-Tank Regiment had asked him to find another posting. Unsuited to the regimented constraints of the regular military, Hislop confessed that he had 'faced the prospect of the future with some misgiving'.

It was the 'freemasonry of the Turf' that had come to his rescue. Upon hearing of his predicament, a jockey friend had invited Hislop to join the Phantoms, a little-known unit that would prove to be the making of him. The GHQ (General Head Quarters) Liaison Regiment, as the Phantoms were more formally known, was a small, secretive outfit tasked with embedding themselves amongst the most forward-fighting troops, relaying vital reports about the state of front-line operations direct to GHQ, via wireless.

As with the SAS, officially the Phantoms remained posted to their parent unit and wore its regimental insignia. The only thing that marked them out as anything different was a distinctive shoulder flash – a white 'P' over a square of black. Hislop had been posted to the Phantoms' A Squadron, which was populated by several high-profile racing acquaintances, including Maurice Macmillan, son of the future British prime minister, and John 'Jackie' Astor, of the super-wealthy and titled Anglo-American Astor clan.

Somehow fittingly, the squadron was commanded by the actor David Niven, who was fast becoming a household name. Niven had been in America when war broke out, working on a clutch of movies. At that stage, America was two years away from joining the conflict, but even so he had returned to England forthwith and signed up with the Phantoms.

Shortly thereafter he'd been dining with a party that had included Winston Churchill. Churchill had placed a companionable hand on the famous actor's shoulder. 'We are all, I am sure, very pleased and proud that this young man should throw up a brilliant and lucrative career in Hollywood to come back to fight for his country – but wouldn't have thought much of him if he hadn't!'

For Hislop, his posting to the Phantoms proved doubly fortunate. The squadron had its 'country headquarters' at the glorious Stourhead House, in Mere, Somerset, then owned by Sir Henry Hoare and his wife. Somehow, the privations of the war seemed to have passed Stourhead by; imperial peacocks strolled the grounds, and lithesome hunters graced the stables. Hislop was soon riding out over the glorious Somerset countryside.

By the spring of 1942 he found himself back in the racing saddle, riding Overseas in a chase at Cheltenham. He coaxed his horse into the lead, only to fall at one of the final fences. Hislop was thrown, badly breaking his leg. Nine months on crutches followed, after which he was invalided out of the Army. But Hislop refused to go quietly. Instead, he fought his way back to physical fitness and rejoined the unit that he was coming to love.

Hislop was taken into F Squadron, commanded by his friend and long-time racing buddy, Jackie Astor. Astor ran a 'happy

Squadron', Hislop remarked, one 'devoid of discontent, mistrust, depression or apathy; a light-hearted enthusiasm pervaded.'

Recently, the men of F Squadron had been asked to join forces with the SAS, which had found itself short of skilled signallers. Since it would doubtless involve parachuting, for which one needed to volunteer, men were asked to step forward.

At the start of the war Hislop had been very much the reluctant soldier. He wasn't any more; he was amongst the majority of the F Squadron men who did step forward.

Time and again the Phantoms had proved themselves superlative wireless operators, especially during exercises on the remote Scottish moors. Unlike the Royal Corps of Signals (the regular Army's communications specialists), the Phantoms combined a relentless training regime with a relaxed attitude, and an *esprit de corps* that encouraged self-starters and those of an independent mind.

There was little saluting or rank-consciousness in the Hon. Jackie Astor's company. Instead, men were given free rein, being urged to experiment with aerial lengths, frequencies, the positioning of wireless sets and so on. No one minded how unorthodox the methods might be, as long as the Phantoms got the message through.

And, on the coming mission in the Vosges, doing just that would prove of paramount importance. In order to arm the Maquis, details of drop zone coordinates, dates and timings of drops, plus weapons requirements, would need to be radioed through to London. Unless effective communications could be established and maintained, Op Loyton would be finished before it had even begun.

Just prior to mission departure, Hislop had been invited to visit the SOE's unremarkable, grey-faced 64 Baker Street headquarters in London to pick up some of the specialized gadgetry that the coming mission might call for. He was introduced to a slight, dark-haired man, who squinted at him from behind thick spectacles.

'Ah, Captain Hislop . . . So very nice to see you! So, you're going on a little foreign trip? Well, let's have a look to see what we've got that might be useful to you . . .'

The SOE's gadget man produced a fountain pen which, upon scratching its paint off, proved to have a tiny compass embedded in one end. Alternatively, Hislop could opt for a compass disguised as a button and sewn onto his shirt. 'It's attached to you, so you won't lose it as easily as a pen,' the SOE man enthused.

Then there was a handkerchief that you had to urinate on and – eureka! – it revealed a map of northern France. Or another in white silk with a number of hidden, coded phrases written upon it, such as: 'Surrounded by the enemy; expect no more messages.'

'They look nice with a dinner jacket,' the gadget man added, somewhat unnecessarily.

Hislop was offered a pen that wrote in invisible ink, paper he could eat 'in case of emergencies', plus an escape pack loaded with 'boiled sweets, Benzedrine and one or two other comforts'. Benzedrine is a potent amphetamine, one that was then popular in London's swankier nightclubs. With its euphoric stimulant effect, it could keep an operator alert and energized for long periods, an obvious advantage for behind-enemy-lines operations.

And so, weighed down with SOE gadgetry, Hislop and the three fellow Phantoms he commanded had joined the Op Loyton advance party. Corporal Gerald Davis, Hislop's second in command, squatted at the Whitley's exit. Davis suffered from a slight speech impediment and he had a somewhat cynical outlook on life, but all of that was offset by a strongly independent nature. He was tall, lean and athletic, and of bulletproof reliability, and he wasn't overawed by anyone, no matter who they might be.

Once Davis had been on an exercise and his military car had broken down. An officer had arrived on the scene, only to find Davis staring at the vehicle, hands on hips. 'Hullo, Corporal Davis, why are you standing about doing f-all?' the officer had asked. Davis had turned and answered casually: ''Cause there's f-all to do!' In short, Davis was calm, steadfast and utterly dependable, and Hislop had come to like and respect the man.

Squatting beside Davis was Private 'Jock' Johnston, a quiet, dour Scot. Johnston was slow of speech but he had a cool, clear head, and he was a demon with a wireless set. No matter what the situation, he could be relied upon to get the signal through, and Hislop could ask no more of the man.

Hislop's third Phantom operator was somewhat less predictable, though through no fault of his own. Prior to joining the Phantoms, Sullivan had seen serious action with the commandos, and it had served to put his nerves on edge. Never lacking in courage, he became noticeably tense and jumpy in moments of real danger, which Hislop found somewhat disconcerting.

And, in truth, Hislop found the entire Op Loyton undertaking rather daunting – largely due to their present company.

His first impression of the SAS had been that they were some kind of rabid, warmongering 'Foreign Legion'. During operations overseas they seemed to have acquired soldiers of every nationality, including a smattering of Germans. Upon the Regiment's 1944 return to the UK, there had proved to be no official record of many of their number ever having served in the British Army.

'All the time I served with the SAS I never quite overcame the impression that I belonged to a species of banditi,' Hislop recalled. 'The enterprise of the SAS troops on exercises shook the local authorities accustomed to the more staid practices of home-based troops. On one occasion they held up a train in order to get a lift.'

Following his racing injuries, Hislop's jockeying exploits had been sadly curtailed. He'd opted instead to start breeding and training racehorses. He'd just started getting serious about it, acquiring two promising steeds, Orama and Milk Bar, when the D-Day landings had taken place, after which he'd been ordered to deploy on the present mission.

Normally, dwelling on such thoughts of 'the Turf' served to put steel into Hislop's soul – a steel that he didn't quite believe was innately his. As he tensed himself at the Whitley's bomb-bay exit, lining up with the SAS 'banditi', the words of a favourite poem flashed through his mind.

> So the coward will dare on the gallant horse
> What he never would dare alone,
> Because he exults in a borrowed force,
> And a hardihood not his own.

All thoughts of cowardice were driven from Hislop's head as the Whitley began its run-in to the DZ. Within moments, a forest clearing hove into view, one marked by a series of blazing fires. Even from this altitude the bonfires looked massive, as if groups of French villagers had somehow decided to celebrate Guy Fawkes.

Hislop found himself wondering whether maybe the Maquis hadn't overdone things a little. Surely, as well as being visible from the bomb bay of the Whitley, the conflagrations would be seen by the enemy, drawing them towards the DZ. He comforted himself with thoughts of their RAF Fairford briefing, at which they'd been told that only a handful of German troops were stationed in the area, and even those were of a low calibre.

The timbre of the twin engines dropped to a throaty grumble as the plane descended. The flames could be seen illuminating the whites of upturned faces, as whoever was below scanned the skies for the aircraft they could now doubtless hear. The pilot began his final approach, the red 'action stations' jump light flickering on. Moments later it switched to green, the dispatcher yelling: 'GO! GO! GO!'

The first stick of six – led by Druce – threw their legs forward, leading with the one weighed down by the leg bag, and, as one, vanished through the floor. The second stick – including Hislop and his Phantoms – lined up beside the windswept, empty grave as the aircraft climbed again, swinging around and aligning itself for a second run.

Hislop felt his heart pounding like a jackhammer as his stick shuffled closer together. The tighter the pack at the moment of the jump, the faster they would get out and the more likely they were not to miss the DZ. The wait seemed to last for an age, and Hislop could feel the tension spiking.

By the time the jump light flashed green for a second time he was shaking with nerves.

Chapter Three

A second row of stick-like figures plummeted through the gaping maw of the bomb bay and tumbled into the dark and howling void. The Whitley's engines had been throttled right back, but still Hislop was sucked into the churning maelstrom of the aircraft's slipstream, the pummelling taking his very breath away.

He was spat out on the far side. Hislop sensed himself falling for just an instant, before the static line pulled taut, ripping away his parapack and releasing his chute. A split second later, there was a distinctive crack in the night sky above him, as if a powerful gust of wind had caught a yacht's mainsail, and a canopy of silk blossomed grey-white in the darkness.

Hislop felt as if a giant hand had pulled him up by the shoulders, leaving him suspended in mid-air. As the oscillations of the chute diminished, he became aware of the vast and arresting silence and stillness of the Vosges night. After several hours cooped up in the aircraft's suffocating hold, the emptiness felt deafening, but at least no one seemed to be shooting at him.

He reached down to pull the cord that was supposed to release his leg bag and let it fall away. Perhaps unsurprisingly, the mechanism failed. One strap unfastened but the other did not, leaving the heavy bag dangling awkwardly, as if a rabid dog had grabbed one trouser leg and would not let go. With over 50 pounds of kit unbalancing him, there was a good chance that he would land badly, breaking a leg.

The flare of the bonfires was growing ever brighter as he reached down, grabbed the release cord and hauled on it for all he was worth, trying to wrench the dead weight into something like a vertical position. But, even as he was doing so, a sharp burst of gunfire cut the night, hot tracer arcing through the dark heavens.

Hislop had little time to worry about whether the shots were aimed at him, or whether it was just some over-excited Maquis loosing off in high spirits. If he didn't get this irksome kitbag under control, he was about to break his leg again – and this time deep inside enemy-occupied France, as opposed to the comparatively benign environment of Cheltenham racecourse.

Hislop was so preoccupied with his bag-wrestling antics that he had little time to steer for the clearing. He crashed into a copse of saplings, which fortunately bent and flattened, serving to break his fall. He tumbled through the last of the branches and was deposited on his backside amidst the dew-kissed undergrowth, with nothing but his pride suffering any form of hurt.

Before he could struggle to his feet, three figures were upon him. From their dress – the odd piece of khaki battledress, interspersed with moth-eaten tweed capes and French-style black berets – Hislop figured this was no Gestapo reception party.

'*Nous sommes les guerriers de Malicoco!*' he blurted out, in his best Wellington schoolboy French.

There was no answering cry of, '*Bamboula vous attend!*'

Instead, the Maquis got to work disentangling his parachute – it constituted dozens of yards of highly prized silk – while trying to cadge some cigarettes. One grabbed Hislop's Bergen, another his helmet, and a third the downright murderous leg bag, and together they made their way towards the firelit muster point, where dozens of excitable figures could be seen flitting through the shadows.

Unbeknown to Hislop, their stick commander, Druce, had suffered a similar, yet far more debilitating equipment malfunction. Druce's leg bag had dropped only as far as his right foot and then become stuck fast. He'd landed heavily, the weight forcing him to fall backwards and suffer a savage blow to his head. In spite of his helmet, Druce had suffered a bad case of concussion, and he could be heard 'babbling nonsense' to anyone who would listen.

On the opposite side of the DZ, one of the stick's 'old sweats', SAS man Ron Crossfield, was also in trouble. Crossfield had joined the Army in 1934 and had several brothers in uniform. While trying to avoid one of the raging bonfires, the veteran operator had landed in a mature stand of trees. As he crashed through the thick branches his helmet and leg bag were torn away, and he came to rest swinging to and fro, with no idea of the extent of the drop below him.

Regardless, Crossfield punched the quick-release catch on his parachute harness . . . and fell. It was a good 15 feet, but at least his landing was cushioned by a thick carpet of pine needles. He came to his feet, only to see a shadowy figure dashing towards him through the trees. He grabbed his pistol, but the cry of '*Très bien, Angleterre!*' (Very good, England!) stayed his hand.

Druce's force represented the first Allied parachutists ever to drop into the Vosges, an area of mountainous terrain of approaching 2,500 square miles. The names of the tallest peaks attest to the mixed Franco-German heritage of the region. The highest basks in the very French moniker of the Grand Ballon, but the next two in line are the entirely Teutonic-sounding Storkenkopf and Hohneck – testifying to just how close the airdrop would bring these men to German soil.

Just 20 miles due east of the drop zone lay the border, marked by the line of the mighty River Rhine. Very few navigable passes cut through the Vosges, but if the British soldiers – together with the Maquis – could sow havoc and confusion here, then they were to switch to a very specific task: they were to seize and hold one of those passes, so enabling Patton's armour to punch through, and to reach the Rhine before the bridges across it could be blown.

Such grand designs were very far from the minds of Hislop, Crossfield and a dazed Druce as they took stock. They found themselves surrounded by a hugely curious and excitable crowd. From the way in which the Maquis poked and fingered them, grabbed and pumped their hands and kept repeating the same enthusiastic greetings – '*Bienvenus! Bonne chance! Bonne chance!*' – it seemed to Hislop that they might as well have been Martians descended from a spacecraft.

It was approaching three o'clock in the morning before some semblance of order was wrestled out of the chaos. As the parachutists mustered, so others reported in with injuries. One SAS man had burned his hand while fighting with the stubborn cord of his leg bag. Another had sprained his knee. But no one – the babbling, incoherent Druce included – seemed incapable of walking, which was of utmost importance right now.

Priorities had to be established, and quickly. Another aircraft was due any minute, so the marker fires had to be re-stoked. Once the second airdrop was complete, the party needed to load up, move off and melt into the hills. Come daybreak, there had to be zero evidence that a force of parachutists had landed here, which meant dragging the silk chutes down from the trees, stamping out and scattering the fires, and clearing away all debris.

The majority of the second aircraft's cargo was to be non-human – weaponry and war materiel for the Maquis. But one of the first signs that the drop was underway was a piercing cry that rang out from the darkness.

A figure had descended under his chute, the cursed leg bag causing him to badly twist his ankle and break his toes upon landing. The injured man was Sergeant Kenneth Seymour, and he found that his pain was so acute that he was unable to move without removing his right boot. He would need to be stretchered if he were to make the journey into the hills.

An even greater concern was that Seymour's radio had been ensconced within his leg bag, and it too had been smashed upon landing. Bereft of a wireless set, Seymour and his fellows' very specific mission here was at risk of being rendered all but redundant.

Seymour was no SAS man. He and his two colleagues – Captain Victor Gough and Frenchman Lieutenant Guy

Boisarrie – constituted a highly specialist team only loosely attached to Druce's force. They were SOE agents, and part of a recently formed unit dubbed 'the Jedburghs'. The 300-strong unit shared its name with the small Scottish town of Jedburgh, but it had been named largely at random, so as to reveal little of its secretive purpose to a watchful enemy.

Seymour, Gough and Boisarrie made up a Jedburgh team code-named JACOB. Their specific mission was to link up with the Maquis leadership, serving as what we might today call 'military advisers', forming an army of resistance to hit the enemy from within, even as the Allied forces broke out of their beachheads. Indeed, Seymour's Bergen, like that of his two fellow 'Jeds', was stuffed full of hundreds of thousands of French francs: money with which to fund the raising of a bloody insurrection across the Vosges.

The DZ they had landed upon was controlled by one Colonel Gilbert Grandval, a man of great local prestige and a renowned Resistance leader. Grandval – code-named 'Maximum' – commanded a band of fighters a few hundred strong, styled the Alsace Maquis. He'd promised the SOE that some 25,000 men were ready to rise up against the hated Boche. All he needed was the raw hardware – weapons, ammunition, explosives – with which to arm such a force. It was Gough, Boisarrie and Seymour's task to ensure that he got it, this being the unique role that the Jedburghs fulfilled within the SOE.

But it wasn't going to be easy. Deprived as they now were of a radio set, the biggest challenge was going to be communicating Grandval's needs to SOE headquarters back in London.

*　　*　　*

Never one to eschew unconventional warfare, Churchill had thrown his weight behind the arming of the French Resistance. In the spring of 1944 he'd ordered arms drops to the Maquis to be greatly increased. He cabled President Roosevelt to inform him that he was keen to raise guerrilla armies across France 'à la Tito' – a reference to the then Yugoslavia's wartime guerrilla leader – and urging the Americans to join the party.

Responding to Churchill's prompting, it was to be the Americans who completed the largest of such airdrops. In Operations Zebra, Cadillac, Buick and Grassy, massed ranks of US bombers with fighter escorts had carried out a series of stunning daylight operations. In Operation Cadillac alone, some 300 American Liberator bombers, with P51 Mustangs as escorts, had dropped 400 tonnes of arms to the Resistance forces ranged across the Dordogne.

Cadillac had taken place on 14 July, Bastille Day – which commemorates the start of the French Revolution and the founding of the French Republic – and the parachutes were symbolically painted in the Tricolour, the colours of the French flag. Brigadier Colin McVean-Gubbins, chief of the SOE, had hailed Cadillac as one of the 'most important parachute drops of the war'.

In 1940 McVean-Gubbins – better known to all simply as 'M' – had fought rearguard actions in Norway, organizing striking companies to wage a guerrilla war to hold up the advancing Germans: blowing bridges, sabotaging railways and mining roads. Both he and Churchill were diehard advocates of such tactics, and in their minds the French Resistance constituted an ideal guerrilla force in the making – one that would help them wage 'total war' against the enemy.

Which is where the Jedburghs came in.

Grassy – the most recent mass airdrop – had taken place just four days previous to the Op Loyton advance party being parachuted in. Gough's Team Jacob had been sent in with clear instructions to launch an Operation GRASSY for the Vosges. They'd been met on the ground by the 800-strong force of the Alsace Maquis, but only fifty of them appeared to be armed, and mostly with obsolete French rifles somehow kept hidden from the Germans during four years of a brutal occupation. There was clearly a great deal of work to be done.

Team Jacob was typical of the Jedburghs' make-up – a three-man unit, including a native French speaker (Boissarie), a radio specialist (Seymour) and an officer, Captain Gough. Many of the Jed teams would be Anglo-American in composition, because the Jedburghs were in part an American innovation. The Americans had recently formed the Office of Strategic Services (OSS), which was loosely based upon the SOE model, and the Jedburghs were a joint SOE-OSS enterprise.

The Jeds – like the SAS and the Phantoms – were a wholly unorthodox lot. One of their oldest recruits was also one of their most renowned. At fifty-something, Lieutenant Colonel Jim Hutchinson had had an eventful war already, being captured and escaping at least once. Fearing the enemy would possess a photo of him, Hutchinson not only adopted a *nom de guerre*, but he went as far as altering his face with plastic surgery, subjecting himself to a 'nose job', and getting a piece of bone removed from his hip and grafted onto his chin to alter his profile. His appearance suitably disguised, Hutchinson would lead one of the first Jed units into action in France.

In essence, the Op Loyton advance party was a classic Special Forces unit of the time: the Jedburghs, tasked to link up with the Maquis; the Phantoms, tasked to establish communications with London; and the SAS, tasked to fight the enemy.

The 26-year-old Captain Gough was a typical Jedburgh. Dark haired, dark eyed and of mesmerizing appearance, Gough had spent the early part of the war in a shadowy force known as the British Resistance Organisation (BRO). The BRO was an early brainchild of McVean-Gubbins, and its remit was to wage a war of resistance should – as had seemed likely in 1940 – the Germans invade mainland Britain.

In essence, the BRO was a very British version of the Maquis. The BRO fighting units were made up of those who knew the countryside intimately – gamekeepers, poachers and agricultural workers – with caches of arms and explosives hidden throughout the forests, dells and dens of the mother country. There were a smattering of professional soldiers serving as a leadership cadre, and Gough – a country lad born and bred – had been one of those.

As the threat of invasion had receded, Gough had cast around for a new role, finding his way into the Jeds. He had received a fine education, first at Hereford Cathedral School and then Temple Technical College, Bristol, where he trained as a mechanical engineer. Something of an amateur cartoonist, it was Gough who had designed the Jedburghs' distinctive cap badge, which consisted of a pair of white parachute wings flanking a red disk, with the letters 'SF' (for Special Forces) stamped in silver across it.

In his recruitment questionnaire Gough had stated his hobbies as 'Wireless, Riding and Shooting'. He also expressed interest in learning foreign languages, undertaking 'outdoor work' and 'going abroad'. In getting recruited into the Jedburghs and deployed on Op Loyton, it seemed as if – for now, at least – all of Gough's Christmases had come at once.

During their rigorous pre-deployment training, the Jeds had adopted their own battle cry: the very un-British sounding 'Some shit!' It had been inspired by a bunch of American recruits who were put through the brutal selection course at the grand, 600-acre country estate of Milton Hall in Cambridgeshire. Jed selection had a very high dropout rate, and anyone stepping out of line was forced to perform rigorous PT exercises. The American recruits had responded to the physical punishment with the comment, 'Some shit!', and it had stuck.

But right now, as the first light of dawn touched the skies over the Vosges, Jedburgh team Jacob was in some degree of 'shit' of its own: no radio; a signaller too injured to walk; and facing a long hike into the high ground, where the Alsace Maquis had sited their remote and most easily defended bases.

Running roughly north–south and parallel to the Rhine, the Vosges constitute a solid barrier of granite and red sandstone barring any easy movement west-to-east or vice versa. Over the aeons, these mountains have been eroded into a series of dome-shaped massifs. Though densely forested, conditions on the highest reaches are so harsh that tree cover tends to peter out, leaving bald patches atop a shaggy mane. Snow sits on the summits for nine months of the year.

It was on one of those inhospitable peaks that Gilbert Grandval had established the local Maquis headquarters. And it was there that Druce's force were to head, carrying the heavy supplies that even now were thumping down all around, as the aircraft made repeated runs over the DZ, dropping dozens of parachute-borne containers.

Those containers were simply constructed and designed to fit into the aircraft's quick-release clamps, which had once unleashed salvoes of bombs. Each was fitted with a shock absorber at the tip, one designed to cushion the landing. The 'C Type' container was a bomb-shaped cylinder 68 inches long by 15 wide, and hinged down its length to aid opening. The 'H Type' was of similar dimensions, but compartmentalized internally, and designed to carry more delicate loads. Each weighed some 500 pounds and came complete with a shovel, so it could be buried and hidden, once emptied of its load.

The containers had codes stencilled on the outside, identifying the contents. The code 'SERA' indicated a load of explosives, comprising 20 pounds of PE, six Lewes bombs, a selection of timers, fuses and detonators, plus non-flaming matches and various other elements necessary for blowing the enemy all to hell. The 'JODI' container was stuffed full of twenty-four-hour ration packs, plus tins of cigarettes, water-sterilization powder and Hexamine cookers, complete with fuel blocks.

Items that didn't particularly need protection – sleeping bags, clothing, boots – were packed into steel wire panniers, and padded out with coir (coconut fibre padding). The panniers proved highly ineffective. Dropped manually, as opposed to using the bomb-release mechanism, they were invariably kicked out last from an aircraft travelling at around 100 metres per second. Being lighter they tended to drift on the breeze, and more often than not ended up a good distance from the drop zone.

As a result of such shortcomings it was approaching dawn by the time the Maquis, together with their Special Forces companions, had gathered up the scattered Op Loyton supplies. This 'stores' airdrop had delivered enough weaponry to arm 200 Maquis, but a great deal more was required.

As the column of mixed SAS, Phantoms, Jeds and Resistance fighters shouldered their heavy loads and set off for the hills, Hislop couldn't help but feel a burning sense of urgency to get away from the open expanse of the DZ. Even as they were swallowed by the beckoning forest, he had the unsettling feeling that it would not be long before the enemy discovered the location of their drop, and came hunting.

Hislop's instinct would prove remarkably prescient.

The Op Loyton war diary makes it clear that the greatest challenge facing these men was one not of their own making: it was timing. 'It had been hoped to mount this operation shortly before or immediately after D-Day, at a time when the area was relatively lightly-held by the enemy and while there were . . . many other areas of partisan activity, which would distract enemy attention from the presence of SAS troops in so sensitive a position.'

But D-Day had been 6 June 1944, over nine long weeks ago. Inserting the Op Loyton force had been delayed by two main factors: one, the inclement weather; and two, the need for the longer hours of darkness that August had brought, to hide the aircraft and parachutists from enemy eyes.

In the interim, conditions had changed irrevocably on the ground. The fifteen Special Forces soldiers now climbing into the hills above La Petite Raon had been told to expect little resistance from the enemy. Sparsely garrisoned with low-calibre troops, the Vosges should have offered them the perfect environment to hit the transport and communications infrastructure that linked the front-line troops to the German heartland.

That may have been the case back in June. It wasn't now. Increasingly, as German forces fell back from the Normandy beachhead, and from the Allied thrust through the soft underbelly of southern Europe, they were being funnelled into the main gateway into Germany – the bottleneck of the Vosges.

In the way of this massive, battle-ravaged German force stood fifteen Special Forces soldiers, plus a few hundred very poorly armed Maquis.

And all too soon now, battle would be joined.

Chapter Four

At first glance the terrain of the Vosges seemed ideal for the kind of covert operations and skulduggery that Druce had in mind. Carpeted in dark and impenetrable forests slashed by deep chasms, brooding lakes and plunging waterfalls, the valleys were perfect for concealing such small, mobile parties.

But those same deep, twisting ravines were also the route-ways for the few roads that snaked through the region, as well as the villages that clung to their length. Away from those sparse settlements, there were just a few isolated farms and lonely foresters' huts scattered amidst the deep woods. And by no means all the inhabitants of the Vosges were guaranteed to be friendly.

A passing visitor might gaze upon the Vosges villages as islands of rural tranquillity. In truth, there was a seething distrust that lay just below the surface. On the western slopes of the mountains most villagers were staunchly French in every sense of the word, forming the heartland of the Resistance. But on the eastern – German – side, many were as Teutonic as your average Berliner, and they still owed their allegiances to the Reich.

For centuries the Vosges had been fought over, a prize sought and alternately claimed by each party. In 1871 the

41

Prussians – loosely speaking, the 'German' side of the divide – defeated Napoleon III and took possession of the Vosges. Less than fifty years later, at the end of the First World War, France claimed the territory back again.

In May 1940 the mighty Nazi war machine had thundered across the border, and Germany claimed the Vosges once more. Most resented the invaders and hungered for some means to fight back and resist. But there were some, especially those living on the steep, eastern flanks of the hills, who viewed the Germans as liberators.

It was in those areas and amongst those inhabitants that the SAS would have to take the very greatest care. One man amongst their number, Robert Lodge, felt this venomous threat most personally. Sergeant 'Lodge' was in truth Rudolf Freidlaender, a German Jew who had had the foresight to flee Germany in the 1930s, even as Hitler had ramped up his hate-fuelled rhetoric against the Jewish population, in preparation for launching his 'Final Solution'.

Friedlaender had settled with his family in west London, but at the outbreak of war he'd felt compelled to fight, and he had already won the Distinguished Conduct Medal on previous operations. He was a comparatively ancient member of Druce's party, being all of thirty-three years of age, but in spite of this and his thick, jam-jar glasses, he'd earned one of the finest fighting reputations in the SAS.

Friedlaender had adopted the typically Anglo-Saxon sounding name of 'Lodge' in the hope that it might obscure his German Jewish origins if he were ever to be captured. But with his big, heavy, kindly looks, he was – to many eyes – clearly from a Jewish background, and he was under no illusions as to what might happen if he were taken captive in the Vosges.

The trek from the DZ to the Maquis' hilltop redoubt proved to be a gruelling, ten-hour affair, crossing terrain as difficult as any the Op Loyton party had ever trained over. The first 2,000-foot ridge was crested in the cool hours of early morning, putting the DZ thankfully out of sight. Even if the enemy did find the DZ, tracing Druce's force would become more and more difficult with their every footfall further into the hills.

The first miles on the trail were almost welcome after the cramped, stuffy confines of the warplane's hold. But as the sun climbed above the horizon, its powerful rays reaching into the deepest valleys and chasing away the shadows, so the heat began to rise. In spite of the dappled shade cast by the ranks of trees that towered on either side, it grew hot and humid, and the men found themselves boiling up as they toiled beneath their crushing loads.

The Maquis guides were as sure-footed as mountain goats. The pace they set was punishing, even for men accustomed to such tough physicality, and especially as the adrenalin of the parachute drop drained from their systems. By mid afternoon they'd completed some 10,000 feet of exhausting ascent and descent, and the Special Forces operators found themselves gasping for breath and sweating rivulets.

Captain Henry Druce had to force effort from limbs that felt like lead. The Op Loyton commander was suffering more than most. Even as they had begun the trek he was still talking (mostly) concussed nonsense. Springs and gushing creeks were on hand at every turn, and at their rest stops Druce splashed cool mountain water over his neck and face, in an effort to try to clear his head.

The forest was thick and verdant: ever-present, crowding in from all sides. Here and there huge granite boulders reared up from the undergrowth, as if hurled down from a distant peak by a giant's hand. In such terrain you could stumble to within 15 feet of an enemy position and still not be able to see it. It was ideal ambush territory.

By the time the Maquis camp was in sight the fierce exertion seemed to have driven most of Druce's concussion away. The base – set just to the west of Lac de la Maix, an upland lake lying at some 2,000 feet of altitude – was of solid timber construction. A log cabin closely surrounded on all sides by dense tracts of woodland, it was rendered all but invisible to anything but an aircraft flying directly overhead.

It was equipped with rough-hewn tables, chairs and sleeping platforms, and Druce was surprised at the neatness and apparent efficiency of the place. There was even a French tricolour flying from an adjacent flagpole, one that would be hauled down at sunset with military precision and raised again at dawn. In the minds of the Alsace Maquis, the Lac de la Maix area was already part of liberated France, and Druce, Hislop, Gough and their men couldn't help but be impressed.

Strictly speaking, the Maquis hadn't been formed as a military force; at least, not to begin with. Under the terms of the humiliating armistice signed between France and Germany in June 1940, 1.6 million French soldiers had been taken into captivity as prisoners of war. In due course the Germans offered to release a great number of them, if for each man thus 'freed' three Frenchmen would 'volunteer' to labour for the Reich.

Initially, this *relève* (relief) applied only to fit young men. But as the German armament factories, mines and defensive projects demanded more and more labour, the *relève* was extended to include all males up to the age of fifty, plus able-bodied women. The *relève* was soon made compulsory and renamed the Service du Travail Obligatoire (STO): the Compulsory Work Service. By the end of 1943 some 650,000 Frenchmen and women had been shipped off to slave for the Reich.

Those who sought to avoid the STO fled into the remoter stretches of the French countryside, becoming maquisards. The name Maquis appears to have been taken from the word for 'bush' or 'scrub', the kind of terrain they tended to hide out in. At first, a Maquis wasn't someone who necessarily took up arms. Many were keen only to avoid being fed into Nazi Germany's vast slave-labour operation, from which few would return. But there were those too who were desperate to fight.

Against this growing body of Maquis, the Reich employed the full panoply of state oppression. France was garrisoned by two types of force: German combat troops, tasked to prevent an Allied landing and liberation; and occupation troops, responsible for keeping iron control over the French population. The former were some of the best fighting soldiers available; the latter were often former prisoners of war – Russians, Ukrainians, and even Indians and North Africans – who had opted to switch sides rather than languish in the POW camps.

The occupation troops were generally ill-disciplined and cruel. Commanded by Germans, they fell under the control of the RSHA (Reich Security Main Office): the Nazi intelligence services and secret police, known more commonly as the *Sicherheitsdienst* (SD) and the Gestapo. They made wide use of informers and quislings, particularly from within the Milice – the pro-Nazi French militia raised under German occupation. The Milice was trained and armed by the SS, Hitler's personal shock troops, and ordered to hunt down the Maquis.

When facing such an array of powerful and unsavoury adversaries, the Alsace Maquis appeared hopelessly outgunned. But if Druce's men could get proper supplies of weaponry airdropped to them, Colonel Grandval's Maquis would doubtless prove a force to be reckoned with. Aided by their Jedburgh advisers, they should be well placed to set the Vosges aflame.

One other thing was crystal clear after the long trek to the Maquis' mountaintop hideout: they couldn't count on covering much ground over such precipitous and punishing terrain. Druce's men had managed to travel just 10 miles in ten hours.

That evening they pooled their rations with the Maquis, whose food supplies consisted mostly of a coffee substitute made from roasted acorns, coarse brown bread, meat and a ready supply of vegetables. Their hosts rustled up a meal and, once the famished and exhausted newcomers had eaten, they settled down to rest, safe in the knowledge that the Maquis had set watch for the night.

In the Op Loyton war diary, Druce described their Lac de la Maix base as being 'well-organised and well-run', and set 'in a good defensive position' on the hilltop. He wrote of being treated to 'an excellent meal' and of 'sleeping the clock around'. For now at least, he and his men felt secure.

Druce awoke early the following morning to fine sunlight lancing through the branches and birdsong serenading the dawn. It was such a peaceful, bracing scene – the mountain air cool and invigorating at such an altitude – that it was hard to believe the world could be at war. Druce found that the climb followed by the long sleep had completely cured any lingering muzzy-headedness, and he figured it was time to get down to the serious business of waging war.

In their rushed pre-departure briefing Colonel Franks had made it clear that time was of the essence with Op Loyton. Druce needed to get the main force in as quickly as possible. Yet, at the same time, he didn't want to signal the all clear until he had a good sense of the lie of the land, and especially of the Maquis' capabilities.

Colonel Grandval's local commander at Lac de la Maix was Lieutenant Félix LeFranc. He was supported by a small nucleus of former French Army officers. There were some eighty Maquis under them, with other groups located at further mountaintop redoubts. Discipline seemed reasonably good, but prior to the airdrop, Lieutenant LeFranc's men had been armed only with a dozen ancient rifles and possessed very limited supplies of ammunition.

The first priority had to be to instruct the Maquis in the use of the new weaponry. Priority number two was to radio in a 'sitrep' – situation report – to London, giving the location and status of the mission. And as soon as possible Druce needed to arrange a meeting with Colonel Grandval to assess the needs of the entire Maquis, then leave Gough and his Jedburghs to call in the bulk of the arms while he got the main body of the SAS flown in.

'So, when will I be able to see Colonel Maximum?' Druce asked Lieutenant LeFranc, over a breakfast of coarse brown bread dunked in bitter acorn coffee. 'When will we be able to start some proper planning?'

Druce's enthusiasm, coupled with his ability to speak French like a native had endeared him to the Maquis commander.

'The colonel will come,' Lieutenant LeFranc reassured him. 'I am told he is at Le Round Table Salon, attending to some important business. But he will come.'

Druce was unsure what the 'Round Table Salon' might signify, but important Maquis business was presumably important Maquis business.

'Right, in the meantime how about we get your men training with the new weaponry?' Druce eyed a patch of trees that would give good cover, but was relatively free of undergrowth. 'Get 'em to fall in over there, and we'll get to it.'

'Right away, Captain,' Lieutenant LeFranc replied. He paused for a moment. 'But you will need to send a radio message to London, no? The colonel has asked that you do not use your radios within 5 miles of the camp, due to the risks of DF. I can send one of my best guides to take your signallers to a place from where they can transmit in safety.'

'DF' stands for direction finding. The Germans had excellent mobile DF units, which could detect a radio signal at distance, triangulate the point from which it was transmitting, and so fix its location.

'Sounds like a very sensible precaution,' Druce agreed. 'I'll send a team out this morning with your man.'

With the Jedburgh signaller, Seymour, out of action owing to his injuries, it would be up to Hislop and his Phantoms to establish first communications. Just a few weeks previously a new type of radio had been issued to all Special Forces, nick-named the 'Jed Set'. It was comparatively lightweight and was powered by turning a handle, which meant that fewer bulky batteries needed to be lugged over the hills.

The Jed Set was simple to operate, the wavelength of trans-mission being set by a 'crystal', a small piece of crystalline mineral, such as galena, that was slotted into the device. This ensured there was no need to 'tune' the set prior to transmis-sion or reception. The Jed Sets were inoperable without their crystals, so it was crucial to get rid of them if a set were ever in danger of falling into enemy hands.

SAS and Phantom signals were routed via Brigade Tactical Headquarters at Moor Park, where a contingent from the Royal Corps of Signals manned five transmitter-receiver sets 24/7. Each team was supposed to transmit two daily 'skeds' (sched-ules) from the field: the first between 08.30 and 09.00 hours and the second at 13.00–14.00 hours. If one or more sked was missed, Special Forces Headquarters (SFHQ) would consider a party compromised and on the run, possibly captured or killed.

Shortly after breakfast Hislop loaded up his Jed Set and headed into the forest, with seventeen-year-old local Roger Souchal acting as his guide. Souchal was definitely one of those who had come to the Maquis to fight. A schoolboy with aspira-tions to train as a lawyer, Souchal had been forced to grow up fast once the Germans took possession of the Vosges. He burned to drive the hated enemy out, and he would prove to be a steadfast ally over the weeks to come.

During the previous day's climb Hislop had suffered almost as much as had the concussed Druce. In the aftermath of his racing accident, Hislop had contracted jaundice and tonsillitis. During the trek he'd found it increasingly difficult to lift his rucksack after each rest period, and he'd practically crawled into the Maquis camp, dripping wet with perspiration. He'd begun to fear that his lingering illness had rendered him unfit for a mission such as this.

But as they set out that morning, Hislop felt like a new man. It seemed as if he'd sweated the sickness out of his system, the purifying mountain air giving him a new lease of life. As Souchal pushed on at a punishing pace, Hislop and his Phantom team stuck right on his shoulder. Souchal led them to a patch of mature deciduous woodland, which spread a high, cathedral-like canopy above the scene. It was less dense and dark than the coniferous forest which predominated in the area, and it was full of noisy bird life.

It should prove far easier amongst such lighter cover to raise a radio signal. As Corporal Davis rigged up their Jed Set, Hislop scanned their surroundings with eye and ear. To their front he could hear a pair of woodsmen working with some oxen, hauling timber out of the forest. Their musical cries, cut by the rhythmic crack of the oxen whip, rose above the forest quiet, providing a bass track to the morning birdsong.

For a Phantom, the moment of making first radio contact on a live mission was always one of high drama. More or less immediately the first letters of the HQ's answering call sign could be heard, loud and clear. Davis punched a thumb into the air to signify success, but just as quickly the Jed Set went dead, a needle-thin wisp of smoke fingering out of the rear of the radio, betraying the fact that it had burnt out.

Luckily, they'd brought a second, back-up set, and Roger Souchal offered to go and fetch it, the 10-mile round-trip being as nothing to the young Maquis guide. While Souchal hurried off, Hislop lay beneath the trees, gazing up at the canopy above him and feeling as if all was well with the world. But still a small part of him sensed that somehow this was the calm before the gathering storm.

Souchal returned with the replacement Jed Set, accompanied by Victor Gough. With an injured signaller and broken radio to contend with, the Jedburgh captain would have to rely upon the Phantoms for communications, at least for now.

The second set functioned perfectly. 'Landed safely. Skye damaged ankle. Fit in seven days. Have contacted Maximum . . . Are with Maquis group 2 kms south of Vexaincourt in Valley Celles-sur-Plaine.'

Vexaincourt was the nearest village of any size, lying in the Celles-sur-Plaine Valley, adjacent to that in which the Op Loyton team had landed. 'Skye' was Seymour's (the injured Jedburgh) code name. From the tenor of the message, the calm and lack of perceived threat is clear.

But even as Hislop, Gough and Davis were making contact with London, Druce himself was becoming apprehensive. That morning a German Storch reconnaissance aircraft had circled over the Lac de la Maix base. Of course, Druce had no proof it was searching for him and his men, or even for the Maquis. But there was a new, and unexpected, arrival at the camp, who was convinced that the plane was on the lookout for the French and British fighters.

Lou Fiddick was a Canadian airman. During a July '44 bombing raid he'd been shot down by a night fighter over Germany. Though injured, he'd spent a week walking out on the same bearing to that on which his bomber had flown in. He'd crossed the French border, made contact with friendly villagers, and they had brought him to the Maquis.

Fiddick could not have been happier to hook up with Druce's force. 'I was finally amongst people I could understand! I was also impressed by the fact that they had dropped into an area so rife with Germans!'

Fiddick had been in the Vosges for long enough to have learned a little about the enemy stationed in the region. He'd had to evade numerous search parties, hiding in dingy cellars, cramped attics and even down a well. At one point he was en route to join the Maquis, but ended up coming face to face with a German patrol. Fortunately, the villagers had dressed him as a local, and the enemy column had marched on by.

In short, Fiddick knew that – contrary to the briefings the SAS men had been given – the area was crawling with the enemy.

Druce had invited Fiddick to join his force, becoming their sixteenth man, and he'd even kitted out the Canadian in a spare SAS uniform. Fiddick was peculiarly suited to operating in an environment like the Vosges. Having grown up on the heavily forested Vancouver Island on Canada's western seaboard, he'd worked as a woodsman before the war, and the Vosges felt almost like a home from home. As Druce remarked, Fiddick 'would turn out to be one of our best soldiers'.

Being an experienced airman – Fiddick had been flying a Lancaster bomber when shot down – he understood the roles played by various warplanes. He feared that the Storch reconnaissance aircraft could only be doing one thing – searching for the Maquis' deep-forest bases. And, bearing in mind how quickly the Germans had come looking for him, Fiddick feared that the enemy must know at least something of the British parachutists' arrival, hence their aerial search.

Fiddick's concerns were soon to be proved correct. As Hislop, Gough and Davis returned from their radio excursion, they discovered a second new arrival at camp. Albert Freine was the *gard-chasse* – chief gamekeeper – of the region. As such, he was of necessity closely involved with the local German commanders, many of whom were keen on a spot of wild boar hunting, or fishing. It made Freine's other role – that of chief intelligence officer of the Alsace Maquis – doubly rewarding and challenging, in equal measure.

Freine was viewed by the Germans as a 'good' Frenchman, one who was loyal to the Nazi cause. As such, he was often privy to their plans, ones betrayed by casual remarks while out on the hunt. But, by mid August 1944, even Freine's 'cover' was starting to wear thin, and the deadly game of duplicity was playing on his nerves. The intelligence chief of any Maquis group would be hunted most actively, for if he were unmasked and forced to talk then the entire network could be rolled up.

Freine introduced himself to Druce. He was a curious-looking figure: slight, sandy-haired and dressed in the traditional beret and rough tweed cloak that Vosges countrymen favoured. He seemed gloomy by nature but fiercely patriotic and loyal, and boastful and fearless in equal measure. In short, he was a bundle of contradictions, but more importantly he had never been known to give inaccurate information, or to say more than he knew.

Right now, Freine had brought alarming news. A force of some 5,000 German soldiers was carrying out an east-to-west 'sweep' of the Celles-sur-Plaine Valley, which was less than 2 miles north of the Maquis camp. It was far too close for comfort, and Freine could only conclude that the influx of enemy troops was connected to the arrival of British paratroopers.

The German soldiers were from the *Wehrmacht*'s 405 Division, part of the 19th Army. Retreating from the Allied advance in southern Europe, the 19th had been charged with defending Germany's eastern border in the Vosges. The 19th Army consisted mostly of 'third-tier' troops: wounded veterans, conscripts and 'Hiwis' – foreign POWs who had 'volunteered' to serve the Nazi cause. (Hiwi is an abbreviation of the German word *Hilfswilliger*, meaning 'those willing to help'.)

Yet, regardless of their calibre, a 5,000-strong force was far too numerous for Druce's unit, plus the poorly armed Maquis, to take on in open battle. Moreover, the 19th Army also included the 11th Panzer Division, which – with its distinctive emblem of a sword-wielding ghost – had seen action on the Eastern Front, where it had fought with distinction around Kiev and

Moscow. Equipped with 140 tanks, this was a battle-hardened and hugely capable force, one that Druce and his men would be well advised to avoid.

In light of Freine's report the guard was doubled around the camp. At just past midnight dark cloud rolled in from the south-east, and ear-splitting peals of thunder were punctuated by searing bolts of lightning. By dawn the storm had blown over, the morning scoured clean by the torrential rains. But the Storch was back in the air, the crystal-clear skies doubtless giving it a perfect view of whatever it was searching for.

Further worrying reports filtered in that morning. The male population of Allarmont, the nearest hamlet, had fled to the forest to avoid the German soldiers storming through their valley. Worryingly, the 19th Army troops had discovered the DZ upon which Druce and his men had landed. They were reported to be moving more soldiers into the region, supported by their battle tanks.

In that morning's radio sked Druce sounded a somewhat harried note: 'Could not get radio contact yesterday. Sent message blind. Expect conference with Maximum . . . today. Must march 5 miles from camp to send messages. Can only manage 1 Sked per day at present.'

He also warned SFHQ that 'between one thousand and five thousand enemy soldiers' were moving through the region, and that he needed to establish a new and secure DZ. For now, the flying in of the main body of the Op Loyton force would have to be put on hold.

Deep in his bones, Captain Henry Druce could sense that the net was closing.

Chapter Five

On 16 August 1944 Hitler gave orders that his forces in southern France should start to withdraw northwards to bolster the defence of the Reich. Their concentration on the eastern approaches to Germany meant that even more men and war machines were headed into the Vosges. By contrast, General Patton's 3rd Army – the nearest friendly force – was still some 300 miles to the west, endeavouring to secure a breakthrough.

Devoid of an immediate enemy to fight, the incoming Vosges garrisons were ordered to concentrate their full might on finding and eliminating the Maquis, and their British parachutist brothers in arms. The overall German security commander in the region, Dr Erich Isselhorst, was no stranger to such anti-partisan operations.

Isselhorst, a trained lawyer, had joined the Nazi party in 1931, rising rapidly through its ranks. He came to Hitler's notice while defending various prominent Nazis on trial, becoming a protégé of the Führer. Shortly after the outbreak of war, he was appointed an SS officer and chief of the Gestapo in Munich, reflecting his meteoric rise to power. Three years later he was sent to the Eastern Front to use his talents hunting down the very active Russian partisans.

Commanding *Einsatzgruppe* B, based at Smolensk, a Russian city 225 miles to the west of Moscow, Isselhorst would earn several decorations for so-called bravery. In truth, Isselhorst's *Einsatzgruppe* was one of the euphemistically named 'special commandos', which were basically death squads, charged with rounding up those earmarked for 'liquidation': Russian resistance fighters, Jews, gypsies and the disabled.

In Smolensk, part of Isselhorst's remit proved to be the merciless 'evacuation' of the Jewish ghettos. In August 1943 he wrote in his diary of one such operation: 'Since there was resistance – great slaughter; 3,100 J [Jews] dead. Only 350 have volunteered for transportation available.' That transportation was, of course, to the concentration camps, and during his time on the Eastern Front, Isselhorst would earn a reputation for being an efficient orchestrator of the machinery of mass murder.

Isselhorst returned to Germany a *Standartenführer* (the equivalent SS rank of colonel) and was appointed the Gestapo chief for the Vosges, based in the city of Strasbourg on the region's eastern border. By the summer of 1944, he was hearing reports of Maquis activity in the region. Then, in mid August, matters became altogether more alarming. Low-flying aircraft had been heard at night, and there were reports that 'English parachutists' had joined the Maquis, bringing weapons to raise an insurrection.

For the staunch Nazi Isselhorst, this was infuriating. Working closely with his triumvirate of deputies, Isselhorst drew up plans for the ironically named Operation Waldfest (which translates as 'party in the forest'). Waldfest was modelled on the type of brutal and bloody operations that he had orchestrated in Smolensk against the Russian partisans.

Isselhorst's deputy on Operation Waldfest was Wilhelm Schneider, a former navy captain from the First World War, and a renowned bully and drunkard. Small of stature, weasel-faced and with a greying, goatee beard, Schneider was largely ineffective without his two partners in crime – one of whom proved to be the real brains behind Waldfest.

Alfonso Uhring, Isselhorst's foreign intelligence chief, was an overweight, balding, jowly tank of a man, who would be responsible for interrogating any captured British operators. Uhring had Schneider's ear, and might be described as the puppet master who pulled his strings. Operationally, Waldfest would be very much his baby.

The third figure in Isselhorst's triumvirate of deputies was Julius Gehrum, a piggy-eyed, triple-chinned bull of a man, one who was said to be inordinately fond both of drink and of his Nazi uniform, and especially of the Iron Cross that adorned his left breast pocket. Gehrum was the chief of the frontier guard force, and he was renowned as a figure of extreme ruthlessness and brutality.

Under stage one of Operation Waldfest, spearheaded by the *Wehrmacht*, a massive military sweep would uncover the arms and ammunition dropped to the Maquis, and find and eliminate their bases in the hills. In stage two, spearheaded by the Gestapo, the surrounding villages would be purged of all Maquis and their supporters, thus draining the Resistance of all backing.

Just as Isselhorst had done in Smolensk, *Einsatzkommandos* would be posted across the Vosges. Most were named after their German commander. *Einsatzkommando* Ernst was commanded by notorious SS officer *Sturmbannführer* (major) Hans Dietrich Ernst, who had recently sent eight hundred French Jews to their deaths at Auschwitz. Ernst was a vicious, sadistic man, and a past master at forcing captives to break under extreme interrogation and torture.

Operation Waldfest received the personal blessing of Heinrich Himmler, *Reichsführer* of the SS, at that time one of the most powerful men in Nazi Germany. With the bulwark of the Vosges forming the German military's key line of defence, Himmler ordered that it be defended at all costs. The area was to be 'cleaned' of all Maquis, a demand that gave Waldfest added urgency and impetus.

By the evening of 16 August 1944 the noose of Waldfest was being drawn ever tighter around Druce's force. Just three days after the British Special Forces had got boots on the ground, Isselhorst's intelligence was already remarkably accurate. He'd split his forces between two valleys – the Rabodeau and Celles-sur-Plaine – leaving the Maquis and their British comrades trapped on the 3,000-foot ridge lying in the middle.

Druce awoke on the morning of 17 August to learn of the dire developments that had occurred overnight. A necklace of German troops had been strung around the base of the mountain. They were moving stealthily upwards, seeking to enclose the British force and the Maquis in a steely embrace. Druce decided to move immediately to stand the best chance of escape. Lieutenant LeFranc concurred, although his orders were to resist abandoning their camp until the last.

There was no time to waste. Weaponry, ammo, supplies and radios – all were loaded up in a hastily prepared mule train of Maquis and Special Forces operators. With the crunch of summer-dry debris underfoot, the columns of men moved out in a tense and apprehensive silence. An advance party led by Lieutenant David Dill, a dashingly handsome SAS man of no more than twenty years of age, took the lead, scouting the way ahead.

Lieutenant Dill was small and slight, with a somewhat impish, almost baby-faced look, and a happy-go-lucky air. In the past few days he'd also shown himself to be astonishingly tough, and calm and cool under pressure. Druce figured he was the perfect man to raise the alarm should they stumble into German forces. They were to hold their fire at all costs. Druce needed to preserve his own men and to bring in the rest of the Op Loyton troops; there was every need to avoid a potentially devastating gun battle.

By around nine o'clock that morning the hundred-odd fighters had been swallowed into the forest shadows. A small rearguard had been left to cover the main party's withdrawal. It included Sergeant Lodge – the German Jew, Freidlaender – and Lou Fiddick. Druce had set a rendezvous (RV) point at a six-figure grid plucked off a map: 470902. This was where they would meet, should they lose each other during whatever was coming.

After two hours of difficult going, Druce's party hit a well-defined track, one used by oxen to haul timber out of the higher reaches of the mountains. The trail didn't appear to have been used for lumberjacking purposes for some time, and a thick carpet of pine needles lay underfoot. It served to deaden the sound of the men's passing. All that could be heard was the occasional clink of metal, plus the groan of a canvas or leather strap under the strain of a crushing load.

Druce led his party along that track for 400 yards, only to see Lieutenant Dill come hurrying back in their direction. A German patrol had been spotted by the trackside. They'd stopped for an early lunch, and luckily neither Dill nor his fellows had been seen. Druce ordered the entire group to secrete themselves in the forest, and to remain utterly silent. The plan was to allow the Germans to pass by, and only then to continue on their way.

At the lower side of the track lay a deep hollow, which provided perfect cover for Druce, Hislop and most of the British force. To either side of them the Maquis melted into the trees. Further downslope the terrain was thickly wooded and precipitous, and uphill lay the track. There were few easy escape routes if the enemy patrol got wise to the British and French presence.

The forest fell utterly silent. The midday sun cut a swathe of blinding light along the length of the track, but to either side the woods were shrouded in semi-darkness. It should be next to impossible for anyone moving in the open to spot those hiding in the thick forest shadows.

A faint chatter of voices announced the enemy's arrival. They moved into view, two columns of grey-uniformed troops marching very much at ease. Doubtless this was one of the Waldfest search parties, but there was nothing about the soldiers' body language or demeanour that suggested they expected to stumble upon their French and British prey any time soon.

The vanguard drew level with the hidden force and proceeded to move on by. Hislop found himself holding his breath as the tension mounted, and he could barely believe their luck as the rear end of the column drew level with their hiding place. But it was then that a disastrously curious Maquis decided to ease his head above cover to get a look at – and draw a bead on – the hated enemy.

A cry rang out, as harsh and guttural as it was unwelcome: '*Achtung!*'

It was followed by the distinctive clink of metal on metal, as a weapon was made ready. But the shot that followed came from the direction of the forest, and it ended in a strangled gurgle, as the German soldier who had issued the challenge was shot dead by the maquisard who had allowed himself to be seen.

As the German patrol was only thirty-strong, Druce ordered an all-out attack, in the hope that they could drive the enemy off. Within seconds the air was cut by bursts of automatic fire, as bullets tore through the vegetation to either side of the path and hammered into the enemy column. Some were hit, but most scattered, diving for a ditch at the edge of the track, from where they could return fire. 'Third-tier' troops they might have been, but they certainly weren't running.

Druce held his men firm, short bursts from Stens and carbines raking the path above them. The two sides traded vicious fire at close quarters, but the enemy had the high ground – Druce having chosen their position for maximum stealth and concealment, not for springing an ambush. Still, if they struck aggressively and hard enough, he felt certain they could break through the enemy ranks and escape.

He was about to order a charge to clear the path when the enemy started yelling for back-up. Druce, who could understand German, heard an answering cry from further up the hill, where a second foresters' track snaked through the vegetation. It was followed moments later by the sounds of dozens of pairs of jackboots thundering downhill towards the firefight.

Seconds later the intensity of the enemy fire redoubled. The Germans on the higher track began to rain down rounds from what could only be a fearsome *Maschinengewehr* 42 'Spandau'.

The Spandau – a bipod-mounted machine gun – unleashed a long series of probing bursts, bullets ricocheting horribly off the trees to all sides. The MG42 could hammer out twice the rate of rounds of any comparable Allied machine gun. So rapid was the rate of fire that the human ear couldn't distinguish between each bullet, the distinctive continuous *brrrrr* of the weapon earning it the nickname 'Hitler's buzz saw'.

'It was frightening,' remarked the otherwise unshakeable Lou Fiddick. 'We didn't have that much ammunition with us. I think we'd fired it all off. I was standing behind a tree with bullets going all around it . . . It was a little unusual to have so many bullets flying all around you. I hadn't expected such a thing, although there were plenty of bullets flying around on the night we got shot down.'

The first of the Maquis broke and ran. They thundered past to either side of the hollow, from where Druce's force was still trying to fight, disappearing in a helter-skelter retreat. Most were laden down with precious items of SAS and Phantom equipment. Hislop and Druce heard agonized cries as the Spandau raked the slope, the buzz saw's rounds scything down the heavily laden Maquis, who were unable to move quickly on the steep slope and made for easy targets.

A long Spandau burst sliced through the vegetation above the hollow, bullets tearing through a tree limb as if it were being unzipped. The British force was heavily outnumbered and outgunned now. Druce ordered his men to ditch all their heavy gear and make a run for it. Moving light and low offered the only hope of escape, but first they would need to booby-trap their Bergens with plastic explosives.

Hislop was forced to abandon his Jed Set, but as he had the crystals and code book on his person, the radio would prove of little use to the enemy. Druce opted to lead one half of the force in one direction, with Hislop taking the other the opposite way, in an effort to fox their pursuers. They gathered at the lip of the hollow, the air beneath the trees thick with the grey smog of cordite fumes.

They broke cover and dashed downslope, keeping bent double to escape the thick bursts of fire ripping through the trees. Hislop figured no horse he had ever ridden had run as fast as he did then, charging through the thick vegetation.

He led his party 400 yards downhill, to a point where the thick bush gave way to another track. The open ground ahead was being raked by sustained bursts of fire from above. Hislop waited for one such salvo to end before leading his men in a mad dash across.

'Now! Go, go, go, go, go!'

He caught a glimpse of the back of Davis – his ultra-reliable fellow Phantom – just ahead of him, as they plunged into the vegetation on the far side. It was the last he was ever to see of him.

Finally Hislop called a halt. In hushed whispers he mustered his force in the thick cover of the undergrowth. He urged them all to keep quiet and to lie low. Any movement or noise would draw the enemy's eye and ear, followed by a savage burst of fire. Their greatest hope lay in concealment, and there was no better cover than the dense bush that surrounded them on all sides.

Hislop did a headcount. Somehow, he'd lost Davis. He'd also gained an additional three, all Maquis: a sixteen-year-old boy who appeared utterly terrified, an old man who seemed to be shell-shocked, plus a young man called Marcel – the only one of the three Frenchmen who still seemed in charge of his wits.

They lay there, catching their breath, bodies pressed into the soft detritus of the forest floor, the cries of their pursuers echoing through the trees. Orders were called back and forth in German, followed by the odd burst of fire. Finally, the noise of the shooting seemed to grow more faint, and eventually the gunshots faded away to nothing. All around them the forest fell silent.

It was early evening by now, and Hislop suspected that the enemy might have left a hidden force behind to keep watch for any survivors. He decided they would stay exactly where they were and try to get some sleep, then move off at first light. Marcel offered to guide them to a neighbouring valley where the villagers were friendly. There, they could scavenge some food and seek news on the whereabouts of the enemy, plus the rest of their scattered party.

It was a plan of sorts, but it did little to disguise the fact that their fortunes had taken a sudden and very dramatic turn for the worse. Some of the men were missing, and Hislop had no idea where Druce was located, or of the fate of their rearguard. He could only hope that they'd reach Druce's RV to find the rest of the party awaiting them, and that they could salvage the mission from there.

During the trek through the midday heat Hislop had stripped down to his para-smock. He'd lost all the rest of his kit during the mad dash to escape. As he settled amongst the undergrowth and the night chill descended, he rued getting rid of his warm clothing. But he figured his discomfort was as nothing compared to those unfortunates who may well have been injured, captured or killed.

Druce's group had fared little better than Hislop's. After charging downhill, they'd run into a German on the lower path wielding a Schmeisser. Fortunately he'd proved to be a hopeless shot, and Druce had managed to lead his men across without anyone being hit. Lieutenant Dill had gone back to try to nail the lone German. Despite a vicious exchange of fire he had proved to be in good cover, and Dill failed to hit him.

By the time Druce stopped to do a proper headcount, he had several Maquis – including Lieutenant LeFranc – with him, but Seymour, the Jedburgh who'd injured his foot on the DZ, was missing. Seymour had had to be carried from the Maquis base by four stretcher-bearing Resistance fighters. No one was about to flee down this precipitous slope laden with a stretcher, and it seemed highly likely that Seymour had been captured or killed.

On Lieutenant LeFranc's advice Druce's force set out for a remote farmstead, positioned in the forests above Moussey village. Their route took them in a southerly direction, sticking to the forested high ground and keeping away from both the Celles Valley and that of the Rabodeau. They marched into the evening. Relieved of their heavy loads they set a punishing pace, seeking to put the battleground and the enemy well behind them.

They arrived at the farmer's run-down homestead in good time. Known to all simply as 'Père George' – *Père*, meaning father, was a respectful reference to his advanced age – he lived on his own in a single barn, with only his cats, pigs, cows and a dog for company. Père George farmed about four acres of rough pastureland, set amidst the crowding forest. More importantly, he was a diehard communist, which made him a natural enemy of the Nazis.

Lieutenant LeFranc had led the force here, relying upon the age-old adage 'the enemy of my enemy is my friend'. Père George was no great fan of Churchill, but as the SAS men had come here to fight the hated Germans, he was happy to offer them a place in his barn.

It was a rough lodging, but after the intensity of the day's firefight and the forced marches, Druce and his men could have slept practically anywhere. Crucially, Père George's farm offered the perfect hideaway from the marauding forces of the enemy. Set in a fold of the hills and surrounded by thick pinewoods, it had never once been visited by the Germans.

There was little food on offer, and what there was seemed borderline edible. When his wife had still been alive, they'd eaten fine potages – thick soups and stews – Père George explained. But since her death there was no one to cook, so he lived off similar fare to his livestock, eating out of a *pot de chambre* and sharing his meals with his animals.

'Like all really good farmers, I feed my livestock very well,' he declared, defiantly.

As Captain Druce, Lieutenants Dill and LeFranc and party settled down to sleep, Père George proceeded to wax lyrical on his favourite topic: politics. He sat in his rough peasant garb and wooden clogs, his enormous moustache twitching as he spoke and animating his deeply lined features.

'*Churchill, il est bien. De Gaulle, bien.* But it was after Churchill visited Moscow that the tide of victory finally turned . . . Stalin: he is the one. Ah, Stalin, he is the great man. It is a pity that Churchill isn't a communist.' And so it continued.

The only response from the soldiers lying prone in the hay was a series of muted snores.

Two or 3 miles to the north-east of Père George's barn, Druce's rearguard had run into the worst trouble of all. Half a mile from the Lac de la Maix base they had stumbled into a ferocious ambush. Robert Lodge was leading, when all of a sudden he froze and signalled for the others to hit the dirt.

Moments later they found themselves in the midst of a savage firefight. Canadian airman Lou Fiddick was armed with only a Colt .45, and facing savage bursts from Schmeissers, plus rifles and Lugers. The enemy was no more than 30 yards away, and firing at them through a thick screen of scrub.

'Neither side could really see each other because of the undergrowth,' Fiddick remarked, 'so we just fired when we saw movement in the bushes and hoped we hit someone.'

The battle proved claustrophobic and confusing, as both sides exchanged fire at close quarters. One of Fiddick's better-armed SAS comrades spotted movement, and raked the bush with his Sten gun. Agonized screams revealed where he'd hit one of the enemy. But then SAS man Wally 'Ginger' Hall, a Grenadier Guardsman with a shock of bright ginger hair, took a blast to the chest.

Hall went down. He was still conscious, but he urged his fellows to leave him. By the time Fiddick and the few survivors managed to extricate themselves in a fiercely fought with-drawal, Sergeant Robert Lodge, the renowned SAS veteran and German Jew, was also found to be missing.

By nightfall, Druce's party had been scattered to the four corners of the Vosges. There were dead, injured and very likely captives on those forested hills and several groups of men were on the run. The bulk of their weaponry, kit and equipment was missing.

Worse still, in their flight from the enemy they'd lost all their radios.

Chapter Six

Stage one of Isselhorst's Waldfest had proved spectacularly successful, capturing a good deal of Maquis weaponry, much SAS kit, and dispersing or wiping out their fighting units. Isselhorst could have wished for no better start. On 18 August, stage two was scheduled to begin: the SS and Gestapo's clampdown on those villages seen to be the breeding ground of the Resistance.

But first, Isselhorst and his fellow commanders had a rich haul of captured equipment and papers to study, plus captives to interrogate. Amongst the most sensitive of all was the so-called 'Forgotten List' – a Maquis document recovered from the Lac de la Maix base, naming some of the key figures in the Vosges Resistance. It included many of those who had been present at the 13 August airdrop onto the Raon L'Etape DZ. Worse still, it identified their home villages. For Isselhorst, Schneider, Uhring and Gehrum, this was dynamite.

At dawn on the morning of 18 August, the *Einsatzkommandos* moved into the villages that had been named – including Raon L'Etape, Allarmont and Moussey – on a seek-and-capture mission. All civilians were warned to keep off the streets, as the German troops proceeded to mount house-to-house searches.

SS commander Lieutenant Karl Fischer set up his headquarters in the Moussey village crèche. He demanded that ten 'hostages', among them Jules Py, the local mayor, and Achilles Gassmann, the village priest, give themselves up. Once they had done so, all males between the ages of seventeen and sixty were made to line up on the village square. Those named on the Forgotten List were told to step forward, or the lives of the hostages would be forfeit.

By the evening of the 18th, eighty-eight males of fighting age had been arrested across the several villages. After a night of interrogation and torture, they were loaded aboard trucks and driven away.

Ten miles to the east of Moussey lay the garrison town of Schirmek, which doubled as the nerve centre for Waldfest. It was from there that Schneider, Uhring and Gehrum were overseeing operations, along with Isselhorst, when he was not working out of his Strasbourg HQ. On the outskirts of Schirmek lay a *Sicherungslager*: a security camp.

The *Sicherungslager* were supposedly the more 'respectable' face of the Nazi concentration and death camp system. Schirmek came complete with ranks of wooden huts, subterranean prison cells, electrified-wire perimeters and watchtowers. It had been put at Isselhorst's disposal, so that the anticipated influx of Waldfest captives could be 'processed'. But for those destined for 'termination' – first and foremost the Maquis – an even darker fate awaited.

A few miles to the south of Schirmek lay a former ski resort. Before the war, Natzweiler had been a place of fun and holidaying. But few visited of their own volition now, or even spoke of it. Under Nazi rule Natzweiler had been transformed into a place of darkness and evil. It was a concentration camp – the only one ever built on French soil – and within its confines tens of thousands would be starved, beaten, tortured and gassed to death.

Natzweiler was one of Hitler's so-called *Nacht und Nebel* camps. In a chilling order issued in response to the rise of the Resistance, Hitler had decreed that all such 'terrorists and enemies of the Reich' were to disappear into the *Nacht und Nebel*, the Night and Fog. They were to be eradicated utterly without trace, so that their loved ones would never learn of their fate. Hitler saw this as the ultimate deterrent to the Maquis: that their every trace would be wiped off the face of the earth.

It was to Schirmek's *Sicherungslager* that the eighty-eight villagers – the Maquis suspects taken captive – were headed. After 'processing' there, many were destined to pass through the dark gates of Natzweiler.

One member of the Op Loyton force had preceded those villagers to Schirmek. The stretcher-bound state of Seymour had made him easy prey. Taken captive in the forest, he had at first faced an execution squad. But a senior German officer had saved him, making it clear that he was wanted alive, for questioning – hence Seymour was the first to arrive at Schirmek's *Sicherungslager*.

He was delivered into the hands of the notorious camp commandant, *Hauptsturmführer* Karl Buck. Buck, a civil engineer by training, had overseen the construction of the camp, and it was very much his baby. He had fought and been wounded in the First World War, losing a leg. Still troubled by his injuries, and a gangrenous infection that refused to heal, Buck used morphine to dull the pain. His tempers were the stuff of legend, and with his pristine white uniform and pencil-thin moustache he cut an unmistakable figure as he stomped around the camp on his false leg, plagued by unpredictable mood swings.

Upon arrival in Karl Buck's domain, Seymour was asked to explain what his winged SF Jedburgh badge might signify. He answered that he was one of a group of paratroopers, making up a 'recce party'. He had no idea what had become of his fellow Special Forces operators, and little sense of what fate awaited him. As a soldier captured in uniform, by rights he should have enjoyed all the protections afforded by the Geneva Convention.

But for now Seymour was presented with a collection of captured radios, code books and explosives, and told to explain exactly what it all might signify. Seymour was left in little doubt what would happen if he refused to talk: life would become very unpleasant for him. As he was left to think things over for a short while, a second British captive was driven through the camp gates.

Injured, but still very much alive, it was Corporal Gerald Davis – Hislop's bulletproof and reliable Phantom operator. Having lost the others during the firefight in the forest, Davis had had the misfortune to place his trust in one of the least trustworthy of locals. He had approached a church and asked for help. The priest, Clement Colin, had offered to contact the Maquis. Instead, he had returned leading a force of Gestapo – hence Davis joining Seymour at Schirmek camp.

Both men were presented with the same ultimatum: tell us all you know, or darkness, pain and bitter death will follow.

Captain Victor Gough – Seymour's fellow Jedburgh – had managed to escape the 17 August firefights unscathed. Via the Alsace Maquis he got a radio message sent back to London, reporting on the devastating impact that Waldfest had had so far, and reflecting what desperate straits he now found himself in as the hunt for the Maquis continued.

'Have no W/T set. Contacted SAS team Loyton here. Got them to arrange arms drop on *Pedal* with you. Could not receive arms – were attacked on DZ – many casualties . . .'

The situation was fast moving and horribly confused. Just five days after parachuting into the Vosges, Captain Gough was on the run with the Maquis and being remorselessly pursued. He'd requested an airdrop of arms onto Pedal – codename for one of their isolated DZs – but they'd been attacked there. And at Druce's hideout, equally dire news would filter in about the fate of his missing men.

Faced with sharing the uncertain food supplies of Père George's chamber pot, Lieutenant LeFranc had suggested they move to an altogether more beneficent protector. Madame Rossi lived with her daughter, Odette, in a tall, shuttered house on the outskirts of Moussey village – the last before the forest took over. Mme Rossi's abode came complete with a giant iron waterwheel, and an unqualified welcome for all who might resist the despised Germans.

Mme Rossi and her daughter were generous of physique, larger than life, and indomitable. They didn't baulk at hiding and feeding Druce and his fellows, in spite of the fact that some

500 German troops were camped out in the village nearby. So high-spirited and full of vitality was Mme Rossi, that Druce suspected she actually thrilled to the danger that sheltering British parachutists inevitably brought.

Her house lay at the confluence of the main valley with a narrow, V-shaped gorge. Beside it ran a path that snaked into the hidden reaches of the forest, making it a perfect hiding place for both Maquis and British soldiers. Mme Rossi was incapable of hiding how much she loathed the enemy. Mirthful and forthright, her house had been searched by the Gestapo numerous times, yet she never once suggested that Druce and his fellows shouldn't hole up there.

'*Oh, la! Les Boches!*' she would trumpet, as she stood over a freshly baked quiche, beefy arms crossed and blue eyes sparkling. 'Boh! Those filthy creatures! They're brutes, that's what they are.'

Then she'd dissolve into peals of laughter. If anyone ever suggested she might be a little quieter, for fear of attracting unwanted attention, she'd roll her eyes and quiver. '*Mon Dieu!*' she'd cry, with renewed indignation. '*Les salauds! A bas les Doryphores!*'

'*Les Doryphores*' were a potato-infesting bug, one of her favourite nicknames for the Germans. '*A bas les Doryphores!*' Down with the potato bugs! And '*Les salauds!*' The bastards.

Mme Rossi was irrepressible and she would not be cowed. Right now her house offered a vital refuge for Druce and the rump of the Op Loyton force. The forests all about were being scoured by the enemy, so there was no way that Druce and party could make for the agreed RV. It was time to lie low.

'The Germans were in and out of there all the time,' Druce remarked of Mme Rossi's abode. 'But she was literally getting us hot food three times a day. She really didn't give a damn about the Germans and she had absolutely no fear, no thought as to her own safety, her own security, and she looked after us better that you'd look after your own children. She was superb.'

With movement largely impossible for British soldiers in uniform, Lieutenant LeFranc offered to make his way to Colonel Grandval's location to try to get a radio message through to London. LeFranc's papers were in order, so he stood a chance of making it. Druce asked him to explain the reasons for the delay in calling in the main body of the Op Loyton force. At the same time he wanted SFHQ to stand by for coordinates for a new DZ, so those reinforcements could be parachuted in.

Nothing seemed to faze Druce, and he had far from given up on Operation Loyton. He viewed the predations of Waldfest as a temporary setback. To his way of thinking, the Vosges remained ideal for launching hit-and-run attacks, and with the influx of enemy troops it had become a wonderfully target-rich environment.

In most battlefield situations, one of the key objectives of any commander is to disrupt the enemy's supply and communications lines, without which no army can function for long. Such attacks fall into two broad categories: either flanking man-oeuvres by the main force, or long-range penetrations by small-scale, independent units. The SAS had been formed in 1941 to fulfil the latter role, hitting enemy supply lines in the North African desert.

At that time, news had been grim for the Allies on all fronts, but the SAS had helped turn those fortunes around. Enemy headquarters camps, transport convoys and aerodromes were hit by surprise, and with enormous success. With the arrival of the American jeep in theatre, such efforts were redoubled, the jeep being an ideal cross-country load carrier and gun plat-form, and perfect for launching the SAS's speciality: the hit-and-run attack.

In the Vosges, Druce's force, scattered and battle-scarred though it might be, sat astride the few road and rail routes that linked the German front line to the heartland of the Reich. Though newly recruited to the Regiment, Druce was no stranger to the SAS's means of waging war. He remained determined to get the right men, machines and weaponry dropped in, so as to wreak havoc.

Following Lieutenant LeFranc's departure on his vital mission, news reached Druce that Robert Lodge was dead. There was some confusion as to how exactly the German-Jew-turned-SAS-veteran had died. His body had been delivered by the enemy to the house of the local priest, Abbé Gassman, who was ordered to dispose of the corpse.

A second body was brought to the priest. As yet unidentified, Abbé Gassman feared it was also that of a British parachutist. Druce decided he needed to go and see for himself. With Mme Rossi's help he dressed himself in the kind of worn and work-manlike clothes a local might wear, and set off on the quarter-mile journey into the village.

Druce had walked these hills before. He spoke French like a native and he figured he could talk his way out of most trouble.

More to the point, the dead and the missing men were *his men*. He may not have known them for more than a few days, but they were soldiers in a unit under his command. Druce felt a burning sense of responsibility; plus he needed to know exactly how many fighters he had left alive.

Druce was also spurred to act by Mme Rossi's description of the key role that Abbé Gassman fulfilled in the village. As with Albert Freine, the gamekeeper-cum-Maquis intelligence chief, the Moussey priest was playing a dangerous and duplicitous game. Ostensibly a 'good Frenchman' and a friend to Nazi Germany, Gassman was in reality the linchpin of the Moussey Resistance.

'Without him,' Mme Rossi commented, darkly, 'things might have turned out very differently around here.'

Moving through the woods under cover of night, Druce made it to the rear of Abbé Gassman's house unchallenged. The Moussey priest seemed remarkably unfazed by the SAS captain's arrival at his back door. Cool as a cucumber, he invited Druce in and insisted he be his guest for dinner. Though they conversed mostly in French, Druce learned that Gassman spoke almost perfect English, and he was immediately intrigued by the man.

Gassman had the air of a cleric of ancient times, when the calling of holy man was more often closely allied to that of a warrior. Tall, lean and cadaverous, his warrior-monk demeanour was softened by a merciful and ready smile, and a gentle humour. Gassman was an intensely human individual. This was a man who had witnessed the very heights and the depths of his fellow man's behaviour, making the risks that he was taking in his present role seem paltry by comparison.

Gassman treated Druce to a hearty dinner, after which the grim details of Lodge's death were recounted. On the evening of 20 August, Lodge's body had been delivered to the church for 'disposal'. Gassman had detailed some loyal churchgoers to dig the grave and assist with the burial. He reckoned that Lodge had been dead for less than twenty-four hours, and he noticed bayonet wounds to his stomach, plus a gunshot wound to the head, seemingly inflicted at close quarters.

At first Druce figured that Lodge, wounded and faced by imminent capture, had taken his own life. 'If he was about to be captured, he might well have committed suicide,' Druce mused. 'The talk of bayonet wounds and things . . . I wouldn't have been at all surprised if Lodge had blown his own brains out. He was a Jew. He knew . . . and I think he would have decided that, *well, it's time to blow my own brains out.*'

From Gassman's description of the second body, it appeared to be that of Gerald Davis, Hislop's fellow Phantom. According to the priest, Davis's corpse had been delivered to the village churchyard after its retrieval from Schirmek. Davis had a small, half-inch-wide bullet hole in the front of his skull, and a large exit wound at the back. Davis too seemed to have been shot in the head at close range.

Druce was beginning to suspect that both men might have been executed under Hitler's top secret and shadowy 'Commando Order', something that had come to the SAS's attention only in recent months.

In the spring of 1944 Lieutenant Quentin Hughes of 2 SAS had parachuted into Italy as part of a team targeting enemy aircraft at San Egido airbase, in the centre of the country. While setting Lewes bombs on the warplanes, one went off prematurely, deafening and blinding him. Hughes was taken captive and treated for his wounds, but once he had recovered his senses he was told that he would be handed over to the Gestapo, for execution as a 'saboteur'.

One of the doctors at the hospital, assisted by a recovering German staff officer – both of whom had befriended Hughes – managed to sneak him aboard a train bound for the main German clearing camp for prisoners of war. They hoped that the long arm of the Gestapo would fail to reach him there. But Hughes, still only partially recovered, had other ideas. Together with an American POW, he jumped the train and they made their way back to the Allied lines.

Hughes had written a report about his experiences, warning in particular about Allied parachutists being branded as 'saboteurs' and handed over to the Gestapo to be shot. That report had landed on the desk of Bill Barkworth, 2 SAS's intelligence officer – the same individual who had given Druce his eleventh-hour briefing. Barkworth had alerted Colonel Franks, and Franks in turn had warned his officers about what fate might await their men if they were ever captured.

But Hughes' report gave only an *inkling* of what might befall those who ended up in enemy hands. In the late summer of 1944, the Allies knew precious little about the machinery of death implemented by the Nazis across so much of occupied Europe. Few had any concept of what a 'concentration camp' might be, other than that these were places where Hitler gathered together and incarcerated those opposed to his regime.

All the same, it made the wearing of a clearly identifiable uniform absolutely vital for those dropped behind enemy lines. Hughes had deployed in old-style battle dress, plus plimsolls and a balaclava. His 'non-standard' appearance had allowed the Gestapo to argue that he had gone into action out of uniform, and thus could not be afforded the treatment extended to bona fide prisoners of war.

If Druce was caught dressed as a villager wandering the streets of Moussey, or dining at the priest's house, he knew he faced almost certain death.

'I realized that if I was caught in civilian clothes, I would have my head chopped,' Druce remarked. 'And frankly, we were all brought up knowing that if you were caught spying you were going to get shot. Of course, the crime of being caught is . . . to get caught.'

It struck Druce that the bodies of Lodge and Davis had been dumped in Moussey almost as a warning to any would-be Maquis: *pour encourager les autres*. But, under Abbé Gassman's guiding hand, the villagers were not about to be turned aside from their path. The Moussey priest proved to be fervently pro-British, and over dinner it became ever more clear why.

'You know I would do anything for the English,' Gassman announced. 'You see, I have only once been to England and it was there that I was made your debtor . . . The English are a very formidable people. I recognised in a flash that we must be formidable too, and that it was possible; above all, that is was possible.'

Serving as a priest in the French Army, Gassman had been at Dunkirk. It was on those war-blasted beaches that he had first witnessed and come to admire the dogged British spirit of resistance; the '*flegme britannique*': the British phlegm, or stiff upper lip, as he called it.

He'd seen British troops under withering fire, but waiting calmly in line on the beach, and he'd begun to wonder whether perhaps all was not lost. He'd waded towards one of the waiting boats as German warplanes tore into them, only to see the private soldier in front of him calmly trying to light his pipe as he stood in the chest-deep water. It was but one of many such examples, and each had helped give Gassman the strength to continue the fight.

But in Britain Gassman had found himself torn. On the one hand he wanted to join the struggle to liberate France, as a soldier; on the other, he felt drawn to his flock: the Moussey parishioners. His loyalty to the village and the Church had finally won through, and Gassman had quietly returned to the Vosges and to his calling. It had been then that he had set about founding the local Resistance.

In truth, Gassman was the linchpin of the Maquis, together with the village mayor, Jules Py. The two men had likewise established a ratline: a network through which downed Allied airmen could be smuggled back to Britain. Few French villagers ever played more of an active role in these two endeavours than did those of Moussey.

But for the war, few outsiders might ever have heard of Moussey. Tucked away from all major roads, its houses trace the course of a small mountain stream running along the valley floor. Before the war some 1,100 villagers lived there, subsisting on farming, forestry and the local textile factory. There was a *mairie* (the mayor's office), a few shops and one or two cafés lining the village street, and Abbé Gassman's church.

On the surface there was nothing to mark this place out as the abode of heroes.

Chapter Seven

It wasn't until 22 August – approaching a week after the launch of Waldfest – that matters began to take a turn for the better for Druce and his men. As Moussey was the heartland of the Resistance, sooner or later the scattered remnants of the Op Loyton advance party were drawn into its embrace.

At dusk, Druce said a fond – and, he suspected, temporary – farewell to Mme Rossi, and set off once more for the forest. Guided by a recently returned Lieutenant LeFranc, he was taken to a midnight rendezvous in the hills above the sleeping village. Camped in the deep woods were the operation's survivors, including downed Canadian airman and now honorary SAS man Lou Fiddick, Jedburgh Victor Gough, Hislop and the baby-faced but fearless SAS Lieutenant, David Dill.

Three men were missing: Lodge and Davis, who Druce knew for sure were dead and buried in the Moussey churchyard, and Hall, who had been killed in the initial firefight by a burst of fire to his chest. With the addition of Fiddick, Druce's party stood at thirteen. It could have been far worse. With thousands of German troops scouring the valleys and the woodlands, it was a wonder that this many had escaped death or capture.

Lou Fiddick sums up the feelings of those gathered in the forest: 'After we came down from the hills after being ambushed . . . I felt fear, attached to a desperation really. Sitting in the woods just outside of Moussey not really knowing which way to turn. David Dill and I lay there for about two days not knowing whether to go ahead or to go back. I think that was one of the worst moments.'

Their forest camp was a rough-and-ready affair, compared to the Maquis log cabin base at Lac de la Maix. It consisted of little more than some branches woven together at head height, with a tarpaulin thrown over for shelter. Vegetation laid on the ground formed a sleeping platform and kept the worst of the chill away. In the damp early morning, and especially after rain, a fire could be kept burning, the smoke mingling with the low cloud and mist.

But there had been little chance to tend such cheering fires over the past few days. Ever since the first attack, Hislop and his group had been on the run, flitting from one makeshift camp to another. They had moved only at night so as to avoid the German troops, who seemed unwilling to set foot in the forests after dark. A Maquis guide would lead the way as they formed a human chain, each holding on to the man in front's belt and shuffling ahead into the impenetrable moon shadows.

This would be the way of things for several days now. Since they were bereft of radios to make direct contact with London, all messages had to be routed via the French underground, who had a wireless set secreted at a top-secret location. After his visit to Abbé Gassman, Druce had every confidence in the ability of the local Resistance to hold firm under Waldfest; sure enough, confirmation was duly received via the Maquis' radio of a planned resupply airdrop.

This time, Druce had chosen a DZ set some 10 miles to the west of Moussey – at Veney, a tiny hamlet just to the east of the village of Neufmaisons – in the hope that this area might be less heavily patrolled by the enemy. He was given the date and time of the airdrop, plus details of a series of coded signals to pass to the aircraft, using torch flashes, to confirm that the DZ was in friendly hands.

For five nights in succession Druce's party waited in the thick tension and darkness on the Veney DZ, flashlights at the ready – but the only aircraft to pass anywhere near them were identified as being German. Lou Fiddick could recognize an Allied warplane by its engine beat alone, and likewise one of the enemy. The sense of disappointment and frustration was becoming unbearable for Druce and his men.

The unfortunate truth – one of which the SAS captain was painfully unaware – was that this vital airdrop had already gone ahead. The much-needed resupply, plus a stick of fresh SAS fighters, had been parachuted in – only they'd been released over a DZ positioned 20 miles to the west of where Druce's force was presently waiting.

Veteran SAS Major Peter Power had landed with his nine men in a clearing set on the fringes of the Meurthe-et-Moselle region, which borders the Vosges. Major Power was a renowned SAS operator with a full squadron of sixty men under his command. He'd picked a crack force for what was supposed to be a crucial resupply mission for Operation Loyton, but he'd ended up being dropped in completely the wrong location.

According to the mission's war diary, the confusion was caused by a series of conflicting messages passed via the French underground to London. 'Captain Druce had requested reinforcements, but . . . his message was confused with another received the same day . . . We had decided to act on the last, as this was the DZ mentioned in the later signal, although it was considerably further from the area where Capt. Druce was thought to be.'

Of course, none of this would prove much consolation to Druce, Hislop, Gough, Fiddick et al, waiting on the Veney DZ for an airdrop that would never materialize.

Major Power's SAS stick, plus the dozens of containers carrying weaponry, food and radios, had landed in a forest clearing, to be received with enormous surprise by the assembled Maquis. They had ringed their DZ with signal fires, anticipating a three-man SOE team to drop from the darkened skies. Instead, they'd got ten SAS and several tonnes of war materiel.

Major Power and his stick had been mistakenly released over a Jedburgh drop zone. This was confirmed fairly shortly when a second aircraft flew overhead and three figures descended by parachute. One, a twenty-stone, bearded giant of a man turned out to be Major Oliver Brown, the commander of Jedburgh Team Alastair and the former chief training instructor of the unit.

Having gathered the scattered resupply containers, Major Power rendezvoused with another Jedburgh officer, Arthur 'Denny' Denning, whose team had long been embedded with the local Maquis. With the Jedburgh officers' help, Major Power took stock of the unexpected situation that he now found himself in.

Druce's force, he knew, was in dire straits. He had a reasonable fix on their location: they were camped out in the forests somewhere around Veney. While he and his men could hardly manhandle the supplies across the rugged mountains that lay in between, they could at least try to get to Druce, so as to bolster his beleaguered party.

Sensing perhaps how difficult that push eastwards might prove, Colonel Franks sent a radio message ordering Major Power to make the best of a bad job. He was to stay put and to work with the local Maquis to sow chaos in the enemy's rear. That signal was never received. Leaving Major Denning to sort out the vast heap of weaponry and stores, and to distribute it around a very eager Maquis, Major Power prepared to lead his force east into the forest.

The 32-year-old Major Power's full name was Peter Lancelot John Le Poer Power. A former tea planter from what was then Ceylon (modern-day Sri Lanka), he'd already been awarded a Mention in Dispatches during SAS operations in Italy and a Military Cross (MC) during a more recent mission in Normandy. He sported a scar on one cheek, the result of a bullet wound received in North Africa, which made his features seem both stronger and more inscrutable. If anyone could get through to relieve Druce, it was Major Power MC, but in pushing eastwards he would be heading into the jaws of Waldfest.

Prior to setting out, the SAS major decided to strike a first blow. Working on information supplied by the Maquis, he 'selected as the two best bombing targets an SS HQ at Vincey, and a dump of 3 million litres of petrol, at Nomexy'. He radioed through their coordinates to London, and each was hit by an RAF bombing raid.

'Four hundred SS were killed while parading to move out,' Major Power reported of the first target in the mission war diary. And of the second: 'The petrol was all destroyed, and the glows of the fires could be seen over two successive nights.'

Op Loyton had drawn its first blood. The second strike wasn't long in coming.

Using the plastic explosives and timers delivered in the misplaced airdrop, Major Denning and his Maquis began to make mischief. Under cover of darkness, small charges were dropped into the petrol tanks of German ammunition trucks parked up at a nearby military depot. Fitted with twelve-hour delays, they detonated the following morning, the powerful blasts transforming the now-busy base into a seething fireball.

In the blistering conflagration – the burning petrol 'cooked-off' the ammunition in a series of massive explosions – and the firefight that followed, the Germans suffered some eighty casualties. By way of retaliation, their forces surrounded the nearby village of St Remy-aux-Bois, which they suspected of being a hotbed of Maquis activity, and torched it.

Meanwhile, Major Power and his nine SAS men were pushing eastwards on foot. Driven by a burning sense of urgency, the major had managed to borrow enough bicycles from the Maquis to enable his force to up their pace considerably, but taking to the open road while dressed in British uniform increased the risk factor exponentially.

What Major Power needed right now was a reliable guide,

one who knew the back routes and the forest tracks that might lead his party safely through the mountains. While camped in the thick cover of the forest some 20 miles west of Druce's Veney hideout, Major Power met up with a young Maquis girl called Simone, whose reputation amongst the Vosges Resistance had come to rival that of the legendary Jeanne d'Arc.

Barely seventeen years of age, with golden hair and delicate features, Simone combined the grace of a deer with the strength of an ox. Her stunning looks, legendary endurance over the hills, plus her courage and skills as a mountain woman, were coupled with the kind of innate sense for danger more commonly found in a wild animal. Simone offered to guide Major Power through the forests of Baccarat, over the closely guarded River Meurthe, and into the very heart of the Vosges highlands.

With Simone taking up the lead, Major Power's force struck eastwards with a renewed sense of purpose. But it was now that they received a surprise radio message. According to the war diary, it ordered their force 'to blow up railway Lunéville – St. Dié at all costs'. *At all costs*: such a missive could not be ignored, no matter how pressing the rendezvous with Druce might be.

The town of St. Dié lay 20 miles south-west of Druce's area of operations, and the railway offered the enemy a major resupply route through the Vosges Mountains. Major Power decided to split his force. He sent a team of four under one of his best operators, Lieutenant J. McGregor, to sabotage the railway and to block it with a blown-up train. He was to follow on only once that had been achieved. Major Power would continue to push east, to RV with Druce.

By the time McGregor's force had laid multiple charges along the Lunéville–St. Dié railway line, German units with machine gun posts had taken up positions guarding every bridge spanning the River Meurthe. The route east was now closed to them. Thus McGregor resorted to doing what came naturally to many an SAS operator: causing havoc to the enemy wherever his small band of warriors might find them.

In one instance they felled a massive pine tree to block a major road. The SAS were trained to target high-ranking German officers, for little spreads more terror and confusion amongst the ranks than witnessing your commanding officer getting blown away. In the ensuing ambush McGregor's force wiped out a senior German commander and his entire entourage. 'Carbines scored a ½ inch group in the officer's head,' McGregor reported, reflecting how accurately he had been targeted.

But McGregor's supplies were running desperately low. 'Tightened our belts and took Benzedrine,' reads his classic war diary entry.

Hunted by an enraged enemy, running low on ammo and explosives, and constantly weakened by lack of food, the tiny force seemed to stumble into Germans at every turn. McGregor decided he had no option but to lead his men towards the only place of relative safety, if they could make it: west towards the Allied lines.

Meanwhile, under Simone's guidance, Major Power was still pressing eastwards in an effort to reach the beleaguered Op

Loyton force. And at their Veney DZ things were looking black indeed for Druce and his men.

There had still been no resupply airdrop, and Druce's force was constantly being harried by the enemy. Far from chasing a rag-tag army of soldiers retreating in disarray across the German border, the SAS found they were very much the hunted in the Vosges.

'We were really boxed in trying to save our own skins,' Druce remarked. 'The Germans had sent a division from Strasbourg to find us and we were pretty oppressed . . . I was only twenty-three and at that age you don't really think too hard about what you are doing. But pressure affects men in different ways.'

Matters weren't helped by the fact that the ranks of the Maquis were awash with wild rumour, much of which was terribly dark. 'There were fantastic reports of dead, wounded and prisoners,' recorded Druce in the war diary. 'Also horrible rumours of Sergeant Seymour having (a) shot himself, (b) been shot and (c) been bayoneted to death. All these stories put us all on our guard.'

And the pressure kept mounting. At a 24 August meeting, *Standartenführer* Isselhorst and his deputies decided to 'industrialize' Waldfest: the deportations of the 18th were to be expanded across all villages of the high Vosges, until the Resistance had been utterly crushed. Such a policy was driven by a directive issued by Himmler to his SS and *Wehrmacht* chiefs of staff, in which they were ordered to defend the western wall of the Vosges to the last man.

On the night of 26–27 August, Druce was certain he heard

an aircraft flying over the Veney DZ at low altitude. He consulted Lou Fiddick, who assured him it was a Stirling – a four-engined heavy-lift bomber often used for glider-towing and resupply duties. The men rushed into the open with their torches and signalled for all they were worth, but no parachutes came drifting out of the clear, starlit skies.

Following night after night of repeated no-shows, morale was reaching an all-time low. It was even affecting Druce – a commander possessing otherwise unshakeable self-possession and poise. Druce was desperate to hit back and strike a blow against the enemy, and to turn the hunters into the hunted.

'Feeling very depressed and very helpless,' Druce recorded in his 29 August war diary entry, 'and with strong temptation of going off and shooting up whatever we could find'.

Druce wasn't alone in feeling so disempowered. Jedburgh Captain Gough had been tasked to arm and equip the Maquis for war, but with the skies above the Vosges remaining stubbornly empty of Allied aircraft, he had failed to deliver on his mission. Understandably, the pressure – and the sense of disappointment – was getting to him, as reflected in the increasingly desperate messages he was sending to SOE headquarters.

'Arms, ammunition, grenades urgently needed for 600 men. Can take maximum of 70 containers. Send also Jed Set, 2 rucksacks. Area getting hotter daily.'

'Have no W/T set . . . Could not receive arms – were attacked on DZ – many casualties. Team Loyton having resupply drop here in few days. Please contact them and send me rucksack and further 100,000 Francs. Food difficult.'

'Do not drop . . . tonight. DZ in Boche hands.'

The Op Loyton force had been on the ground for well over two weeks now, and Druce and his men were beginning to starve. Under the iron fist of Waldfest, free movement was banned, which meant that there were few opportunities for villagers to bring food to those in the forests.

More to the point, the villagers had little to spare and they too were going hungry. 'You could go down and ask for a couple of potatoes from a dear old lady,' Druce remarked, 'but that doesn't go far when trying to feed eighty to one hundred men.'

Eventually, Druce and his fellows managed to corral an ancient-looking and emaciated cow. They shot the wretched beast and tried to gut and joint it, but none amongst their number was much of a butcher. It was the toughest meat any had ever had to chew on, but at least it was food.

With no reliable means of making radio contact, Druce couldn't even be certain which of his reports were getting through to SF Headquarters. Just how much did Colonel Franks know? Did he understand how mission expectations and the reality on the ground had proved so utterly mismatched? Did he realize what his men would be getting into if further SAS were dropped into the Vosges? Druce remained convinced that their mission was achievable, but he wanted his commanding officer to be fully in the picture before committing more men and materiel to such a challenging theatre of war.

'What he was coming to and what he expected to come to were two quite different things,' Druce remarked. In a sense, he felt he had failed in the task that his colonel had set him. 'He was expecting to come to an organized headquarters, some-where in the hills away from the Germans, which he could use, which could be supplied and re-supplied and which he could operate out of.'

The reality was far different. 'We had to be on the move all the time . . . If you had a parachute drop of arms in the valley, to get it up the hill was a major operation in itself. Then to move it again would have been totally impossible.'

In an effort to get a clear message through, Druce sent one of his French SAS officers, Captain Lesseps, east on foot to cross over to the Allied lines. He was to give Colonel Franks a full briefing on what he would be committing to in the Vosges, for Druce felt that the 2 SAS Commanding Officer had to be forewarned.

But events were about to overtake such efforts in the most unexpected of ways.

Chapter Eight

On the evening of 30 August 1944 a suspicious figure was spotted by Druce and his men. What drew their attention was his decidedly odd behaviour. He was carrying a basket and kept bending to inspect the undergrowth, as if collecting mushrooms. Nothing so unusual there: the forests of the Vosges were rich in edible fungi, if you knew how to identify them. What made it all so bizarre was what followed on the man's heels: *a German patrol.*

It looked to Druce almost as if the 'mushroom collector' was leading the enemy towards his makeshift camp. A short and savage exchange of fire ensued, but with the SAS in the cover of the forest and with darkness falling, the enemy showed little inclination to venture further into the uncertain woodland. Druce grabbed the chance to send some of his men around the flanks to seize the 'mushroom picker' and to hold him for questioning.

He claimed to be a Frenchman called Fouch, though the name sounded more German to Druce. Fouch swore blind he was a local villager and a bona fide 'mushroomer', but before the SAS captain could question him fully some Maquis arrived with urgent news. Breathless, they came with an important message from Colonel Grandval (Maximum): an airdrop was due that very night, for sure.

With a German patrol in the vicinity, Druce reasoned that great care would need to be taken to defend the Veney DZ. A wall of steel would have to be thrown around it. The location of their camp was clearly compromised, so he ordered his men to abandon it, pack everything and to make directly for the DZ. The Maquis, who were located in a sister encampment, were to follow as soon as they could strike camp and move.

The suspect, Fouch, was placed under guard and marched towards the DZ. Recently, Druce's force had been bolstered by the arrival of a handful of escaped Russian prisoners of war. They were tasked with keeping a close watch over Fouch. Druce and Fiddick went forward to recce the DZ – an open, grassy area lying between two dark fingers of forest. They crawled around the grassland in the gathering darkness, but could detect no obvious signs of an enemy presence.

'I was very anxious to get clear of the field as quickly as possible,' Druce remarked. 'It was dangerously close to the Germans, but it was all that we had.'

At three o'clock on the morning of 1 September the faint drone of an approaching aircraft was heard. To Fiddick's finely attuned ear it was most definitely British. The shadowy form appeared overhead, like a great black bat swooping out of the night. Hurriedly, the agreed recognition signal was beamed to the aircraft, and an answering signal was seen flashing from its hold. With a mounting sense of excitement the beleaguered soldiers figured that the long-awaited airdrop was finally on.

The lone aircraft made a ponderous turn and came around for its run-in. Druce, Hislop, Gough, Fiddick, Dill and all waited anxiously as the tension built to unbearable levels. All it would take was for the Germans to attack the DZ and the aircraft might abort the drop, or the resupply be captured. Not a man amongst Druce's force was willing to give up these precious supplies: they would fight to the death to get them in.

As the aircraft passed overhead there was a distinctive crack in the skies above, and the first chute blossomed silver-white in the moonlight. Dark silhouettes floated earthwards, but to the surprise of the waiting soldiers the initial drop didn't consist of resupply containers at all. Instead, one of the first shadowy shapes turned out to be Colonel Brian Franks, leading a stick of SAS reinforcements.

Franks had jumped with twenty-three men. It was a hugely daring move by the 2 SAS Commander. Leaving veteran SAS man Major Sandy Scratchely in charge at headquarters, he'd opted to parachute into a volatile region deep behind enemy lines, with no transport and surrounded by the enemy. He'd done so as good as blind, for few of Druce's warning messages had got through.

Colonel Franks landed in a heap pretty much at Lou Fiddick's feet. He righted himself, gathered in his chute and eyed the Canadian-airman-turned-SAS-fighter suspiciously. This certainly wasn't a figure that Colonel Franks recognized, though he did appear to be wearing the SAS insignia.

'Hello, who the hell are you?' Franks demanded of Fiddick.

Fiddick gave a hurried explanation as to how he'd ended up with Druce's force, whereupon Franks formally invited him to join 2 SAS.

'Don't worry, you'll learn as you go along,' Franks told him. 'Now, where are the porters?'

In a sense it was a fair question: tonnes of supplies were even now being kicked out of the aircraft, as it made another pass over the DZ. Figures dashed about, searching for the resupply containers as they fell. Druce ordered his men to redouble their vigilance, while he took Colonel Franks into the cover of the trees to give him a hurried heads-up.

Druce was gripped by a certain sense of unease. 'I felt we'd let him down pretty badly,' Druce recounted. 'We were sent in to do a job, which was to bring in a large number of people to operate, and we had failed dismally. We had not achieved any of the objectives . . . Whether it was our fault or not wasn't the point.'

Druce was being overly harsh on himself, and he needn't have worried about his commanding officer's reaction. Franks – tall, lean, athletic and the archetypal unflappable commander – would prove clear-headed and decisive, and he instantly comprehended the situation. It was the measure of the man.

'He quickly appreciated we had been given a bum steer right from the start,' Druce remarked. 'He was imaginative, quick to understand and ready to do anything. He understood the picture and was always cool; always ready to listen.'

The arrival of Colonel Franks massively boosted morale, and galvanized all of the men ahead of the coming action. But for now, things were about to go seriously awry at the Veney DZ.

As the resupply containers started to thud and thump into the grassy terrain, one promptly exploded. Carrying a load of PE, fuses and detonators, it proceeded to cook-off, spontaneously combusting in a massive fireworks display. On the opposite side of the DZ, one of the panniers collided with some trees and it too burst into flames.

If the Germans weren't aware of the drop before, they most certainly would be now. Worse still, amidst all the confusion caused by the explosions, Fouch – the 'mushroomer' and suspected German spy – grabbed a Sten gun and made a run for it. Fouch's Russian guards yelled out a warning in German – the only language they spoke apart from their native Russian.

At the cries of, '*Achtung! Achtung!*' the Maquis feared the enemy had discovered the DZ, and they opened fire. In the ensuing melee one of their men was injured. As Fouch tried to make good his escape, bolting for the open ground, Druce knew for sure that he couldn't be allowed to make it to the German lines.

'One couldn't allow him to escape,' Druce remarked. 'By that time not only was he the suspect traitor, but he also knew exactly what had gone on with this landing. Clearly he had to be removed . . . I have no qualms about having shot him.'

Druce had charged after Fouch and gunned him down. That done, he'd just about managed to calm things and restore order at the DZ, when a horrifying series of screams rent the darkness. It turned out that one of the Maquis – who, like Druce's men, were starving hungry – had mistaken a lump of plastic explosives wrapped in greaseproof paper for some type of cheese. He'd torn off a ravenous mouthful and swallowed it, before realizing his mistake.

Wartime PE contained arsenic. The maquisard was in a terrible state. He'd consumed a lethal dose, and in his death throes he was writhing and twisting with agony.

'It was terminal for him,' Druce recounted, 'and he was screaming like nothing on earth. It was really very uncomfortable . . .'

That maquisard was the second man that Druce had to shoot dead that evening. The first he had gunned down as a suspected traitor; the second was a mercy killing.

With dawn fast approaching, it was of utmost urgency that they vacate the DZ and find somewhere safe to establish a new base. The last of the parachutes were got rid of and Druce began to muster his greatly enlarged force in preparation for moving out. With the new contingent of SAS, there were some thirty-five Special Forces fighters on the ground now. This was a force to be reckoned with.

The food, ammunition, explosives, warm clothing and sleeping bags would transform the lives of those who had been on the ground for approaching three weeks. But, almost of more importance, Colonel Franks had brought several new Jed Sets with him, which meant that direct and reliable radio communications could once again be established with London.

Captain Hislop's Phantoms had been reinforced by a three-man unit, commanded by Lieutenant Peter Johnsen, who had already seen action in occupied France. In the immediate aftermath of D-Day, Johnsen had parachuted into Normandy to call in Typhoon ground attack aircraft, so as to hit German trucks and trains. He'd ended up rescuing one hundred Allied POWs, for which he had won a Mention in Dispatches.

In light of the earlier loss of all their radios, Hislop decided that they would disassemble the Jed Sets and carry them on their person, stuffed deep in pockets and secured in their webbing. That way, if they did have to go on the run and ditch their heavy packs, they wouldn't risk leaving their precious radios behind.

At dawn Druce's force got on the move. They hurried across the open expanse of the road leading into Veney, pushing east towards the dense, rolling woodlands of the Forêt de Reclos. Even as they moved out, the terrain to their backs resounded to the crump of powerful explosions. The enemy had brought up heavy armour to shell the camp that the SAS had just vacated, at the fringes of the Veney DZ. The force had got moving in the nick of time.

They climbed steadily, taking to the high ground above Celles-sur-Plaine village. There Druce figured they could establish a new base in some degree of safety. But the Bergen-loads of fresh supplies proved too heavy to haul up the precipitous slopes, and all non-essential kit had to be dumped in the undergrowth. Druce prioritized the bare necessities: food, ammo, warm clothing, radios.

'We had to reconnoitre a new place to go to, to try to set up camp,' Druce remarked, 'and there were always Germans on the main roads to make us be wary. When we were at the top of the hill it was five miles down to the bottom. It felt like fifty by the time you'd climbed up to the top of that hill, where we had somewhere considered safe from the Germans.'

Their new mountaintop base was chosen with the help of Roger Souchal, the seventeen-year-old aspiring-lawyer-turned-SAS-guide. Souchal had attached himself to Colonel Franks, seemingly irrevocably. Franks appeared to have that kind of effect on people: inspiring loyalty, courage and selfless devotion, largely by example.

Colonel Franks had only been with the SAS a matter of months, but he'd fought alongside them in Italy when serving with the commandos, winning the Military Cross (MC). Neither hidebound nor constrained by convention, he'd also served with the Phantoms, and was another close friend of the Phantom and actor, David Niven.

Niven and Franks had grown up together on the Isle of Wight, forming a sailing club in their teens. They'd made a decent profit in the first year, investing it all in booze, and had been found one morning face-down in a patch of nettles. Crucially, Franks had a combination of bravery and maverick daring that suited the Regiment. And, in his command of 2 SAS, Franks seemed to encapsulate the Regiment's motto, first coined by their founder, David Stirling, three years earlier: 'Who Dares, Wins.'

In theory, Franks could have called off Operation Loyton in light of the adverse conditions encountered on the ground. Operation Instruction No. 38 – the order that defined Loyton – stated the following, regarding Druce's advance force: 'If this party were successful and targets were available and aircraft re-supply proved easy, permission to increase the party up to one Squadron would almost certainly be given.'

By Druce's own admission the advance party had been far from successful, and while there were targets aplenty on the ground, resupply by air had proved hugely problematic. Franks would have had every excuse to cancel Op Loyton, but it wasn't in the man's nature to take a backward step. Quite the contrary; by going in to lead things himself, Franks had signalled what a massive personal investment he was making in the present mission.

On the high ground above Celles-sur-Plaine, a makeshift base was hewn out of the bush. The SAS colonel called a conference with the Maquis leaders, as a result of which several maquisards were attached to the SAS to act as porters, cooks and general helpers. It was agreed that the Maquis would operate separately from the SAS, but work in close collaboration wherever practicable.

The Jedburgh officer, Captain Victor Gough, was to serve as the link between the two outfits. Colonel Franks had also brought with him Captain Chris Sykes, one of 2 SAS's most experienced intelligence officers. Sykes would be Franks' liaison with the Maquis, working closely with their gamekeeper-cum-intelligence-officer, Albert Freine.

The Op Loyton war diary makes it clear how good the SAS's intelligence network in the region was. 'There is a group of about 20 natives in this area who are trustworthy, intelligent and working under SAS direction gathering intelligence. With this net and other means, it is believed that any enemy information requested from the area can be supplied.'

Captain Sykes was particularly suited to this task. Recruited into the SOE in June 1940, Sykes was posted to Tehran under the cover of being a diplomat. He'd worked before the war as a diplomat in the British embassy in Berlin, so was well prepared for the role. In 1942 he was sent to Cairo and found himself largely without work, so he volunteered for the SAS.

Before the war he'd studied in France, spending a year in Paris, writing – he was also a novelist in civilian life – and he spoke fluent French. For the past several months prior to deploying to the Vosges, he'd worked with a group of French officers, helping form and then shape the operations of one of the French SAS squadrons. He'd also won a Mention in Dispatches immediately after the Normandy landings.

Sykes considered himself to be a true friend of France. As he knew well, the French longed for there to be an uprising of the Maquis so widespread that they would play a major role in liberating the country, constituting an act of Gallic defiance that would enable the French to rediscover their pride and self-respect.

Sykes hoped to make that a reality here in the Vosges, but his initial impressions of the Maquis weren't overly positive. 'We were greeted by a host of untrained, unarmed, expectant and physically exhausted young men,' Sykes remarked. Their only idea of military strategy was to assemble in large groups and to start 'firing what few weapons they possessed at every rustle of a rabbit.'

Yet in spite of this, Sykes felt that the Maquis were being surprisingly effective in keeping the forests free of German troops. In fact, they were doing so largely *because* they were so untrained.

'Having no concept of "fieldcraft" they continued to fire their weapons at every starting rabbit or hare.' As a result the crackle of automatic weapons was heard daily and across a wide swathe of territory. 'This persuaded the Germans that the Maquis were an immense and heavily armed force, and in consequences they did not enter the woods.'

Sykes homed in on two Maquis bands that he considered to possess the most promise. The first was led by a former professional soldier called Joubert. A simple, unassuming, modest young man, Joubert had drawn a band of like-minded fighters to him. In spite of their youth they were remarkably well disciplined, and they chose their time and place of attack most carefully. Whenever morale flagged, Joubert would opt to launch a stinging ambush to lift the spirits of his young guns.

The second Maquis leader could not have been more different. Etienne was twice Joubert's age and he had the most villainous appearance imaginable. He spoke French with a terrible, guttural German accent, walked with an ape-like gait, and wore a peaked black cap pulled low over his eyes. His Maquis band was shaped in his image. None looked younger than fifty, and they seemed more like an assemblage of tramps and wizened wizards than the remarkably effective maquisards that they were.

Etienne's men were very fond of the bottle. Their actions were often drink-fuelled and spontaneous, though no less effective because of it. They roamed the hills incessantly, they knew the forest like the back of their hands, and no German was ever safe from their murderous intent. It was due in large part to Joubert and Etienne's operations that the enemy believed they were living in the midst of a massive uprising.

With Franks and his reinforcements having parachuted in, it was time for the Op Loyton force to go on the offensive. The first actions consisted of tentative, probing missions, as the SAS colonel sought to get a feel for the enemy. Across the Vosges all motorized transport had been requisitioned by the Germans, so anything moving on the roads was bound to be enemy. Franks sent out small parties of four to lay explosives on the key thoroughfares that cut through the mountains.

The SAS used devices euphemistically named 'tyre-bursters' by their inventors – the gadget people at the SOE. SOE agents had retrieved samples of rock types from key areas of planned Maquis and SAS activity. Working from those samples, the SOE boffins had manufactured plastic explosive charges that mimicked the texture, colour and shape of the rocks commonly found in each region. Laid on a road, they appeared to be nothing more than a few scattered stones, until a tyre or track passed over them, detonating the powerful charge.

Reluctant to stop there, the SOE had even produced tyre-bursters that mimicked dog turds and horse droppings, reasoning that no self-respecting German would want to stop their vehicles to remove a pile of poo from the road. But arguably the most infamous such device was the 'exploding rat', about which the SOE instruction manual is largely self-explanatory:

'A rat is skinned, the skin being sewn up and filled with PE to assume the shape of a dead rat. A standard No. 8 primer is set in the PE...' The exploding rat was actually designed to be dropped into the coal supply of a steam train. The stoker would shovel the 'dead rat' into the furnace, along with the coal. The rat would then detonate, and the blast would penetrate the high-pressure steam boiler, which in turn would create a devastating explosion.

Equipped with their tyre-bursters, four-man recce parties were sent to find and identify the enemy's armour, fuel dumps and rail links. Franks urged his commanders to launch whatever opportunistic strikes they could against 'the grey lice', as he'd nicknamed the enemy – for so they appeared, from his mountaintop vantage point, as they moved along the valley floor.

The radio messages sent through to London during that first week of September reflected how the newly invigorated Special Forces operators were gearing up for action, and how wide-ranging were their patrols.

Observed line railway St. Dié–Saales completely blocked with stationary trains. Ideal target RAF.

7 troop trains at Jarville sheet 14G 8709 11.00 hrs 3 Sept.

Source Alsace agent, second September. German counter-attack using GAS planned for ten September. Troops at Colmar exercising in MASKS. 3,500 troops Mutzig. Further information . . . 700 Gestapo arrived tunnel Ste. Marie-aux-Mines. Hitler Jugend digging in area. 50 petrol tankers road Châtenois-Selestat.

That last message alerted London to a suspected poison gas attack. During the war the Nazis had developed the fearsome nerve agents sarin, tabun and toman. Even in the autumn of 1944 the Allies still had no effective defences against such agents – largely because they didn't even know that they existed. So advanced were these deadly chemical weapons that they are still stockpiled by the world's major powers, although their use is supposedly banned under international treaties.

As the Allied advance threatened the Fatherland itself, so the fear grew that Hitler would resort to using such weapons in a desperate last stand. The radio message warning of the gas attack also warned that the 'Hitler Jugend' – the Hitler Youth – were digging defences in the area, which was all part of Himmler's initiative to bolster the western wall of the Vosges.

John Hislop was one of those tasked by Franks to go out and ensure that Himmler's defences could be breached.

'If you and Peter would like a bit of variety you can go out this evening and mine a road,' Franks suggested. By 'Peter' he was referring to Lieutenant Peter Johnsen, Hislop's fellow Phantom who had recently rescued the hundred Allied POWs.

By a 'bit of variety', Franks meant a break from signals work. And in truth, Hislop was bored of being tied to his Jed Set and sending the regular morning and evening skeds. Hislop – not long ago accused of having *a regrettable lack of military aptitude* – jumped at the chance of a bit of action. Franks showed him and Lieutenant Johnsen the exact point on the map where he wanted the charges laid.

A quick lesson from an SAS sapper refreshed Hislop and Johnsen's knowledge of how to lay the explosives, fuses and wires. Bergens packed, they set out into a clear, crisp night. As they took the rough, winding track that led in the direction of Moussey, Hislop found he was remarkably relaxed. By now he was a comparative veteran of the Vosges, and he'd also developed a constant background alertness of mind – a vigilance that was a ever-present companion for those fighting in such territory.

They passed an area where some woodcutters had been at work. The scent of freshly cut pine was rich in their nostrils: tangy, clean, lemony. It reminded Hislop of riding through such woodland at home, before Europe was consumed by war. It seemed an unimaginably long time ago, and a world away from where they were now.

As they wended their way down from the hills, their route took them close to Mme Rossi's place of abode. They made their way carefully around her property and tapped gently at the rear entrance. Mme Rossi opened cautiously, but once she realized who it was she threw the door wide.

'At first we thought it was the Germans,' she declared, as – unbidden – she went about warming some food on the stove. 'They were here earlier, asking a lot of questions and looking around . . . But they won't come back now it is dark!'

The kitchen was dimly lit and the windows shuttered tight, so that not a chink of light escaped: no outsider would be able to spy on the Madame and her daughter, and whatever company they might be keeping. Many had been the time when the two redoubtable Frenchwomen had had to hurry their British guests out of the back door, as German visitors hammered on the front.

With their Bergens of explosives propped by the kitchen table, Hislop and Johnsen awaited the inevitable meal. Over a dish of potatoes – simple fare, but delicious to those surviving on sparse military rations heated over an open fire in the mountains – Hislop and Johnsen were given the low-down on German troop dispositions, checkpoints and places of particular danger, plus any obvious targets.

Once they'd eaten their fill, the two men gathered up their means of waging war and slipped out quietly, with Mme Rossi's whispers of '*Bon courage!*' ringing in their ears.

The night was still and quiet. Hislop and Johnsen flitted through the deserted streets of Moussey as silent as ghosts. Two miles out of the village, they came to a halt. To their left they could hear the pounding of metal on metal. There was the glimmer of arc lamps breaking through a skeletal black lattice-work of trees.

The two men crept closer, sticking to dense patches of under-growth and the thickest darkness. Once they were near enough for voices to be heard, they settled down to listen. Soon enough they recognized the language as German. A maintenance unit was at work carrying our repairs to some heavy armour. Position duly noted, Hislop and Johnsen made their careful way back to the road.

They pressed on. Eventually, only the sounds of nature broke the night. It was the early hours of morning by the time they reached the target location – a road junction.

Hurriedly, they laid their explosive charges, before melting back into the darkness.

Chapter Nine

Twenty-five miles to the west of Colonel Franks' mountaintop base, Jedburgh Team Archibald's Major Arthur 'Denny' Denning had been waging a highly successful form of guerrilla warfare. Having armed his Maquis with the weaponry dropped with SAS Major Peter Power's stick, the Jedburgh major and the local Maquis had fought a series of running battles in the western foothills of the Vosges.

General Patton's forces were presently some way to their west, and bogged down in vicious warfare. At one stage Denning and the Maquis had seized the village of Charmes, killing some forty Germans. They'd taken possession of the bridge over the River Moselle, intending to hold it until Patton's armour could punch their way through and cross this major waterway.

But at the last minute, Denning and the Maquis were driven back by 400 German infantry, supported by tanks. The worst of their injured had to be abandoned.

'One or two wounded were left behind, and were later found with their heads crushed in, probably by rifle butt,' Major Denning recorded in the Team Archibald war diary. The dead had been left for all to see, to 'show what happened to terrorists' – which was what the Germans had branded the Maquis.

Should one of the Jedburghs fall into enemy hands, doubtless he would also be branded a 'terrorist', and face a similar fate. During the fierce fighting Major Denning had been shot in the thigh, but he had carried on regardless, earning a fearsome reputation amongst the Maquis.

Of course, he was fortunate enough to be operating in an area where the allegiances of the locals were mostly with the Allies. Even so, in recent days Major Denning and his Maquis had been forced onto the back foot. 'Conditions became so impossible that [Maquis] activity, other than information services, was instantly and ruthlessly quelled,' Denning wrote, in the war diary.

As the Germans grew increasingly desperate, so their responses to Resistance activity became ever more brutal. In particular, Denning feared that any attempts at operating further east – moving into Op Loyton territory – would prove disastrous. 'Reprisals, shootings, burning and deportations became too common to attempt to arm any men further east.'

But somewhere further east, and sandwiched between Major Denning's Maquis and the Op Loyton force, were SAS Major Power and his unit, although nothing had been heard of them for approaching two weeks now. In the depths of the Vosges Mountains, Major Power and his small band of SAS men seemed to have fallen off the face of the earth.

Colonel Franks' Op Loyton force was about to elicit a similarly violent reaction to that faced by Major Denning and his Resistance fighters. Their road-mining activities, small-scale hit-and-run attacks, plus the RAF air strikes that his men had called in, had stirred the cauldron of Waldfest mightily.

Standartenführer Isselhorst's SS and Gestapo units were determined to ensure that any Resistance activity was 'instantly and ruthlessly quelled'.

On 4 September Colonel Franks and Captain Druce were busy arranging a major airdrop of arms for the Maquis. With Colonel Grandval's help they'd worked out exactly what was needed to equip an initial force in excess of 1,000 men. Once that many Maquis were armed and trained to use their weaponry, Franks would be ready to switch to more daring, large-scale sabotage and guerrilla operations.

But before that airdrop could happen, the Alsace Maquis made a fatal move. While Joubert's young fighters were far too shrewd to launch themselves into such a rash endeavour, and Etienne's old drunkards far too wise and canny, there were still plenty of partisans whose trigger fingers remained decidedly itchy. On the afternoon of 4 September several hundred men of the Alsace Maquis launched an ambush that was to have devastating consequences. They hit a lone German truck on the road into Veney, raking it with fire and killing eight soldiers.

The ambush was well executed, apart from the fact that the Maquis had ignored the 'golden rule' of such an attack: always be certain of your route of escape, and always cover your tracks. After destroying the German truck, the Maquis had returned to their base of operations – a deserted farm at Viambois, on the outskirts of the Forêt de Reclos. The Germans tracked them to it, and their response was swift and decisive.

They threw a cordon of steel around the Maquis' position, trapping hundreds – and so a bitter fight to the death began. In the battle for Viambois the Maquis were caught utterly by surprise. The German forces positioned machine guns in the fringes of the forest, and when they opened up on the tumble-down farm, the Maquis were torn apart by intense bursts of fire. Those with weapons tried to fight back, but they were still only lightly armed.

The Alsace Maquis were hopelessly outgunned. It was only by a stroke of good fortune that they weren't utterly annihilated. By chance, a flight of passing Allied aircraft was drawn to the firefight. Seeing the 'grey lice' in action they dived to attack, strafing and bombing the German positions. Those Maquis who could, escaped in the resulting confusion, but scores of wounded were left behind – and they were finished off wherever they had fallen.

Captain Gough – Jedburgh Team Jacob's commander – was one of those who managed to get away. But his Jedburgh colleague, Frenchman Lieutenant Guy Boisarrie, was killed. He suffered a single shot to the head, suggesting that he too may have been captured and summarily executed.

Gough's subsequent radio message reflected the desperate straits he found himself in: the sole member of Team Jacob still at large, harried by a determined and remorseless enemy.

Skye captured 17th August. Reported shot as reprisal . . . Please check with Red Cross. Connaught killed. I am now sole member of Team Jacob. 100 Maquis killed. 100 captured in same battle. Rest dispersed . . .

'Skye' was the code name of Gough's signaller, Seymour. Of course, Seymour had been captured on 17 August, and Gough had heard reports that he had since been executed. 'Connaught' was Boisarrie's code name. Approximately 200 men from the Alsace Maquis were dead or captured – and under Waldfest, 'captured' was as good as dead.

As the Maquis had tried to escape the trap, weapons were thrown into the bush and abandoned. In the eyes of the SAS, the Alsace Maquis had jumped the gun in launching their ill-fated ambush, and they had been punished accordingly. The way the French saw it, their young and spirited fighters were understandably desperate to hit back against the enemy, and the ambush was a natural – if perhaps not entirely prudent – course of action to have taken.

Either way, the results were the same. The effect on the Alsace Maquis – the main body of the Resistance in the area – was little short of disastrous. The Loyton war diary doesn't pull any punches: 'This decisive defeat, due . . . to a poorly conceived commitment of a partially-armed force is believed to have completely broken their spirit and rendered them useless for future efforts.'

The effects of the battle for Viambois spread across the region like ripples from a stone dropped into a still pool. Some Maquis were forced to talk before they were executed. That very evening a company of 'grey lice' was spotted, approaching Colonel Franks' hilltop base. The fifty-odd soldiers were 600 yards away and advancing with great care, which at least gave the Special Forces operators and their Maquis helpers time to make their getaway.

Colonel Franks and his men knew their role here. It wasn't to stand and fight pitched battles with scores of German troops, as the Alsace Maquis had been forced to do; it was better to vanish into the dusk forest to live to fight another day.

Fortunately, that very morning Captain Druce, again dressed in civilian attire – it was becoming something of a habit with him – had crossed the hills heading north, to visit the isolated village of Pierre-Percée. It consisted of a clutch of houses lying at the end of a V-shaped, dead-end valley, with steeply forested slopes crowding in from all sides. At its western edge the village clustered along the shoreline of a beautiful expanse of water – the Lac de la Pierre-Percée – with verdant forest sweeping down to the waterline.

In peacetime Pierre-Percée had been a popular holiday spot, but of course the war had changed all that. Druce met with the village mayor, Monsieur Michel, who confirmed that no Germans had been seen in the area for a month or more. The mayor made it clear to Druce that he and his band of SAS fighters would be very welcome there.

En route back to base Druce tried to steal the car belonging to Fouch, the suspected German spy that he'd shot dead at the Veney DZ. By now it had been confirmed that Fouch had indeed been working for the enemy – which would explain why he'd still possessed a car, when all other motor vehicles had been requisitioned by the Germans.

Druce had failed to nab Fouch's wheels, but did succeed in making it back to Colonel Franks in time to deliver the good news about Pierre-Percée. Franks set out, leading his force north across country toward their planned new base of operations. Behind them, a thick pall of smoke rose from the location they had just vacated, the Germans having torched what remained of their camp.

The men marched all night. It was one of brilliant and ethereal moonlight, so there was little need this time to hold on to the belt of the man in front. The light cast the forest into stark patterns of silver and ebony, tree trunks assuming grotesque shapes as the men passed, their shadows seeming to writhe on the ground.

The new camp was hewn out of the living bush above the lake of Pierre-Percée. Franks' force knocked down a couple of trees, propped them at a 45-degree angle across a horizontal bough, and threw a few canvas groundsheets over the top, forming a makeshift roof. The camp was small-scale, primitive and impermanent – they didn't even bother to dig a latrine – for at any moment the grey lice might appear, at which point they would be on the run again.

For now, Hislop made contact with London headquarters, and sent the prearranged code word, 'Wren' – the signal for the planned arms drop to go ahead. Two Stirlings flew in that night, the first releasing dozens of para-containers over an open field above Pierre-Percée. Each aircraft was packed with enough weaponry to equip a hundred fighters, but with the Alsace Maquis having been decimated in the battle for Viambois, had the arms arrived too late to be of use?

No one knew for sure. It remained to be seen whether the Alsace Maquis would regroup and re-energize themselves, or not. And in the meantime, there were targets aplenty for the SAS.

By the time the first aircraft had finished releasing its load, fingers of ground fog had reached out of the forest and gripped the isolated DZ. The mist thickened, obscuring the lights that

118

Franks' men were using to mark the rallying point. A stick of fourteen SAS reinforcements – led by Colonel Franks' intended second-in-command on Op Loyton, Major Dennis Reynolds – dropped with the supplies, but three men must have been driven off course owing to the terrible visibility. Sergeant Fitzpatrick, plus Troopers John Conway and John Elliot were nowhere to be found. It was as if they had been swallowed up by the cold and clammy fog.

The following morning there were reports that a German patrol had recovered parachutes from the forest to the west of the DZ. Presumably these were the missing men's chutes, as all other debris from the airdrop had been cleared away before daybreak. The three parachutists must have got lost in the fog, and the hope was that they would find their way to the SAS base in due course.

In fact, Trooper Elliot had drifted off course, landing badly and breaking one of his legs. Fitzpatrick and Conway had carried him to what appeared to be the nearest place of sanctuary – a farmhouse on the outskirts of the village of Pexonne. It lay on the far edge of Bois de Bon Repos – the wood of good rest – on the opposite side of the Pierre-Percée lake. But those three men were betrayed by a local Frenchwoman, and captured by one of Isselhorst's infamous *Einsatzkommandos*.

Colonel Franks and Major Reynolds remained unsure of what had happened to them, but there was little time to dwell on their fate. There was a war to fight, and right now, with approaching fifty SAS operators on the ground, well stocked with arms, explosives and ammo, they were a force to be reckoned with.

The day after the airdrop, Franks sent out his first serious ambush party. It was commanded by Lieutenant Ralph 'Karl' Marx, a striking individual whom even Captain Druce – the past master of nonchalance – described as being 'as cool as a cucumber'. At barely eighteen years of age, Marx – a captain both of boxing and tennis at school – had turned down a place at Cambridge University, signing up instead to join the Army at the outbreak of war.

His leadership qualities were quickly recognized and he was sent to Sandhurst for officer training. Posted to the 9th/12th Lancers, he'd been deployed to North Africa and fought in the battles for El Alamein, where he'd first got to hear about the exploits of the SAS. Twenty-two years old by the time he parachuted into the Vosges, Lieutenant Marx was a perfect example of the type whom 'you least expected to be cool and calm, yet turns out to be . . . cool and calm and operated well', remarked Druce.

Lieutenant Marx left the SAS's Pierre-Percée base with nine men armed with their personal weapons, plus two Bren guns – a .303 light machine gun – and eighteen 'tyre-bursters'. They threaded their way south through the Pierre-Percée forest – passing close to their former camp, now burnt out – and at dusk they descended towards the village of Celles-sur-Plaine.

With Allied aircraft controlling the skies over occupied Europe, the Germans had taken to making road movements at night and showing no lights, in an effort to hide from marauding warplanes. One of the main trans-Vosges highways ran through the Celles Valley, constituting a major German supply line. Just to the north of Celles-sur-Plaine lay a major junction, where a side road branched north-west towards the town of Badonviller, some 5 miles away. Come nightfall, six tyre-bursters were laid on all three branches of the T-junction, so that each was covered by a charge.

At ten o'clock that evening two explosions rang out across the Celles Valley. A pair of German troop transports had driven over some innocent-looking rocks scattered across the highway, only for their undersides to be torn apart by the resulting blasts.

By then Marx and his men were well on their way, marching north-west through the night towards their next target. They were making for La Chapelotte, a tiny hamlet lying due north of Celles-sur-Plaine, on the winding road to Badonviller. The site of a major battle during the First World War, the Col de la Chapelotte – the 1,500-foot forested peak that rises above the hamlet – was peppered with heavily fortified bunkers and gun emplacements. Marx figured it would be an ideal spot to find some enemy and ambush them.

Having paused in the dawn forest to eat, and to strip and clean their Bren guns, they approached La Chapelotte to carry out a recce. The SAS soldiers were moving along a path to one side of the road, when quite unexpectedly a German foot patrol emerged from the forest on the far side. Thinking fast, Marx dived into a nearby slit trench, his men piling in after him.

Cries rang out through the still dawn air. '*Kommen Sie hierher! Kommen Sie hierher! Schnell! Schnell!*'

Marx and his party refused to leave their cover. The German troops opened fire. Rounds tore into the wall of trees to the rear of the trench, tearing off chunks of bark and scattering it over the men below. They kept their heads well down and their weapons trained on the enemy. If the Germans advanced across the open ground and got to within killing range, Marx and his men would let rip.

But for now they held their fire. Eventually the Germans must have decided that discretion was the better part of valour. The firing petered out and the grey lice disappeared noisily into the woods heading back towards La Chapelotte.

Marx took to the shelter of the trees, splitting his patrol into two groups. Seven men were to set an ambush on the approach into La Chapelotte, with the two Brens covering the road. He ordered his remaining two fighters to shadow the German patrol, in the hope of springing an ambush on them with their tommy guns.

Marx and the main force slipped into the trench position, which was set some 10 yards back from the road. With their two Brens set firmly on their tripods on the lip, they had a perfect firing position. The road was steep here as it climbed towards the Col de la Chapelotte. Any vehicles coming this way should make for easy targets, as long as that pesky German patrol didn't raise the alarm.

The men waited, hunkered down behind their Brens. 'Fire on my fire,' Marx hissed. 'Fire on my gun.'

There were a series of whispered acknowledgements. Five minutes dragged by. The five became ten, and the tension kept mounting. At any moment the SAS men expected to see an enemy force heading out from La Chapelotte, looking to hunt them down. But then Marx and his men heard it – the faint strains of a struggling diesel engine and the ponderous crunch of gears. A vehicle was approaching.

Shoulders hunched tighter behind the Brens as the distinctive shape of a five-tonne German Army truck crawled around the bend, belching thick diesel fumes. Marx fixed the iron sights of his weapon above the long, raking nose of the truck and its high grill, targeting the centre of the single, flat windscreen. When he opened fire the bullets would tear through the glass and rip into the soft rear of the truck – a combination of wooden planking topped by canvas.

The ambush force waited. The truck crawled closer. Fingers tensed on triggers. Any moment now.

The truck was no more than 30 yards away when Marx let rip. The entire magazine of the Bren – some thirty rounds of .303 inch bullets – was emptied into the cab of the vehicle, shattered glass and debris spinning through the crisp dawn air. The truck slewed to an abrupt halt, lying half off the road, but it came to rest shielded by a mound of earth.

Marx led his men in a dash for higher ground, to bring the shattered vehicle back into their line of fire. By the time they were in position, a few grey-uniformed figures were seen darting into the woods on the far side of the road. Marx and his men covered the truck with their Brens, but there was no further movement or sign of life.

Knowing that the noise of the ambush would have been heard in La Chapelotte, Marx ordered his men back into the cover of the woodland. They moved quickly, heading towards an RV point where they'd stashed their heavy Bergens. Reunited with their packs, the force turned south, pushing along an open track, aiming to put as much distance as they could between themselves and the enemy.

They'd been moving for no more than five minutes before the feared counter-attack came. A force of German troops opened fire from the valley bottom. The range was too great for the fire to be accurate, but a worrying noise could be heard echoing through the trees. It was the baying of dogs.

'Make for the high ground!' Marx ordered. 'Make for the hills!'

He turned due west, aiming to head across country direct to the SAS base, and hoping to lose their pursuers in the thick woodland and over the rugged hills. But as his men dashed into the dark embrace of the forest, three seemed to have misheard him. They rushed off straight down the track that they had been following, and no amount of yelling could bring them back.

Once Marx and his remaining men had covered a few hundred yards, they hit a clearing. He ordered a halt. Below, they could still see the track, and every now and again his three errant men were visible, running hell for leather into the distance. The party on the run consisted of Sergeant Terry-Hall, and Troopers Iveson and Crozier. At their heels were German troops with dogs baying for their blood.

The effective range of the Bren is 600 yards. The Germans were well beyond that, and even if Marx did open fire it would give away their position. He had no option but to set a compass bearing for the SAS base and lead his men west, making for the high ground.

At dusk Marx called a halt. He didn't want to enter the SAS camp before doing a recce, and it would be too dark by the time they got there. The pause was fortunate. Two hours later, long bursts of heavy machine-gun fire cut the air. The noise was coming from what could only be the direction of their base. An hour after that, Marx received a message from Colonel Franks on his Jed Set.

'Do not return to Camp. Further instructions later.'

By dawn the following morning their predicament was clear. Trucks could be heard moving through the Pierre-Percée Valley below, and the hamlet was crawling with the enemy. On the opposite side of their hilltop position, at Celles-sur-Plaine, there were yet more Germans. The enemy was also visible on the road running west to Raon L'Etape, and on their fourth side lay La Chapelotte, where they'd just stirred up a hornets' nest of enemy activity.

Marx and his small force were surrounded on all sides.

Chapter Ten

The heavy machine-gun fire that Lieutenant Marx had heard had indeed signalled an assault on the SAS base. Once again it was largely due to an extraordinary piece of bluff that the Op Loyton force had escaped the trap set for them, and Captain Henry Carey Druce was again at the forefront of it.

On the morning of 9 September Druce had headed into Pierre-Percée on a recce mission, dressed as a local. As he moved into the streets of the tiny hamlet, he found that they were crawling with enemy troops. This was barely five days after moving into an area that the village mayor had confirmed hadn't seen German soldiers for many weeks. It was obvious what the grey-uniformed troops had to be there for.

At one point Druce asked for a light for a cigarette, offering one to the German soldier that he feared was about to challenge him. His apparent self-confidence and 'friendly' demeanour had seen him through.

Recce done, he hurried back to the SAS camp, whereupon Franks ordered the immediate collapse of the base. Barely had the SAS men begun to move when German troops were detected closing in from all sides. Franks' rearguard started taking heavy fire, and it was only due to Druce's early warning that the Op Loyton force managed to make their getaway, and without suffering any casualties.

Only one possible route of escape lay open to them: south across the Celles Valley, towards the DZ upon which Druce and his advance unit had originally landed. From there, the Op Loyton party was repeatedly forced to move, as they looped eastwards through the Lac de la Maix region – the site of their first, 17 August brush with the enemy. They were being chased in circles, and barely managing to remain one step ahead of the enemy.

Finally, on 14 September, they moved into the hills east of Moussey, establishing a firm base in a high-walled gully set to the south of Les Bois Sauvages – the Wild Woods. This densely forested and steep-sided valley is called the Basse de Lieumont – the base of the place of mountains. Basse de Lieumont would become the closest the SAS would have to a permanent operational headquarters in the Vosges.

In an effort to scope out an alternative safe haven, Colonel Franks had dispatched his recently arrived second in command, Major Dennis Reynolds, to check out the area north of Pierre-Percée. Remote, forest-bound and almost devoid of any roads, it seemed to offer the perfect terrain in which to hide a fifty-strong SAS party, plus Maquis guides and helpers. The recently arrived Captain Anthony 'Andy' Whately-Smith – Franks' adjutant – accompanied Major Reynolds on that mission.

But as they had skirted around Pierre-Percée, Reynolds and Whately-Smith ran into a German patrol. In the firefight that followed, the two SAS officers managed to escape, but Major

Reynolds was shot in the forearm. In an incredible act of bravery a French couple sheltered the two British officers, one of whom was seriously weakened by blood loss.

Freddy and Myrhiam Le Rolland were Parisians who had retired to a pretty house in scenic Pierre-Percée. They led Reynolds and Whately-Smith to a woodland cave within walking distance of their home. There the two SAS men would manage to hide under the very noses of the Germans. In a stroke of good fortune, Myrhiam was a former nurse. She managed to treat Major Reynolds' wound and arrest the gangrene, which had fast started to take hold.

Colonel Franks radioed through several RVs to the two men, but Major Reynolds proved too weak to make a move. Eventually, Franks decided to fetch his two officers in person, once he'd got the new Basse de Lieumont base firmly established, and his men firmly on the offensive once more.

Lieutenant Karl Marx was also trying to find his way to Colonel Franks' new Moussey base. His unit had suffered no casualties, and even the three men last seen running from the Germans with their search dogs had managed to shake them off. But for forty-eight hours Marx and his men had had nothing to eat bar a few scavenged potatoes, and they had been burning through the Benzedrine in an effort to stay one step ahead of the enemy.

Unfazed by such hardships, when Lieutenant Marx made it to the new Basse de Lieumont base he proved keen to be dispatched on offensive operations again. Colonel Franks decided to entrust the young lieutenant with one of the most audacious missions of the war, an act designed to serve as the ultimate provocation to the enemy. Carrying some very special demolitions equipment, Marx was to lead his force east across the border into Germany to blow up a train on German soil.

Marx chose to take with him three tried-and-trusted men from his previous mission – Lance-Corporals Garth and Pritchard, plus Trooper Ferrandi – along with a new addition, Trooper Salthouse. Between them they were carrying 5 pounds of plastic explosives per man, four pressure switches, detonators, primers, a dozen tyre-bursters and two boxes of the so-called 'fog signals', which was a very particular piece of kit indeed.

Experience had taught the SAS that there was little point in simply blowing up a railway. An approaching train driver might well spot the break in the tracks and bring his locomotive to a halt. The buckled and twisted tracks could be removed relatively easily and new rails slotted into place. It might only disrupt rail transport for a few hours. What was needed was a much more significant interruption to services, and the 'fog signal' was the answer.

In developing this cunning piece of kit, the SOE had opted to adapt a well-proven device to their purpose, one that was already half a century old. The original 'fog signal' was designed to warn a locomotive whenever a stop sign ahead was obscured by fog – hence the name. It consisted of a metal bowl attached to a pressure plate, which clamped onto the top of the rail. The bowl was filled with black powder and percussion caps. Whenever the fog came down the signalman would fix three onto a rail ahead of a stop sign. An approaching locomotive would detonate the signals as it went over them, each exploding with a loud bang and warning the driver to slow down.

Otherwise of similar design, the SOE's version had an added 'snout' protruding from the metal bowl, set to the outside edge of the track and attached to a length of detonation cord. The hot gases from the exploding powder would rush through the snout, igniting the detonation cord, which was connected to an explosive charge set several dozen feet in front.

As detonation cord 'burns' at 23,000 feet per second, the fog signal and the main charge would explode bare microseconds apart, giving the train driver no time to take evasive action. Unable to stop, the train would be derailed, causing massive destruction and significant delays as a result.

In an effort to counter the fog signal, the Germans had fitted their locomotives with wire brushes to 'sweep' the track ahead of an engine. The 'Torpedo A3' version of the standard SOE fog signal was the answer to that: it was an American-designed improved version, which gripped the track so firmly it could not be dislodged.

With fog signals at the ready, Lieutenant Marx and his four-man team set out heading east, towards Hitler's Germany. It was some 15 miles as the crow flies to their intended target, the railway line leading north-east from the French town of Saales into the German Rhineland, forming a vital artery to bring war materiel to the embattled German front on the Vosges.

Their target lay well beyond Schirmek, the location of *Standartenführer* Isselhorst and his deputies' field headquarters. If Marx and his men could reach the railroad and destroy it, it would help give the lie to Isselhorst's ability to achieve Himmler's bidding and crush the forces of insurrection in the Vosges. In short, striking into Germany itself would constitute a massive psychological blow.

No one figured the mission was going to be easy. The rail track was guarded by pairs of sentries set at 100-yard intervals on a round-the-clock watch rotation. Presumably their vigilance would be greater the further Lieutenant Marx was able to push on to German soil, prior to launching his attack.

En route, Marx took the opportunity to sow chaos in his wake. He and his four-man team laid tyre-bursters boosted with lumps of PE on the first major road junction they encountered. A German troop transporter was blown up, losing a wheel and careering into a roadside ditch. They laid a pressure switch-operated charge on another road, complete with a one-pound lump of PE. A German half-track – an armoured troop carrier, with wheels at the front and tank-like tracks at the rear – triggered the device, with the resulting explosion tearing apart the vehicle.

At Champanay, just south of Schirmek, Lieutenant Marx paid a visit to a particular house in an effort to contact the local Resistance leader. But the SAS lieutenant was warned that the Maquis chief had been arrested, along with several of his deputies. And the further east that Marx and his men pressed, the less willing anyone seemed to support their efforts or give them any kind of sanctuary.

They went in search of that ever-pressing need: food. Marx and Ferrandi turned up at a household they had been led to believe was friendly. They only managed to escape by the skin of their teeth. Marx revealed himself to be a master of sangfroid and understatement when he wrote about the incident in the war diary.

'We walked out of the back door as the Germans walked in the front. We had been sold by the woman in the house.'

Moving further east, he and his team were involved in an incident that was clearly seen as being of sufficient controversy post-war to warrant the censoring of the Operation Loyton war diary. Originally marked 'CLOSED UNTIL 2019' on the front cover, a version of the war diary was released in 1994, but certain sections had been redacted.

One of those concerns the actions taken by Lieutenant Marx and his men, as they prepared to hit the railroad around the 'German' town of Wildersbach. Needing to cross the then border – following the outbreak of war, much of the eastern Vosges had been 'reincorporated' into Germany, the border moving some way west of the Rhine – Marx sent Lance-Corporal Pritchard and two men to recce the way ahead.

Pritchard returned with more than Marx had bargained for. The section censored from the 1994 war diary reads: 'They returned at 1500 hours with food, and a German Sergeant Major. Pct. [Parachutist] Ferrandi and Salthouse took him into the woods and shot him.'

It appears that Pritchard had grabbed a German border guard, so they could interrogate him and gain intelligence about the planned border crossing. For whatever reason – and presumably at some time during his interrogation – the man was shot dead. No further explanation is given in the war diary, or any other available documentation.

Perhaps he'd tried to escape; perhaps he'd tried to resist; perhaps he'd tried to give the SAS men away; or maybe they'd shot him in cold-blooded revenge. Or could it have been that they couldn't afford to take a prisoner with them on the onward mission, but nor could they afford to set him free and thus disclose their whereabouts and strength?

The war diary offers no answer. But what is abundantly clear is that the absence of the German soldier was duly noted, for the frontier guard force was immediately strengthened from fourteen to twenty-one. Yet by then Lieutenant Marx and his men had slipped across the border anyway. Under cover of darkness they'd made their way onto German soil, pressing onwards towards their target.

They chose to hit a rail junction just to the west of Wildersbach, where three separate tracks converge. On each was clamped a fog signal, attached to a one-pound charge of PE. At fifteen minutes past ten that night a train hit one of the fog signals, triggered the PE charge ahead of it, and careered into the length of blown-up track.

Moving at speed, the locomotive ploughed across the broken section of rails, tearing up further lengths of track as it slid along uncontrollably, before eventually tumbling down the embankment's steep slope. It came to rest lying on its side, a steaming, wheezing wreck, with scores of broken and buckled carriages concertinaed up behind it. Marx and his fog signals had done their work; the train was destroyed, the track was blocked and a long length of line was left in utter ruin.

By first light Marx and his team had slipped back across the border into France, and called in a flight of RAF ground-attack aircraft. They proceeded to strafe and bomb whatever remained of the train and its cargo, which might otherwise have been salvageable. It was a perfect outcome to the mission devised by Colonel Franks, if one ignores the mysterious shooting of the German border guard.

The response from the enemy was immediate and extreme. Teams of German troops began combing every conceivable stretch of woodland in which the saboteurs might have gone to ground, wreaking revenge on the local French villagers. At one hamlet where Marx and his men tried to scavenge for food, they learned that the Gestapo had arrived to cart off all the male residents, and in their place had billeted six truckloads of German troops.

One such sweep made by those soldiers came very close to cornering Marx and his force. But – 'cool as a cucumber' – Marx decided that he was far from done. He and his men still had PE and detonators to get rid of. Splitting his unit into two, they laid 12 pounds of PE on the roads in the neighbouring area. The first charge was triggered when a German Army truck set off one of the tyre-bursters. Sympathetic detonations – the triggering of further explosions by the first – 'scattered the truck everywhere', Marx recorded.

In a final act of sabotage, the last of their explosives were used to take out a sleek-looking German staff car – one used to ferry officers about their business. Hopefully, it contained the senior commanders who had been sent into the area to coordinate the hunt for Marx and his fellow saboteurs.

With noticeably lighter Bergens, Marx led his men in a forced march west, heading fast towards the SAS's Moussey base.

Behind them they could hear German forces searching the woodlands they had just vacated, and the odd burst of probing gunfire, but the enemy was shooting at ghosts.

For his command of this singular mission, Lieutenant Marx would be awarded the Military Cross. The citation would state of his actions: 'Throughout this operation Lieutenant Marx showed himself to be imbued with a determination to cause damage to the enemy. His skill and personal courage during the whole period were an example to all ranks and deserving of high praise.'

But for now, Marx led his team west through the Wild Woods, heading towards the SAS base set in the hills above Moussey. There was worrying news to greet him when he got there. While en route to their rendezvous with Colonel Franks, the three men from his previous mission – those last seen running from the Germans' search dogs – had taken shelter in a sawmill, the Scierie de la Turbine, in the Celles Valley.

Five other SAS men had joined them there – a sabotage party led by a Lieutenant James Black. Sadly, they had been betrayed. Their presence was reported to the local Gestapo, and the forces of the enemy had surrounded the sawmill. In the firefight that followed, the eight-strong SAS force, already running low on ammunition, had run out of bullets with which to fight. All had been taken captive, with at least one – Lieutenant Black – being wounded.

Chris Sykes – the 2 SAS intelligence officer – had managed to glean as much detail as possible from his contacts in the Resistance. Foremost amongst those was Albert Freine – the gamekeeper-cum-Maquis-intelligence-chief – who had become

Sykes' most trusted source. Ominously, Freine had learned that the eight captured SAS men had been taken to Schirmek's *Sicherungslager* – the security camp where the one-legged, morphine-addicted Karl Buck held sway. As to their fate thereafter, that was in the lap of the gods.

Sykes and Freine had taken to meeting daily beneath a certain tree. By mid September the weather in the Vosges was starting to turn, the balmy days of late summer giving way to those conditions so much more common in the region – incessant drizzle and rain. 'Weeks of shared misery made us life-long friends,' Sykes remarked of his relations with Freine.

The gamekeeper's knowledge of enemy movements proved encyclopaedic and invaluable; on several occasions it would prove a lifesaver. In the damp conditions of early autumn the ground was wetter underfoot, and the SAS's boots left imprints on muddy tracks and paths. The Germans had learned to recognize the distinctive markings made by their rubber-soled footwear, so as to better track the Op Loyton force. Alerted to this by Freine, the SAS men opted to cut away their boots' tread pattern, but still the heels remained as conspicuous as ever.

Sykes could tell that Freine was under pressure. His nerves were stretched to breaking point. In the aftermath of Lieutenant Marx's strike onto German soil, the iron fist of Waldfest was grinding ever harder into the valleys of the Vosges. Chief amongst its targets were those like Freine, from whom a confession extracted by torture would yield a bonanza of intelligence.

In the neighbouring Celles Valley, a *garde de forêt* (state forester) was playing a similar role to Freine. He was serving as the go-between for Colonel Franks and Major Reynolds, the wounded SAS officer ensconced in the Pierre-Percée cave, along with Captain Whately-Smith. Strong and absolutely silent, the forester was imbued with a very different kind of courage to the chest-thumping Freine. Indeed, he exhibited the type of '*flegme britannique*' that had so impressed the Moussey priest, Abbé Gassman, on the beaches of Dunkirk.

Sykes had taken to meeting with this forester regularly, seeking news of the two SAS officers. In response, the lean and weather-beaten man would remove his wooden clog and, without a word, withdraw a tiny note secreted between his toes: a message from Major Reynolds. Sykes would scribble a reply, the forester would insert it between his toes again, and quietly slip his clog back on. His silence was eloquent: it spoke of a rock-like firmness in the face of adversity.

In truth, these pillars of the local Resistance were up against it now. The indomitable Mme Rossi had suffered her own predations, but typically she remained tight-lipped on the matter, and unbowed. Of course, Sykes had made her acquaintance, and amazingly her loud laughter and merriment remained undimmed, as did her desire to feed, shelter and assist the SAS men at every turn.

The Germans had come to suspect that Mme Rossi's house lay beside the path that led to the new SAS base, which indeed it did. The Gestapo paid ever more frequent visits to her home. On one occasion they searched it from top to bottom, while the redoubtable madame had six SAS men hidden there, some of whom were lying beneath the water wheel at the rear. Such experiences would have tested the toughest of nerves, but she never once baulked at her house being used as a refuge and a rendezvous for the SAS and the Maquis.

A second redoubtable Moussey woman also served the cause of the Resistance. In many ways Mlle Bergeron was the opposite of Mme Rossi; she was a severe-looking, middle-aged spinster living in a farm set some distance from the village. She was also the chief message-bearer for the Maquis. There was little she could not have told the Germans, had they managed to break her. But in one respect she and Mme Rossi proved exactly similar: they were *unbreakable*.

The Gestapo piled upon Mlle Bergeron every humiliation and terror imaginable. They beat her and tortured her. They turned her lovely farmhouse into a brothel. This silent, prim and proper woman – who was always smartly dressed and immaculate – proved to have the courage of a lioness. When they realized they could not make her crack, they turned upon her eighty-year-old aunt. One night they dragged her out of her bed and forced the octogenarian to dance for them in her nightgown. She died of the shock.

Still Mlle Bergeron would not talk. If anything, such outrages made her stronger.

Yet by mid September 1944, the forces of Waldfest had closed in on one of their key targets – gamekeeper Albert Freine. If the Gestapo could break Freine, the consequences would be utterly disastrous for the SAS. Freine knew as much as there was to tell. As the grey autumn rains settled over the Vosges, the Gestapo came for the gamekeeper's wife. For twenty-four hours Mme Freine was beaten, abused and interrogated. She knew almost as much as her husband, but she gave nothing away.

The Gestapo marched her into the forest. At gunpoint, they demanded to be shown the location of the 'British parachutists' base'. She passed so close to its actual location, one that she knew very well, that Sykes saw the party she led move by. But somehow she convinced the Gestapo that she was a simple, ignorant woman, and that her husband was likewise an innocent *garde-chasse*. They let her go, but not before they had smashed up the Freine household as a warning.

Albert Freine remained unbowed. He was full, as always, of outspoken defiance. 'Death for me is a trifle!' he declared to Sykes. 'Me, a prisoner? Never! Even if the death stroke had to be delivered by my own hand!' Sykes believed him, too. Freine's open boastfulness hid a heart of steely fortitude.

The climate that autumn over the Vosges proved unseasonably cold. With Waldfest biting deeper and the weather conditions worsening, it was hard for the Op Loyton men to keep positive and retain morale. A blanket of mist and fog descended over the hills, making flying resupply missions nightmarishly difficult. Several had to be cancelled, and Franks' force was soon running short of ammunition, explosives and food.

An SAS report on Op Loyton sums up the plethora of problems Franks' men faced. 'The bad weather and impossible flying conditions which hindered the dispatch of supply aircraft, coupled with the difficulty of selecting DZs free of enemy supervision in such unsuitable terrain added . . . to the difficulties of the operation.'

When it rained, and it was doing so pretty much constantly now, the men had to wrap themselves in their sleeping bags and cover themselves from head to toe in a waterproof cape, as they tried to get through the dark, damp night hours. When wet, their down-filled sleeping bags became useless, and they proved near impossible to dry. The SAS men's cotton para-smocks – perfect for jumping with, and for keeping warm in dry conditions – became sodden in the incessant rain.

Captain Druce's advance party had been on the ground for approaching five weeks now, on a mission initially scheduled to last two to three weeks at most. That was the time it was supposed to have taken for Patton's 3rd Army to break through the German defences and advance into the Vosges. Unfortunately there was little sign of that happening any time soon and, as the weather worsened, it appeared increasingly less likely.

An Op Loyton intelligence report smuggled back to London made the situation crystal clear. 'Valleys are becoming very soggy and would probably not be passable for trucks and tanks. There is a local saying: "When it starts raining it stays raining." Rains sometimes hold on for nearly a week with only slight let-ups. Streams due to rainfall are often in flood . . .'

'That was not a happy period,' remarked Captain Druce, a man not normally accustomed to complaining. 'I think perhaps one had one's worst moments when wet, dirty, tired, exhausted and with no chance of getting into a nice warm bed . . . Always trying to sleep under some sort of cover, usually not with any sleeping bag or anything. And September in that area can be damned cold at night. Those are the sort of moments when your morale is really at its lowest, when you're trying to get to sleep but you can't sleep . . . It's bloody cold, and you're wet and you can't get dry and you're possibly quite hungry, because we had periods where we really didn't have very much to eat.'

Under such circumstances, receiving 'comfort loads' – special para-containers packed with letters from home, chocolate, cigarettes and alcohol – attained an even greater significance for the men on the ground. Aside from scoring successes against the enemy, these proved the biggest boost to morale of all. Unfortunately, SAS headquarters had encountered some difficulty in arranging such deliveries to their suffering fighters.

Britain's HM Commissioners for Customs and Excise had long argued that they couldn't permit bulk supplies of cigarettes and booze to be dropped to SAS units deep behind enemy lines. Their reasoning seemed to hinge upon the fact that the men were being provided such comforts at 'duty free' prices, when they did not possess an official Army address outside the UK.

By mid September 1944 SAS headquarters had just about won that battle, but by then the bad weather had closed in over the Vosges. Three Handley Page Halifax four-engined heavy bombers had been assigned to permanent duties in support of Op Loyton, in an effort to get the vital supplies through. 'Comforts' were to be spread across every load, so that if only a few containers were retrieved the men would still enjoy that vital boost to their flagging spirits.

Such matters may appear as trifles at a time when these soldiers were being hunted by a force as formidable as that deployed under Operation Waldfest, but if they could not maintain their morale, Franks knew that his men were lost.

Fortunately, he was about to take delivery of the single biggest morale booster of all.

It would prove a total game-changer in terms of his men's ability to wage war across the Vosges.

Chapter Eleven

Operation Loyton had never been conceived of purely as a foot-borne mission. In the deserts of North Africa the SAS had first learned the vital importance of mobility – both in terms of being able to strike the enemy hard and fast with sufficient firepower, and to make a clean getaway. This was crucial to the practice of land-based hit-and-run warfare.

The American jeep was the key. Designated the '¼ tonne 4×4 truck', but more commonly known as the Willys MB, it was a general-purpose (GP) vehicle – hence the nickname: GP, or 'jeep'. Solid, reliable, relatively fast and manoeuvrable, the Willys seemed purpose-built for SAS operations. Stripped of all 'non-essentials' – including windscreen, radiator grille and front bumper – the jeep was able to carry sufficient fuel, water, weaponry and ammo for the kind of long-distance raids that would become the Regiment's trademark.

With its all-round visibility, the open-topped vehicle also made for an excellent gun platform. Most were mounted with the Vickers 'K' machine gun. The rapid-firing Vickers – a .303-inch calibre light machine gun – could deliver devastating firepower, especially when loaded with a mixture of standard ball, armour-piercing and tracer rounds.

Usually fitted in pairs, a jeep could carry up to five Vickers (with one mounted singly). Equipped thus, the SAS, supported by the Long Range Desert Group (LRDG), had penetrated the North African desert carrying out recce, capture and sabotage missions, hitting enemy supply lines, fuel dumps, airfields and ammunition stores. In September 1942 they had launched perhaps their most celebrated mission: Operation Caravan.

Seventeen vehicles carrying forty-seven men had travelled 1,162 miles across the sand-blasted desert. Upon reaching their objective – the Italian-held Libyan town of Barce – the patrol had split up, one half attacking the enemy barracks, the other the airfield. During the latter assault some thirty aircraft – mainly three-engined Italian Air Force bombers – had been hit. In another similar mission, twelve enemy aircraft were destroyed during a five-minute shoot-'em-up raid.

The Vosges had been chosen as an 'ideal' area of SAS operations because in theory the rugged, wild terrain suited such mobile jeep-borne missions. If he could get jeeps onto the ground, Colonel Franks figured it would revolutionize the war they were waging here. As the third week of September blew in cold, wet and biting, the SAS colonel tried on successive occasions to get a major airdrop scheduled. Each was defeated by the ever-worsening conditions.

A report by Captain T. Burt, 2 SAS's UK-based quartermaster, provided a flavour of the kind of problems encountered when trying to resupply the Loyton force. 'The weather was against us, and the aircraft had to be recalled while over the Channel, and even back here the ground mist was so bad that the load had to be jettisoned near and around the aerodrome.'

At his Basse de Lieumont base, Franks felt doubly frustrated. In recent months a technique had been developed to enable jeeps to be dropped by air into remote areas like the high Vosges. Number 38 Group RAF – a unit more used to the delivery of airborne troops – had been given the tricky job of developing and perfecting this process. Slung in a specially designed metal 'cradle', the jeep could be hung from the main support beam of a Halifax heavy bomber, half-tucked into its bomb bay. When released it would drop beneath four, 60-foot-diameter parachutes, one attached to each of the corners of the vehicle.

That at least was the theory. In practice, if the jeep tumbled upon release, the rigging lines would snag, and if one chute didn't open the drop was doomed. The cradles were vital for cushioning the load. The front and rear wheels were protected by two crash pans, designed to flatten upon impact, and the Vickers machine guns were removed and stowed safely inside the vehicle.

The four chutes were packed into two special 'valises', which sat on the back seat. Upon the jeep's release, a static line attached to the Halifax would haul the valises free and the chutes would deploy. A small explosive charge would detonate upon landing, cutting the four chutes free of the vehicle, and making it easier for the retrieval party to get the jeep up and running.

When first used operationally – parachuting jeeps to SAS parties in the immediate aftermath of D-Day – up to 50 per cent of the vehicles hadn't survived the drop. Colonel Franks was hoping for better success over the Vosges and praying for a weather window. Six jeeps were scheduled to be airlifted to him, which should enable a good half of his force to head out on jeep-mounted operations, all guns blazing.

In the meantime, the missions on foot continued.

On 17 September, Major Peter Lancelot John Le Poer Power finally made it through to Colonel Franks' base. In doing so, he and his small band of men had marched through dozens of miles of hostile and mountainous terrain, evading the predations of Waldfest and tracking the colonel's main force from Pierre-Percée through a dozen different locations, always seeming to be one step behind them.

'Although he set out eastwards to try to contact Capt. Druce, he was out of touch for four weeks,' the war diary records of Major Power and his men. Throughout that time the SAS major had never given up, nor missed an opportunity to hit back against the enemy. And, in spite of the worsening conditions, neither did Colonel Franks and his main force.

The very day of Major Power's arrival at the SAS's Moussey headquarters, Druce had been out on operations. He'd discovered that four trains loaded with tanks had become immobilized at St. Dié station, 8 miles south of their Basse de Lieumont camp. He radioed through the coordinates to SFHQ, requesting an RAF air strike to hit them.

The following day he was charged with capturing two agents of the Milice – the French pro-Nazi militia – who were of 'Arab' origin (most likely Algerians). In another section of the Op Loyton war diary that was originally censored, Druce reported: 'Managed to round those up after considerable difficulty and they were both shot.' Again, the sensitivity appears to have revolved around Druce and his fellows' ruthless suppression of those who might betray the SAS or otherwise jeopardize their mission.

Another of Franks' sabotage parties had blown up a train on the Celle to Allarmont railway line, which was carrying vital supplies to the front. That same party had gone on to ambush a German staff car using an American bazooka – once again, targeting the enemy's commanders. The bazooka round had cut through the vehicle without exploding, but still succeeded in stopping it.

But such missions were becoming increasingly fraught; what the SAS men needed was speed and firepower. On the evening of 19 September they would finally get it. In guiding the flight of Halifax aircraft to the chosen DZ, Colonel Franks was aided by a new piece of equipment – a Eureka air beacon, which was designed to 'steer' aircraft blind through thick cloud and fog.

More accurately known as the 'Rebecca/Eureka transponding radar', it consisted of an airborne receiver and antenna system (the Rebecca) which was used by an in-bound aircraft to pick up a radio signal transmitting from the ground-based Eureka unit. The Rebecca calculated the range and position of the Eureka, based upon the timings and direction of the return signal. It was accurate up to 50 miles in clear conditions and, even under cloud or thick vegetation, it was still detectable from up to 5 miles away.

On the night of 18–19 September, Colonel Franks' Eureka would come up trumps. So, too, would the long-suffering inhabitants of Moussey.

The only feasible DZ not then in enemy hands was a small field lying on the northern outskirts of Moussey village, one surrounded on all sides by the beckoning forest. Immediately to the north lay the 2,500-foot ridge that dominates the Moussey skyline, one more often than not shrouded in grey mist and rain. To the south and east lay further peaks and ridges – Côte du Mont, Côte des Chênes, le Roitelet – of a similar height.

The RAF aircrews were going to have to fly into a patch of grassland less than 500 foot square, sandwiched between high and glowering peaks on all sides. It would be a feat of flying just to get the Halifaxes in there safely, let alone to make several passes at 1,000 feet, dropping supplies and jeeps by parachute.

The Moussey villagers knew that a '*parachutage*' or a '*droppage*' was in the offing, and that the SAS required volunteers to help retrieve the loads and carry them into their rocky fastness. In spite of the risks, they turned out in their droves. The villagers were chivvied along by Etienne and the rest of his band of gnarled and aged warriors.

According to Captain Druce, who'd worked closely with Etienne's Maquis, 'Etienne and his thirty men were first class. Etienne himself was a really good leader.'

Tonight, Etienne seemed to have outdone even himself. The entire population of Moussey appeared to be streaming across the silver moonlit grass, disregarding the fact that there were German troops billeted no more than a mile away. This demonstration of the villagers' solidarity served to lift the SAS men's spirits enormously. They knew how the people of the Vosges were being made to suffer, and it troubled many of them mightily.

Typically, Etienne and his men had brought with them several bottles of *eau de vie* ('water of life') a locally distilled raw spirit, for 'keeping out the damp and the cold'. They yelled their greetings to friends and family across the night-dark expanse of the DZ as the bottles were passed around.

There was nothing the British force could do to quell the high spirits, even had they wanted to. At one point Chris Sykes warned Etienne that the noise really had to stop. The Maquis leader promptly agreed that it should.

'*Silence!*' he bellowed across the field. '*Tais-toi! Un peu de discipline, ou je te claque!*' (Shut up! A little discipline or I'll slap you!)

His threat was met by a round of raucous applause.

But with the first beat of the approaching aircraft's engines, the DZ fell still. An expectant hush settled as the signallers flashed their torches from the ground, and the first of the Halifaxes responded, circling back around at a lower altitude. As the first parachutes were released, the villagers began to remark: '*Ce sont des hommes.*' '*Ce sont des conteneurs.*' '*Ce sont . . . un jim!*'

Men (*hommes*) and containers they were expecting, but seeing the first *jim* (a jeep) drifting to earth beneath its four parachutes was a truly miraculous sight to behold. As loads landed with a sharp crackling of branches and a lone jeep drifted earthwards, figures darted in all directions to retrieve the war materiel.

Moments later, Etienne's voice rang out again. '*Mon Colonel! Ici il y a un jim suspendu dans les arbres!*' (Colonel! Here's a jeep stuck in the trees!)

By the second and third pass of the aircraft, the repeated drops had spread chaos across the field. Figures darted hither and thither, seeking missing chutes. The clang of hammers rang out as containers were split open, the noise echoing back and forth across the still valley. And to the northern end of the DZ, a human snake could be seen slithering into the forest, moving in the direction of the SAS base, each ant-like figure laden down with a crushing load.

As the hours wore on, tiredness killed discretion. Etienne and his fellows' cries grew more brazen and arresting as they sought those loads that had drifted deeper into the woods. Exhausted figures staggered uphill under their fourth or fifth load. And, at one end of the DZ, the first of the prized jeeps was being loaded to the gunwales with the heaviest equipment of all.

Six jeeps had been expected, but the drop was limited to three, owing to the adverse flying conditions. Of those three, one had touched down perfectly in the very centre of the DZ. The second had drifted slightly, landing in a side valley. But the third had ploughed deep into the woodlands. It had come to rest at a crazy angle, snagged in some branches, and all its oil had drained out.

Lou Fiddick was sent to try to retrieve it. 'We had quite a chore. I had a number of French people with me to try to salvage this jeep . . . We eventually managed to get it down, but it was hard work . . . But even worse was getting rid of the parachute, so the Germans wouldn't know we had been there. It was all tangled in the branches.'

As the first of the three vehicles was driven up the winding track leading towards the SAS's Basse de Lieumont redoubt, the door to an isolated house opened and a hot meal was offered to the famished soldiers.

Every villager knew about the *droppages*. And there were few in Moussey who weren't aware of where Colonel Franks had made his new headquarters. What was incredible was that nobody in this village had thought to give the British force away.

Once the jeeps were safely ensconced in the thick and rugged forest, there was much to be done to make them ready. Guns had to be cleaned and tested, for they'd been stowed, greased-up, in the rear of the vehicles. Magazines had to be reloaded, as some of the ammo had been fouled. The jeep that had landed in the trees needed a shot of replacement oil, and even then its brakes needed to be got working again.

With the first of his vehicles in place, Colonel Franks was keen to launch shoot-'n'-scoot attacks across the widest possible expanse of the Vosges. In doing so he aimed to give the impression that the vanguard of the American forces had broken through the German lines. This would sow panic and fear amongst the ranks of the enemy, and so help contribute to the crumbling of their lines.

That, at least, was the theory, and it was supported by a radio message just in. 'A signal had been received that the Americans were expected to reach our area by the 19th,' Colonel Franks recorded in the war diary. 'I therefore decided to deploy my forces as follows . . .'

Two six-man patrols were to be sent out to harry the enemy on foot. The remainder of his force – bar a small headquarters element – was to take to the jeeps under Franks' direct command, and drive out to war.

The nineteenth of September was the day the first jeeps had arrived. If the intelligence was correct, then the American forces should be on Moussey's very doorstep. Now was the time to set forth on a highly visible offensive. Franks warned his men to prepare for the coming American breakthrough, and to be alert for friendly forces; they didn't want to shoot up their own side.

But, in truth, there had been a major breakdown in either intelligence or communications – quite possibly both. Following a rapid advance over the previous few days, General Patton's forces were once more well and truly stalled. Right now, at the end of the third week of September, the tanks, personnel carriers, trucks and self-propelled guns of the 3rd and 7th Armies were actually going nowhere, for resistance along the western wall of the Vosges had proved far more ferocious than Allied commanders had ever anticipated.

'The Germans appear to want to prevent at all costs a crossing of the crest of the Vosges,' a US 7th Army document recorded. 'They have set up a fortifications plan . . . Thousands of youths belonging to the Hitler Jugend, plus young men from Alsace 12–15 years old and conscripted by force, have been made to work on the first trenches . . .'

The Todt Organization – a notorious 'civil engineering' outfit, named after its founder, senior Nazi Fritz Todt – had overseen the building of the Vosges defences. By September 1944, the Todt Organization had 1.4 million forced labourers under its control, of which 1 per cent were Germans rejected for military service, 1.5 per cent were concentration camp prisoners, and the rest were POWs and compulsory labourers from occupied territories, including children.

'Numerous artillery pieces have been brought forward,' the US 7th Army report continued. 'All the bridges and footbridges over the Meurthe have been mined. Sentries guard those bridges both day and night. All the roads crossing the Meurthe are . . . cut across in two and sometimes three places by large and deep trenches covered by heavy planks, thus forming anti-tank barriers. Even these second bridges are mined and guarded.

'New troops numbering three Divisions – one armoured, one motorised and one infantry – have been brought into the sector. Traffic has occurred almost exclusively at night and it has been heavy in men, material and supply columns. The arrival of heavy tanks (Panther and Tiger) indicate that the Germans will not be content to stay on the defensive, but will seize the right moment to push to the offensive.'

By late September 1944, Patton's armies had come up against a second enemy, in addition to the defences strung along the Vosges. For weeks after D-Day an extraordinary American initiative had kept Patton's gas-guzzling armoured columns on the move. The Red Ball Express – named after a railroad expression; to 'red-ball' something was to speed it through – was a truck convoy system designed to keep supplies rolling post D-Day, no matter what.

Priority routes marked with the Red Ball symbol had been strung across liberated France, each closed to all but military traffic. Some 6,000 trucks similarly marked worked to the Red Ball slogan – 'Keep 'em rolling!' – driving day and night to and from the front lines.

But on an average day of operations Patton's forces consumed some 800,000 US gallons of fuel. By late September 1944 they had outrun the reach of even the Red Ball truckers.

In the final push for the Vosges, General Patton's forces had ground to a halt owing to a lack of fuel. Yet for some reason – most likely the ever-present 'fog of war' – Colonel Franks and his men had received no warnings about this. Quite the contrary; they had been told to expect the US cavalry to come riding over the hills at any moment.

'Liaison between the different Intelligence branches was markedly imperfect,' remarked Chris Sykes. 'In consequence we got instructions to prepare for an advance which had, in fact, been cancelled.'

In truth, General Patton's forces wouldn't cross the Vosges for more than a month. And in the interim, Colonel Franks and his men were driving out to a very lonely and one-sided war.

Chapter Twelve

At six o'clock on the evening of 21 September Colonel Franks led the first jeep-mounted sortie out of the SAS's 'bandit' base. The colonel was behind the wheel of the first vehicle, with Major Power serving as his front gunner and Roger Souchal as guide. Lieutenant Dill drove the second jeep, with three gunners poised over the menacing forms of the Vickers twin machine guns.

As darkness fell they sneaked through Moussey village, turned left and then right, snaking their way between knife-cut hills on a narrow, winding road. They were making for La Petite Raon and Vieux-Moulin, where Druce's advance force had originally parachuted in. They'd received reports that the Germans had a tank unit positioned in the woodlands, and Colonel Franks was keen on hunting down those high-value targets.

Sure enough, the distinctive tracks of Tiger tanks were found on the road leading into Vieux-Moulin. The German Tiger was a 55-tonne behemoth boasting a fearsome 88mm main gun, 7.92mm machine guns, plus 120mm-thick armour. There was nothing the two jeeps carried which could so much as put a dent in that, not unless the SAS men could get close enough to hurl a Gammon bomb through the tank's open turret, or stuff it full of grenades.

Colonel Franks halted in Vieux-Moulin to get some directions from the locals. He was told that five Tiger tanks were parked up nearby, hidden amongst the thick woodland. The only way to attack such a formidable target was to launch an ambush while the tanks were powered down – their engines switched off and their crews at ease. If they could kill or scatter enough of the German 'tankies', they might just get close enough to blow up their armour.

Colonel Franks and Major Power headed off into the woods on a foot recce, to see if the Tigers could be hit from the rear. From the cover of the trees they spotted what seemed to be German sentries and the silhouette of a well-camouflaged Tiger tank. The faint noise of hammering echoed out of the darkened woodland. Steel was slamming against steel as the tank crews carried out what sounded like running repairs. Here and there the glow of cigarettes could be seen through the trees.

The two SAS commanders returned to their jeeps. Working from what they'd just seen, they steered their two vehicles towards where they figured the first Tiger was situated. The jeeps crawled along a forest track, moving barely above walking pace to mask the noise of their approach. When they'd got to within 100 yards of the German position, they parked up with their guns brought to bear and switched on both sets of headlamps, full-beam.

In the glare of the illumination they hoped to spot movement as the tank crews reacted to the sudden, blinding light. Most likely they would presume it was a friendly force, for the very idea that British soldiers might be driving around in the Vosges would appear preposterous to the Germans right now.

The twin sets of headlamps lanced into the gloom. Behind them in the darkness, figures crouched over their twin-Vickers, expectantly. Twice Franks' force repeated this manoeuvre, but each time no movement was spotted amongst the trees, nor any response. The Tiger tank unit was proving remarkably elusive; it just seemed to have disappeared.

Eventually, the colonel had to signal the withdrawal. They were needed back at the Moussey DZ. A second airdrop was scheduled that night, this one bringing in three further jeeps, to up their number to the six that the SAS colonel had asked for.

As they withdrew, Franks took note of the position of the Tiger tanks. He would radio it in to SFHQ, requesting a flight of RAF bombers to hit the woodland in which the heavy armour was concealed. They motored back to the Moussey DZ, and the three further jeeps were dropped without too much drama or incident. The SAS colonel now had enough vehicles to make his force truly mobile.

At dusk the following day, the men of Op Loyton removed the screen of cut branches with which they'd camouflaged their jeeps and set off in convoy. Six vehicles manned by twenty-one fighters pulled out of their hidden base, engines grumbling and gears grinding as they nosed down the rough and muddy track. They pushed south towards Moussey, petrol fumes hanging thick and heavy in the cold, damp air.

Colonel Franks was driving the lead vehicle, with Corporal Kubiski serving as his front gunner, Trooper Mason as his fitter and Chris Sykes as his rear gunner and navigator. Lieutenant David Dill commanded the next jeep in line, with Squadron

Sergeant Major 'Chalky' White behind the front Vickers and Corporal Austin as his rear gunner. Major Peter Power and Captain Druce were at the wheels of two further vehicles, each with their own complement of gunners and wireless operators.

'All six jeeps set out together at 17.00 hrs and crossed the valley via Moussey and made for the Celles woods,' Colonel Franks recorded in the war diary. 'We harboured for the night at V 447841.'

The following morning Colonel Franks split his force into three units. He sent two jeeps under Druce's command to recce the road leading into Moyenmoutier, a town lying some 19 miles to the west of Moussey. Major Power, with another two jeeps, was sent north, to recce the main supply route that ran through the Celles Valley, while Colonel Franks remained with the final two vehicles.

Major Power's force was the first to strike. They reached the road that cuts through the Celles Valley, pausing at a major meeting of the ways. It was a prime place for an ambush, as any passing traffic would be forced to slow to negotiate the junction.

They drew into a clearing where they could conceal the jeeps behind thick undergrowth but still bring the Vickers to bear, and killed the engines. They waited, their seven .303-inch rapid-fire machine guns trained on the road, plus a Bren gun for good measure.

Major Power had spent the best part of a hellish month trying to join the Op Loyton party deep in the Vosges. As he hunched over the front-mounted twin Vickers, his eyeline down the gunsights positioned above the flat cylinders of ammo perched atop the machine gun, he sensed that today all his persistence was about to pay off.

Out of sight somewhere an engine whined. A driver was shifting down through the gears as he slowed ahead of the junction. Major Power tensed. The vehicle was approaching from the east, heading towards Raon l'Etape, which was 8 kilometres away. It could only be the enemy, for the locals had been reduced to travelling in horse- and ox-drawn carts during the four long years of occupation.

A slender and stylish bonnet nosed around the far corner, sleek and gleaming in the early morning light. A staff car hove into view, a black cross superimposed over a white one adorning the nearside door – the symbol of the *Wehrmacht*. Major Power's fingers tightened bone-white on the Vickers' twin triggers.

Soon now.

He tracked the vehicle's approach in his gunsights. It slowed to a bare 10 miles an hour to negotiate the junction, making it a sitting target. It was then that the SAS major heard the sound of further vehicles approaching from the same direction. His heart skipped a beat. Unbelievably, a second staff car crawled around the bend. It was clearly travelling in convoy with the first.

Major Power let the lead vehicle crawl past his hidden position. Set well back beneath the trees and in deep shadow, he and his men would be invisible to those on the road. As he menaced the first vehicle with his twin gun barrels, he signalled for others to take the one behind. And then, as if by magic, a third staff car rounded the corner – fat and gleaming, and just asking to take a hit.

What were the chances? For their first ever jeep-mounted ambush in the Vosges, three vehicles stuffed full of German officers had stumbled into the SAS's clutches, like lambs to the slaughter.

The growl of a heavier, diesel engine alerted Major Power to the fact that a fourth vehicle was approaching. The 'tail-end charlie' of the convoy turned out to be a three-tonne German Army truck – no doubt carrying troops as escort for the officers up front. The SAS major calculated that the first staff car could still be hit in the time it took for the truck to come within range.

He held his fire until the very last moment. All his men knew to open up on his gun, so no words of command needed to be spoken. When the lead vehicle was poised to round the far bend and disappear from view, Major Power let rip. The twin muzzles spat fire, the first rounds taking a mere fifth of a second to cross the 200 yards that lay between his jeep and the lead staff car.

Bullets tore through bodywork and shattered glass. Major Power kept his finger hard on the trigger as all around him the Vickers roared and sparked in anger. Swinging the Vickers around on their swivel mount, he raked the lead vehicle from bonnet to boot with a devastating barrage of fire. By the time he'd emptied his two sixty-round magazines, not a figure could be seen moving in that stricken vehicle.

Within moments, all three staff cars had been brought to a halt. Each had been punched through with ragged, jagged holes, like a proverbial sieve. Major Power reached forward, unclipped the empty ammo drums and slotted on replacements. By the time he'd unleashed half of the second two magazines, the lead staff car was a broken wreck, slumped low on the road on flattened tyres and with flames licking out of its ruptured rear.

Tracer rounds had cut through the fuel tank. At any moment now the vehicle was going to burst into flames. The two staff cars behind it, plus the truck, had fared little better. Only one figure was seen to emerge from any of the vehicles, and he was cut down immediately by the force's lone Bren gunner. Major Power signalled to his men to cease fire.

By now, approaching 2,000 rounds had been hammered into the four vehicles, many unleashed at close range, and the staff cars and truck had been torn to pieces. In the deafening silence that followed, the grunt of engines further to the convoy's rear could be heard. The second SAS jeep was set a little higher than the first, and the rear gunner raised the alarm. Behind the stricken vehicles he could make out four more trucks, and there were very likely more to the rear of those.

Major Power figured they'd done their shoot most admirably. But all surprise had been lost now, and it was time to effect the scoot. He lowered his weapon, fired up the jeep's engine and floored the throttle, leading the other vehicle on a mad dash through the mountains, back towards their lie-up in the forest. As it happened, a twenty-five truck convoy had been following the staff cars; Major Power was wise indeed to have led his jeeps out of there when he had.

Behind them, a pall of oily smoke rose above the Celles Valley road, where four vehicles riddled with fire were burning.

En route to their hideout, Major Power met up with Colonel Franks and delivered the good news: three German staff cars destroyed. Captain Druce's two jeeps also rendezvoused with them safely. Druce had likewise been in action, though his target left something to be desired.

In addition to requisitioning any motorized vehicles, the Germans had seized bicycles from the French, to form cycling patrols. Thus, any cyclist on the roads was likely to be German, just as any motor vehicle was most definitely going to be driven by the enemy. Or so the SAS men had thought. But in Moussey there was one exception.

Possibly because he so rarely used it, which meant the Germans never realized he had it, the mayor of Moussey had managed to keep an automobile . . . of sorts. It was an ancient and diminutive Detroit Electric Brougham, which resembled a horse and carriage with an electric motor taking the place of four horses in harness. Designed in 1907, it was one of the first electric cars ever built, with a rechargeable sealed lead-acid battery giving an 80-mile range at a steady 20 miles per hour.

When mounting ambushes, especially on the tight and enclosed roads of the Vosges, there was precious little time in which to study an oncoming vehicle. Decisions had to be made in a snap of the fingers. Druce had done exactly that on the morning of 23 September, the oncoming vehicle taking the full brunt of eight Vickers machineguns. Within seconds the mayor's Brougham had ceased to exist, as it was cut to pieces by a barrage of armour-piercing and tracer rounds.

By some incredible miracle, the mayor had managed to roll from the disintegrating wreckage and dive into a roadside ditch. When he realized who it was that had attacked him, he took out his white handkerchief and waved it above the rim of the gully. But by that time Druce had got his force under way, having hit and now run from the scene of the attack.

It was evening at the SAS's forest hideout when Sykes learnt about the true nature of Druce's target. He was speaking with Albert Freine, and he pulled in Colonel Franks just as soon as the gamekeeper mentioned what had happened. Albert repeated the story in full gory detail, the demeanour of both Franks and Sykes growing ever more concerned. The Moussey mayor was one of their staunchest allies; heaven forbid that Druce had killed him.

Freine's discourse – one replete with dire warnings – was broken by a hiss from one of the sentries. A figure had been spotted plodding uphill towards their position. Freine declared that he recognized the man and went down to bring him in. It was a messenger from the mayor who, it seemed, was very much alive.

He had sent two bottles of his finest champagne, together with the following note. '*Merci pour la salve tirée en mon honneur ce matin!*' (Many thanks for the salvo fired in my honour this morning!) As far as the mayor was concerned there were no hard feelings, particularly since he didn't have a scratch upon him.

The chances of ambushing the mayor's Brougham were about as high as those of Major Power's force taking out three German staff cars in the one hit; both were utterly fortuitous moments – at least in the mayor's case, for he had escaped unscathed and with his good humour so obviously intact.

But Major Power's devastating hit on the road north of Celles-sur-Plaine had stirred up a hornets' nest. You didn't go destroying three staff cars stuffed full of German commanders without some significant ramifications. Practically speaking, that route of attack was now closed to any 'jeeping', as the SAS men called it, at least until the heat died down.

But Colonel Franks was itching for some action. He decided to head cross-country, using the forest tracks to skirt around Major Power's ambush point in an effort to reach Allarmont, which lay at the Celles Valley's far north-eastern end. That way, he could hit the main supply road for a second time, before melting back into the hills.

He picked his route off the Club Alpin de France map that the SAS men were using. Those maps, produced by the well-known French mountaineering club, had proved the most detailed and accurate that could be found. But the forest tracks they'd chosen were at best borderline navigable. As the two jeeps crawled downhill after a very difficult journey across the high ground, they hit the main road, only to realize that there was no way back again.

'The track down which we had come was too steep to return,' Colonel Franks records in the war diary. 'The village of Allarmont was strongly occupied by the enemy, and my track led out onto the main road only about 3 kms from where Major Power had effected his ambush.'

Colonel Franks now found himself on the main resupply route with two jeeps, unable to return cross-country and sandwiched between a heavily garrisoned village on the one side, and the site of the Major Power's devastating ambush on the other. Their position was fine to launch an ambush, but first they needed to locate that most vital of ambush priorities: a viable escape route.

Franks picked a track off his map that looked promising. They drove west up the main road, found it and recced it for quarter of a mile. The track seemed in fairly good order and certainly jeep-navigable. Escape route sorted, they returned to the main road and took up ambush positions. But they must have been spotted as they were doing so, for bursts of fire erupted from a house on the opposite side of the road.

Eight Vickers machine guns swung in that direction and unleashed hell. Armour-piercing rounds sliced through the building's rough-hewn stonework, stitching fist-sized holes in window frames and doors. By the time the jeeps had ceased firing, the enemy guns had fallen silent. But in the quiet that followed, the SAS men could hear German infantry dismounting from vehicles to either side of their position.

They'd had their hit; it was time to run.

They headed for their escape route at high speed. The two jeeps turned onto the track, but the rear wheels of Franks' vehicle skidded on the wet mud. Knobby tyres found their grip momentarily, before the entire rear end lost traction and swung around completely, slamming into a ditch and flipping the vehicle. Moments later it came to rest lying on its non-existent roof, wheels spinning uselessly in the air.

Fortunately, Franks and his three men had been thrown clear. But there was little time to hang around and try to right the stricken vehicle. The cries of enemy troops in pursuit could be heard, as could the ring of hobnailed boots on the road.

Franks and his men clambered onto the bonnet of the one serviceable jeep and, with Lieutenant Dill at the wheel, they headed up the track into the highlands, hanging on for dear life to whatever they could find. The heavily ribbed tyres tore through the dirt, eating up the terrain.

In spite of having lost a jeep, all was going passably well until Dill rounded a corner and was forced to slam on the brakes. Ahead, the track was blocked by fallen trees. Behind, their route was crawling with the enemy. Colonel Franks, Lieutenant Dill and their men had no choice but to abandon their one remaining vehicle.

They took off on foot with the enemy at their heels, running for the uncertain safety of the high ground.

Chapter Thirteen

As the Commander of 2 SAS and his small band of men raced for the heights above the Celles Valley, so Operation Waldfest was about to wreak terrible vengeance on the villagers of the Vosges. Following on the heels of Lieutenant Marx's strike onto German soil, Major Power's brazen attack was as a red rag to a bull. If anything gave the lie to Waldfest's effectiveness, it was a bunch of British parachutists driving around the Vosges in jeeps, blasting apart whatever they chose.

By now the SAS had been on the ground for six weeks, which was time enough for the SS and Gestapo to have hunted them down. In this they had failed. But they had done their homework well, and they had a good idea of exactly who they were up against. German intelligence reports from the time show how Isselhorst and his cronies had got to know their enemy in some considerable detail.

From captured . . . orders and papers it has been learned that the enemy intelligence service has tried to infiltrate single agents and teams and to build up Resistance groups in the rear of the present German front. In this work the SAS troops will share the principal role with special espionage agents.

When the troops jump they are equipped with everything they need for this penetration. Besides the equipment and weapons which the paratrooper carries with him in his jump bag, containers are dropped holding the usual supplies of food, extra weapons, ammunition, explosives . . . The intention is the interruption of railway lines, the blowing up of bridges, traffic junctions and telephone communications.

The architects of Waldfest had also come to know exactly who their adversaries in the Vosges were. 'There are at the moment 3 SAS Regiments which belong to the 1st SAS Brigade,' the German intelligence report stated. 'The Commander of the Brigade is a certain McLeod. The commander of the 1st SAS Regiment is Col. Kaine. The Commander of the 2nd SAS Regiment is Col. Franks.'

Brigadier-General Roderick McLeod was indeed the SAS Brigade Commander. The 1st SAS Regiment was commanded by Colonel Blair 'Paddy' Mayne – not the 'Kaine' of the German report, but close enough. And of course 'Col. Franks' was indeed the commander of 2 SAS, and the man on the ground in the Vosges orchestrating all the shoot-'em-up mayhem.

From captured documents and prisoner interrogations, *Standartenführer* Isselhorst had reached an assessment of just how real was the threat he was facing. 'Experience gained in the campaigns in ITALY and FRANCE shows that members of the SAS are specially trained for this type of work. Their activities are extremely dangerous. The presence of SAS units is to be reported immediately to the divisions concerned.'

In a sense, Isselhorst and his people had overemphasized the danger posed by the SAS in the Vosges. Fifty-odd Special Forces could only cause so much havoc and ruin. But it was that very fear and uncertainty – the myth of the winged-dagger-wearing avengers – which was perhaps their single greatest asset in the Vosges. Thousands of German troops had been drafted in to hunt down a few dozen SAS operators, and that kept them away from bolstering the Vosges defences and resisting Patton's advance.

As Franks noted in the war diary: 'On the whole the Germans seemed very scared of us. Judging by local reports our numbers had been much exaggerated . . . Before we had been found in the Moussey area they started visiting all the farms in the [Celles] woods and then billeting soldiers in them. If they had any suspicions, they razed the house to the ground and shot the occupants.'

The adoption of jeep-borne operations had been a master-stroke. In the eyes of the enemy, the SAS had to be a large and potent force, for how else could they risk driving about launching shoot-'em-up raids in the heart of enemy territory? Surely only a force acting from a position of strength would do such a thing. It was so blatant, it spoke of a serious military potency, or so it would seem.

As Franks noted in the war diary: 'It is quite certain that the appearance of the jeeps astounded and irritated the Germans, and made them redouble their efforts to destroy our party.'

For those orchestrating Waldfest it stood to reason that those jeeps would need to have a base of operations. And it stood to reason that some of the inhabitants of the Vosges *must* know who these brazen operators were and exactly where they were operating from.

As the SAS had not been found by 'normal' means – troop searches, aircraft overflights, tracing their radio signals and interrogations of prisoners – the fist of Waldfest was about to fall heaviest on those suspected of 'harbouring' this 'extremely dangerous' enemy. Thus the village of Moussey found itself bang in *Standartenführer* Isselhorst's sights.

The first the Op Loyton force knew of the savage clamp-down at Moussey was when Captain Henry Carey Druce unwittingly drove into the midst of it. It was the afternoon of 24 September 1944, and Druce was returning in a jeep from La Petite Raon, where he'd been searching for opportune targets. At three locations – La Petite Raon, Le Puid and Le Vermont – his jeeping patrol had encountered the enemy, unleashing fire from the Vickers Ks and killing a dozen or so German soldiers.

Speaking of Druce's jeep-borne operations, on which Fiddick served as one of his gunners, the Canadian airman remarked simply: 'His job was to create havoc, which he did.'

But the day was waning and Druce was yearning to return to SAS's Basse de Lieumont base. He had a special reason to want to get back there; en route, he'd managed to obtain a very tasty-looking French cheese. It was about the size and shape of a large car tyre, and having nowhere else to put it, Druce had strapped it to the leading jeep's bonnet. It struck him as lending their party a very Gallic air.

'I paid for it at some address someone had given me,' Druce noted of the cheese, 'and it was a huge thing. Where the hell do you put a cheese like that? I was very proud of myself, so we put it on the bonnet of the jeep.'

As the two jeeps neared Moussey, Druce had not the slightest inkling how badly things were amiss in their 'home' village. Just to be sure they could pass through unmolested, he stopped a woman on the outskirts. He asked if there were any Germans on the streets. The woman told him there were none. She had either lied to him or was mistaken, and Druce never was to discover which.

The pair of jeeps pushed into the centre of the village, rounding a slight bend leading into the square. All of a sudden, Druce realized just what they had stumbled into here. Sandwiched between the village churchyard and the war memorial there were several dozen SS troopers in full uniform. They were standing to attention, with a senior officer addressing them.

Lou Fiddick was driving the second jeep, and he was right on Druce's tail. 'The German commander was just assembling his men when we appeared,' he remarked. To one side stood the village school: it was crammed full of frightened-looking and cowed civilians. The SS had to be rounding up the Moussey villagers in preparation for yet another round of brutal reprisals.

'I wasn't expecting to see them, but they weren't expecting to see me,' Druce commented of the SS soldiers. At the front of the school were two large gateposts, with a sentry standing guard. He was the first to lay eyes on the British jeeps. He raised his arm to give the Nazi salute, clearly thinking that the jeep-borne force had to be a German. He would be the first to die.

Druce was at the leading jeep's wheel. He stamped on the gas, gunning the vehicle towards the ranks of enemy troops. Even as he accelerated, his men swung around their weapons and prepared to open fire. His gunner in the jeep's rear – Corporal 'Boris King'; in truth a Russian called Boris Kasperovitch – hunched over his twin Vickers and took aim. He opened fire on the sentry at the school gates, blasting him off his feet with a savage burst.

Seven Vickers spat long tongues of flame, the .303-inch rounds tearing into the SS parade at some 40 yards range, and fast closing. The Vickers K has a maximum rate of fire of 1,200 rounds per minute. In Druce's jeep they unleashed three magazines of ammo – 180 bullets – at the target, raking the ranks of the enemy from end to end. It took bare seconds to do so, and by the time of the final shots they were hammering into their targets at close to point-blank range.

The parade disintegrated. SS soldiers were blown off their feet by the intense barrage, the few survivors diving for whatever cover they could find. In the second jeep Lou Fiddick's crew followed suit, raking the enemy lines with rounds.

For a brief moment bullets cut the air around Druce's vehicle, as someone managed to return fire. Druce spotted the enemy gunners. The mayor's house was set a good way back from the road, and a pair of German soldiers were positioned on the roof.

Druce's rear and passenger-seat gunners were busy hammering fire into the devastated SS parade. Only Druce's gun was free. He slammed on the brakes, slowing his jeep to snail's pace, at which speed he was just about able to operate the gun. He grabbed the single Vickers one-handed, swung it around on its pivot mount, nailed the gunners on the mayor's roof in his iron sights and opened fire.

No sane soldier armed with a rifle chooses to stand firm against a Vickers K. Druce saw one figure get hit and fall as the other dived for cover. He dropped his gun, got both hands on the wheel again and got the jeep going at full speed, steering for their exit. By the time they were thundering around the right-hand turn at the far side of the square, they had left bloody chaos and carnage in their wake.

Druce figured some fifteen to twenty SS troopers had been killed or injured in the onslaught. There had been one significant casualty on the SAS side: the cheese.

'When we got to this group in the centre of Moussey we were shooting through this cheese,' Druce remarked. 'The gun that went through the cheese was on the driver's side, my side . . . So it really looked like a Swiss cheese by the end of it!'

As the two jeeps powered away, Druce and his fellow jeepers hoped that, amidst all the chaos, the bulk of the Moussey villagers had been able to make a break for it and escape. By the time their two jeeps reached the Op Loyton base, word seemed to have reached it about what was happening at Moussey, but the details remained sketchy and unclear.

'We heard that a lot of people had been rounded up,' remarked Druce. 'But I don't think even Brian [Franks] knew at that stage. I don't think it clicked with us that indeed there was a big German round-up taking place, and that these people were all being taken away.' Even when the SAS men did learn of the massive scale of the deportations, 'we had no idea where they were being taken, or whether they were being held permanent hostage or under what circumstances.'

Of course, *Standartenführer* Isselhorst knew exactly what fate awaited the 210 villagers seized in Moussey that day. In light of his failure to halt the operations of the SAS, or those of their allies in the Maquis, Isselhorst had unleashed his dogs of war. As Waldfest documents from the time noted, the aim of this Sunday 24 September mass round-up was to 'exterminate this alarming terrorist band' once and for all.

Einsatzkommando Ernst – commanded by *Sturmbannführer* Hans-Dietrich Ernst, fresh from sending 800 French Jews to the Auschwitz gas chambers – had been tasked to spearhead this new Waldfest crackdown. All across the villages of the Rabodeau Valley, able-bodied males were being rounded up and shipped off to the fearsome hellhole that was Schirmek's *Sicherungslager*.

The action had started at dawn, when *Einsatzkommando* Ernst, working with units from the SS and the *Wehrmacht*, had 'hit' Moussey. All those villagers not at first mass were dragged from their homes and herded towards the village school. Men, women and children were packed into the courtyard, opposite the crèche, where the Gestapo had made their temporary head-quarters. Those attending Abbé Gassman's service were dragged from the church into the square.

At neighbouring villages – La Petite Raon, Le Harcholet, Belval, Le Saulcy and Le Vermont – similar dawn raids were underway. In Moussey, it was only due to the efforts of Abbé Gassman and his cohort, the mayor, that the Germans were persuaded not to torch the village and to spare the women and children. The priest and the mayor had offered their lives to save the most vulnerable in their flock.

Even so, all able-bodied males were marched off to the local SS headquarters, situated at the grey-faced, Gothic and sinister-looking Château de Belval, a requisitioned country house lying further east along the valley. After a night of savage interrogations overseen by Commander Ernst, all men between the ages of seventeen and fifty were loaded aboard trucks and driven away. In addition to the 210 rounded up in Moussey, 309 had been taken from the surrounding villages.

Of those 519 deportees, few were destined to return. They would be swallowed up by the *Nacht und Nebel* – the night and the fog.

During the Moussey round-up the Gestapo chief had harangued the villagers, making it clear that the Germans knew there were British parachutists operating in the region, and even driving about in jeeps. The most severe punishment was about to be meted out to the Moussey inhabitants, as a warning to others who might be tempted to harbour 'terrorists'. No mercy would be shown.

'But we will allow for one exception,' the Gestapo chief announced. 'Any man who will step forward with information about these parachutists, he will be allowed to go free.'

Everyone knew where the SAS base was situated. The Gestapo chief repeated his offer. Not a single Moussey villager stepped forward to speak.

Later, during the Château de Belval and Schirmek interrogations, the same offer was put to the men, in more private and undoubtedly more persuasive circumstances. But even under torture, the villagers held firm. No German forces arrived at the SAS's deep mountain base. Indeed, Colonel Franks' men were able to keep operating from their Basse de Lieumont hideout, and there wasn't the slightest suggestion that they had been given away.

Colonel Franks had only made it back to that base by the skin of his teeth. Running from the enemy above the Celles Valley, Franks, Lieutenant Dill and their small force had made for the rough but ready sanctuary of Père George's farm. They'd lain low in the staunchly communist smallholder's barn as the manhunt ran its course all around them. Finally it had petered out, and the 2 SAS commander and his men had been able to return to their Basse de Lieumont redoubt.

They were minus their two jeeps, which meant that only four remained, and the Rabodeau Valley in which they had made their base of operations had lost some 500 of its inhabitants, but Colonel Franks remained undaunted. Indeed, he was burdened by a sense of guilt at the fate visited on the largely innocent villagers, and a part of him felt as if they had to redouble their efforts so that the people of Moussey might be avenged.

Writing immediately after Op Loyton, Colonel Franks made his feelings very clear. 'All the villagers of Moussey were first class . . . In Moussey, where we were welcomed, we were obviously looked upon as the spearhead of the Liberation Force. The fact that we have now left the area and brought such misery and unhappiness to the villagers, is a point which should not be overlooked, and I feel they will consider themselves let down by us.'

In the immediate aftermath of the 24 September mass deportations, Colonel Franks thirsted for one thing only: vengeance.

Henceforth, those who had targeted the French villagers would in turn get hit hard by the SAS. They would cut off the head of the snake. No German officer should be able to sleep soundly in his bed or travel the roads of the Vosges in comfort, as long as the SAS had bullets with which to fight.

First blood came quickly. On 25 September – the day after the mass deportations – one of Franks' foot patrols made it back to base. The force had been running low on explosives, especially tyre-bursters. But a superlative SAS operator and demolitions man named Lieutenant Silly had managed to improvise some DIY tyre-bursters, using plastic explosives combined with fog signals.

Placed on one of the main resupply routes running up the valley, Lieutenant Silly had got lucky. Two vehicles approached his home-made mines; both were German staff cars. He'd used a generous amount of PE. The two vehicles were ripped asunder. Those few who'd escaped death in the explosion were cut down by the patrol's Bren gun, as they stumbled from the burning vehicles. A truck acting as escort was also hit by the blasts and all its occupants killed.

That same day Major Power was back in action, and his 'jeeping activities' were to score another direct hit on the enemy's high command. Travelling in two jeeps they came to a road junction and spotted their prey: a staff car passing west to east. It was travelling at around 65 mph and was 400–500 yards away – at the far end of the Vickers' accurate reach.

They opened fire regardless. Multiple Vickers hammered rounds into the target, Major Power seeing tracer sparking all around the staff car and blanketing it with fire. The vehicle careered around the far bend, disappearing from sight, but already it had been peppered full of holes.

By now, Op Loyton had eight staff cars in the bag, and counting. The message had been sent: no German officer could travel the roads of the Vosges in safety.

And fate was to press another opportunity for revenge into Major Powers' hands. Returning to a temporary hideout in the woods, he was approached by a local Frenchman. He introduced himself as being a Maquis commander called Marcel. Marcel produced a sheaf of documents from deep inside his jacket. It was the entire order of battle (orbat) of the 21 Panzer Division, which had been passed to him just two days before.

The 21 Panzer Division had distinguished itself in the North African Campaign, when it had spearheaded many of Rommel's assaults. Again under Rommel's command, the 21st had been heavily engaged in the fighting on the Normandy beachheads, being the only Panzer division to engage Allied forces on the first day of the landings. And right now, the 21st was one of the key armoured units bolstering Himmler's desperate defence of the Vosges.

The papers listed the division's command structure, its armour, its positions, their major defences, and the distribution of the unit's men-at-arms. This kind of information was priceless. With the papers in hand Major Power thanked Marcel, loaded up the jeeps and headed direct for their Basse de Lieumont base.

Colonel Franks' radio report to London, sent the following morning, reflects the vital import of these papers. 'Have captured documents re order of battle, ammunition stats etc. . . . Two-One Panzer. One and Two Panzer Grenadier regiment. Document . . . states 112 Panzer Brigade has two Panthers, 17 PZ KW, four expecting five Panthers . . . Any hope RV American patrol to hand over.'

The 'PZ KW' was the Panzer IV medium tank, the work-horse of the German armoured divisions; the Panther was its more modern, and potent replacement.

As Franks' message made clear, such a thick wad of papers could not be transmitted via radio. But if they could get the orbat into General Patton's hands, it could prove a game-changing piece of intelligence. Of course, Patton's advance having stalled, no 'American patrols' were anywhere near the Op Loyton party right then – so it would need a volunteer to carry the priceless intel across the lines.

There was only one sensible candidate: Captain Henry Druce, of course.

Chapter Fourteen

Captain Druce had become rather blasé about wandering around the Vosges hoodwinking Germans. He'd taken to riding a bicycle about Moussey and nearby villages, dressed in civvies – battered top hat included – to recce potential targets. Druce believed that bluff and front were all that he needed to ease his way through checkpoints.

On one occasion he'd stopped for a drink in a bar where he had a regular source of intelligence, in the form of the barman. He'd gone to use the loo, only to hear a gun being cocked outside the door. Fearing he was about to get cornered, he'd dived out of the loo window. The only means of escape was a child's bicycle propped against one wall. He'd jumped on it and peddled off as shots rang around his ears, so making his getaway.

From Colonel Franks' note in the war diary, a casual reader could be forgiven for thinking that Druce's new mission to cross enemy lines was going to be a walk in the park: 'I decided to send Cpt. Druce through to contact the Americans, explain our position to them, and to give them . . . the captured documents that Major Power had brought in.'

Druce chose Lou Fiddick – Canadian airman-turned-SAS Vosges veteran – to accompany him on this special mission. These two men were about to attempt to sneak through terrain where two mighty armies were locked into a grim and brutal confrontation, the German forces hunkered down behind massive fortifications, gun emplacements and booby-trapped bridges and roads. But, if anything, Druce was even more offhand about the mission's risks than his colonel.

'I awoke at 0300 hours . . . and prepared to leave for the Americans . . .' Druce noted in the war diary. 'F/O [Flying Officer] Fiddick came with me and we reached St. Prayel by 1900 hours. Here we met two Milice who only had pistols to our Tommy Guns, so they ran away. After dark we bumped into a patrol . . . who heard us but could not find us, although they passed within a yard. We could not shoot them owing to the proximity of the river Meurthe, which we were about to cross.'

Fiddick was slightly more expressive about their desperate attempt to sneak through the enemy lines. 'Suddenly, we were challenged by a couple of sentries. They were armed and we were armed, and so we had this kind of cowboy-style stand-off where we just stared at each other. Then they backed slowly off. The tension levels were pretty high by now.'

'We clung to our guns and were ready to shoot our way out,' Druce conceded of this incident, which occurred on the approach to the bridge over the River Meurthe, 'which I'm glad to say we didn't have to do because we were not very good shots and we couldn't see in the dark. Anyhow, they disappeared and we went on to cross the bridge.'

The Germans had set their heaviest defences along both banks of the River Meurthe. If Druce and Fiddick were challenged while midway across, they would be sandwiched between those two defensive lines, and there would be little chance of escape. As they sneaked onto the bridge, a cry of alarm rang out in the darkness.

'I had a very bad time – fear – when that bloody man on the river challenged us,' Druce admitted. 'I thought we really had had it at that stage . . . We had this patrol walking backwards and forwards; really, they were within a couple of yards of us, and that was a bad moment. But they didn't hear us; they didn't see us. It was mousey-quiet. And anyhow they moved off and we moved over across the bridge.'

Having somehow sneaked across the River Meurthe without getting killed or captured, the two men found themselves in amongst the Germans' main defences in the depths of the night. They only realized that they'd reached the enemy's front-line positions when they tumbled into one of their trenches.

'Stumbling into the German trench was a little bit unsettling,' conceded Fiddick. As he and Druce crouched there in the darkness wondering if they'd been detected, they could hear German patrols moving to either side of them. The labyrinthine trench system was like something out of the First World War, and somehow Druce and Fiddick had to find a way through.

'We retired back into the bush a little distance,' Fiddick recalled. From there the two men tried to work out a safe route. Beyond the trenches lay no-man's-land, on the far side of which lay their second greatest challenge: approaching the Allied lines. It would be a pity to make it past the enemy, only to be shot by their own side.

'A thing I guess I'll always remember was crawling across that open field just on the far side of the trenches,' Fiddick recalled. 'I'm not sure if it was planted with potatoes or whatever it was, but we more or less had to crawl across this open field to avoid being seen by anyone who was in the trench.'

Having slithered through the darkness undetected, Druce and Fiddick stumbled into a second trench system. This, it turned out, was occupied by the 1st Spahis Regiment, part of General Leclerc's Free French forces, known as 'La Division Leclerc'. Leclerc had been one of the first to make his way to Britain under General Charles de Gaulle, raising a French army in exile – which was now fighting shoulder to shoulder with General Patton's 3rd Army.

Against all odds, Druce and Fiddick had made it.

Lou Fiddick's sojourn in the Vosges would end with the handing over of those precious documents to the American high command. He was ordered to return to his Canadian Air Force regiment. Not so Henry Carey Druce. As Colonel Franks' last working radio set had just gone on the blink, he'd had no choice but to ask the ever-resourceful Druce to sneak back across the lines, bringing some radio spare parts to the SAS base set in the heart of the Vosges.

Yet at that base things were looking increasingly troubled. In the forty-eight hours that it had taken Druce and Fiddick to cross the lines, Franks' force had been in action, but not all of it was by any means successful. A foot patrol had returned to base, having derailed a train. They'd struck some 10 miles south of Moussey, to the east of the town of St. Dié – showing how far and wide the SAS were still able to launch such attacks.

Strike one to the SAS.

But a jeep patrol led by Colonel Franks had driven into a savage ambush, and the colonel and his men had been lucky to escape alive. Indeed, they'd barely made it out of their base before the attack had hit them. Franks had been forced to abandon his mission – an attempt to reach Pierre-Percée and link up with Major Dennis Reynolds and Captain Whately-Smith. The two SAS officers – one of whom was still nursing his wounds – had been hidden in their cave for weeks now, and their every effort to reunite with the main force had been stymied.

Strike two to the enemy.

By now – 28 September – it was becoming increasingly clear that mounting further jeeping operations would be tantamount to suicide. Every village along the valley was garrisoned by heavy German forces – amounting to several thousand troops all told.

'All roads . . . were therefore barred to jeeps,' noted the war diary. 'Although jeeps could shoot their way out, they could not return, as presumably Germans would have strong M.G. [machine gun] posts in anticipation.'

Strike three to the enemy.

With 'jeeping' rendered all but impossible, Franks sent out multiple foot patrols – led by Lieutenants Marx, Dill, Silly and others. But the SAS colonel could sense the enemy circling like sharks around a bloody wreck at sea. Sure enough, Corporal Boris Kasperovitch – the Russian SAS man who'd shot up the SS parade in Moussey – was shot dead while out on one of those missions. Trooper Fred Puttick disappeared on the same patrol, either captured or killed.

Strike four to the enemy.

'We were gradually reduced to ambuscading on foot from the woods,' Chris Sykes, the 2 SAS intelligence officer, remarked.

'We had the consolation of knowing we had hurt the enemy and compelled them to withdraw considerable numbers of troops from their front line . . . in order to counter-attack their invisible foe in the Vosges.'

Worse was to come. As the weather grew colder and more bitter, the supplies of both the SAS and the surviving Maquis had dwindled to near zero. Maquis commander Joubert – whose young guns had fought so valiantly – was cornered while out collecting some urgently needed food and ammo. The Germans didn't know for sure that this was the Maquis leader they had so long sought, but with every able-bodied male having been shipped off to the concentration camps, they had their suspicions.

Standartenführer Isselhorst was keen for Joubert to confess quickly. He decided that torture would be the best way to 'persuade' the Frenchman to reveal the location of the SAS base. The Gestapo started on the captive's feet, battering them with a heavy club until all the bones were smashed. Then they worked upon the rest of his body. Joubert never cracked. He knew everything and yet he told nothing. But even so, with his capture, Joubert's Maquis were finished as a fighting force.

A day or two later, Etienne – the seemingly indestructible and ageless leader of the 'old drunkards' Maquis – was found dead in the woods. No mortal enemy had vanquished him. He'd fallen victim to a sudden stroke. But, like Joubert, his wonderfully irreverent and unorthodox band of Maquis died with him.

And, high in the hills above Moussey, the Gestapo finally paid a visit to Père George's isolated farmstead. The gnarled and moustachioed farmer and diehard communist was duly arrested and carted off to Natzweiler. Although Père George would never break or talk, in two fell strokes Colonel Franks' force had been deprived of much of their operational infrastructure in the Vosges: the two local Resistance groups that had proved such steadfast allies, and one of their key points of sanctuary.

The Op Loyton war diary records their situation thus: 'area full of enemy, food short and the French too frightened to help'. No doubt about it, Isselhorst's Waldfest appeared to be working.

On 30 September, Captain Gough turned up at Colonel Franks' Basse de Lieumont base. Gough had been forced to accept that the Maquis were a spent force, which meant that the Jedburghs' role had become largely redundant. He was about to depart on a similar journey to that undertaken by Fiddick and Druce and attempt to make his way through to the American (and French) lines.

Gough's last radio message reflected the kind of difficulties he'd faced in the past days. 'Gave ground. SAS will liaise with you. Great difficulty working alone. Can't come up on regular skeds. Will come up on emergency channel when can . . .'

After bidding a farewell to Colonel Franks and his men, Gough set out westwards. At some stage in the next few days he was captured by the men of *Einsatzkommando* Ernst. Following violent interrogations by the Gestapo, Gough was shipped out to Schirmek's *Sicherungslager* to join the other Op Loyton captives enjoying Camp Commandant Karl Buck's hospitality, in his underground cells.

It never rains but it pours – especially in the Vosges. On 2 October Lieutenant's Silly's patrol returned from operations. They had succeeded in blowing up two German half-tracks, and better still a staff car, which raised Op Loyton's tally to nine. But they'd had to strike as far east as Belval to score such a rare success, and the terrain on all sides was reported to be crawling with the enemy.

So thick were the grey lice on the ground that Franks had been forced to send a very reluctant message to SFHQ: 'Re-supply impossible until further notice.' With no airdrops possible, and with the Rabodeau villages robbed of their populations, the SAS men were starting to freeze to death, to starve, and to run out of bullets.

The state of Franks' men can be gauged by a message sent in response to their final resupply by air. 'Send what you are asked to send . . . On the last re-supply it must have been obvious that food was the main item required, yet the first two containers opened contained Bazookas and bombs, which had NOT . . . been asked for.'

Hollow-eyed, shivering and with their weight falling off them, Franks could tell that his men were approaching a state in which they would no longer be able to fight. He'd been promised the American cavalry would come riding over the horizon. In fact, by rights they should have reached Moussey days ago. But there was zero sign of them and, as the weather worsened, the chances of a breakthrough plummeted in the increasingly snow-bound Vosges.

Incredibly, Isselhorst wasn't done yet. As September blew through to a freezing October, and fresh falls of snow carpeted the high ground, so a fresh wave of purges was launched in the suffering villages strung along the Rabodeau Valley. Determined to up the incidence of searches, arrests, deportations and executions, the forces of Waldfest struck again and again.

By the end of the first week of October some 1,000 villagers had been seized across the valley, earning it the haunting name of 'the Vale of Tears'. Shipped off to the concentration camps, 661 would never return. At some stage during the process of rounding them up, it seems the location of the SAS base was given away.

On 6 October, what Isselhorst doubtless intended to be his final assault was launched against Colonel Franks' Basse de Lieumont headquarters. Captain John Hislop – Phantom commander, champion jockey, and one of Druce's original advance party – was at the base that late afternoon when the enemy were first detected. From all around, the noise of a force of approaching troops filtered through the thick woodland.

It being pine forest, the trees hadn't lost any of their greenery with the coming of winter, and the pine needles served to deaden the sound. Even so, the telltale clink of metal upon metal, the crunch of a fallen branch underfoot and the faint rustle of bodies forcing a way through thick undergrowth carried clearly to the assembled men. Worse still, they could hear the spine-chilling whine of dogs. Completely surrounded, their only option was to remain utterly still and silent, in the hope of somehow evading the search.

Hislop feared there was no way they could avoid discovery, at which point they 'would be outnumbered beyond reasonable hope of survival . . . I thought, "this looks like the finish," and considered how best I could meet it.' While not greatly fearing death, Hislop doubted if he could stand up to interrogation by the Gestapo. He vowed instead to go down fighting.

He was hunched over a fire, together with fellow Phantom Peter Johnsen and Major Power. The smoke was drifting into the thick rain and fog, so it would hardly be visible. Johnsen was turning his socks over the fire, in an effort to dry them, but the young man's hands had started to tremble with the tension. Over the past few weeks Johnsen had distinguished himself as a cool, level-headed and courageous operator, and it struck Hislop as being an utter waste that such a fine young man should lose his life at a time and place as this.

Hislop felt that to some extent he'd lived his life. He was reconciled now to making a last-ditch stand and meeting a bloody end. As for Major Peter Power, he was leaning back against a tree, as inscrutable as ever. He had a cigarette glued to his lower lip, the tip barely glowing, and his face was as expressionless as if he was scrutinizing a particularly promising hand at poker and awaiting the next play.

The tense quiet was shattered by a noise that was as unexpected as it was unwelcome. Someone had dropped an empty tin. It went clattering downhill, deafeningly. In the ringing silence that followed, everyone expected the enemy to close for the kill. The noise of pursuit continued, and even through the thick screen of trees it sounded as if the hunters were drawing ever closer.

The British soldiers tensed over their weapons. No one could quite believe it when the sound of the approaching force gradually seemed to fade away. The forest all about fell silent once more. It was inconceivable that the German troops hadn't heard that tin clan clanking as it fell. For several long minutes the men remained still and quiet, listening intently. But much as they strained their ears, the enemy force seemed to have departed.

Dusk was upon the forest now, and Colonel Franks ordered his men to collapse the base immediately. Once more they were on the run, only this time they were forced to abandon their much-loved jeeps. They needed to travel light and fast, using the remotest, most inaccessible terrain possible. They moved out at nightfall, flitting through the deepening darkness, and in doing so they escaped all but certain death.

The enemy approach had been a recce, and at first light the following morning they returned in force. They hit the base with overwhelming force, including armour and field guns brought up for the purpose, but by then the SAS had disappeared, ghost-like, into the hills. Or rather, not quite all of Colonel Franks' force had departed. Seven brave and courageous men, commanded by the redoubtable David Dill – the baby-faced but fearsome SAS lieutenant from Druce's original drop – had been left at the base as a rearguard.

Their mission was to wait there for Captain Druce, who was expected to arrive at any moment, having crossed back across the lines with the radio spares. Instead, they were surrounded by a massive force of German troops. In the ferocious firefight that followed, Dill and his men held out for four hours, before the last of their ammunition was exhausted.

The German officer who accepted their surrender shook Dill by the hand. 'You are my prisoner,' he announced. 'You are a soldier and so am I.'

Along with Dill, Sergeant Jock Hay – Druce's long-standing right-hand man –Lance-Corporals George Robinson and Fred Austin, and Troopers Jimmy Bennet and Edwin Weaver, plus their young and indomitable French guide, Roger Souchal, were all taken captive. Sadly, they weren't to be held for long by the *Wehrmacht*. Instead, they were handed over to the men of *Einsatzkommando* Ernst.

Dill and his companions were sent to the same processing centre as the other SAS captives: Schirmek's *Sicherungslager*. In the subterranean cells they were reunited with Captain Victor Gough, plus several other SAS men who had been captured. One of Dill's men, Trooper Edwin Weaver, was to distinguish himself mightily at Schirmek; he refused to stop yelling 'Fucking Germans!' whenever one should enter their cell.

The seventeen-year-old Roger Souchal tried to convince his captors that he was a bona fide member of the SAS Regiment, so he could remain in the company of those with whom he had so faithfully served. He argued that he was a French Canadian member of the unit. Indeed, his details had been radioed through to SAS headquarters, so that his name could be formally recorded on the 2 SAS orbat, as an added form of protection.

But Souchal was soon denounced by a local Frenchwoman who identified him as a member of the Maquis, at which moment he was carted off to a concentration camp. Souchal would survive the horrors that lay ahead, and after the war he was awarded the King's Medal for Service in the Cause of Freedom, given to foreign civilians who had aided the British in the war.

The citation stated: 'Monsieur Roger Souchal . . . served as a courier and guide to a detachment of SAS in the Vosges . . . He took part in ambushes against German convoys . . . and the manner in which he employed his knowledge of the locality was of vital importance to SAS detachments whereby an error in the choice of route could have cost the life of the detachment.'

There had been many times when Roger Souchal had held the lives of Colonel Franks' men in the palm of his hand and the young Frenchman had not been found wanting. Now, bereft of their fearless and spirited guide, the main SAS force was left to fend for itself in the forests of the Vosges as the enemy closed in.

And somewhere in those benighted hills, the lone figure of Captain Henry Druce was making for a camp that had been seized by the enemy.

Chapter Fifteen

True to his word, Druce had returned to the Vosges. He'd used the same route as Fiddick and he had come out on, crossing over from the French lines. If anything, his war diary entry is even shorter than that concerning his outward journey, and downplays things magnificently. 'I decided to return to the Colonel and put him fully in the picture of the situation for our future operations. Also to take Capt. Hislop's badly needed [radio] set and new crystals.'

The 'situation for future operations' was really very simple: no American forces were about to punch through the Vosges any time soon. Just as the weather over the rugged mountains had rendered resupply flights all but impossible, so conventional military operations there had become ever less feasible.

Of recrossing the lines Druce wrote that he was 'escorted by a French patrol as far as the edge of the woods . . . There was a German M.G. post here, but the enemy must have been asleep because it did not fire. We went a mile or so into the woods and waited there until daylight.'

Aware that a rearguard party was awaiting him, he made for the SAS's Basse de Lieumont base, only to discover that it had been overrun, and that Lieutenant Dill and his men had been captured. Druce asked the locals about Père George's farm, hoping that Franks and his men might have gathered there. He was told that German troops had burned it to the ground.

With no way of discovering the present location of the Op Loyton force, Druce could conceive only one course of action: the man who had started it all with that 12 August airdrop turned around and prepared to cross over the lines for a third time, heading back to General Leclerc's forces.

Druce had one other urgent reason to make for the Allied lines. From his contacts around Moussey he had discovered some vital intelligence, information that he believed would radically alter General Patton's plan of attack, and the SAS captain felt a pressing need to get it into the Allied commander's hands.

'Captain Jean [a Maquis leader] had procured information about the arrival of three new German Divisions near St. Dié, where I knew the Americans were supposed to be starting their attack,' Druce noted in the war diary. 'The information I had on the three Divisions was so important that it had to be transmitted to the Americans immediately . . . I set out in the morning on the same route for the third time . . .'

As Druce struck out for Allied lines, matters had reached their lowest ebb for the main body of the Op Loyton force. A few hours' rest in comfort and safety; a nourishing meal; a warm, dry place in which to sleep – these were the kind of things the men could only dream of. The worries of normal civilian life didn't touch these war-weary, harried soldiers any more. The future barely concerned them, for they lived from day to day.

Colonel Franks and his men no longer had a base of operations. They were more or less permanently sodden wet and bitterly cold, and forever on the move. Even so, they weren't quite done with their raiding yet. An SAS Lieutenant Swayne and his patrol had been in action. They'd struck on the road leading south from Neufmaisons – the village lying just to the east of Veney, where Druce and his men had been forced to wait for so long for their resupply airdrop.

Lieutenant Swayne's attack was the last significant action of Op Loyton, and it proved wonderfully apposite; they had hit and destroyed two German staff cars, which meant that the tally now stood at eleven. In large part the SAS's mission in the Vosges had been to target senior enemy commanders: *to decapitate the snake*. After destroying eleven staff cars and their occupants, few could argue that the Nazi serpent hadn't had its head significantly hacked.

Swayne's force was reunited with Franks' nomadic headquarters unit on 8 October 1944. That same day, General Eisenhower himself wrote to SAS headquarters, his letter one of fulsome praise regarding the Regiment's achievements in occupied France:

I wish to send my congratulations to all ranks of the Special Air Service Brigade on the contribution which they have made to the success of the Allied Expeditionary Force.

The ruthlessness with which the enemy have attacked Special Air Service troops has been an indication of the injury which you were able to cause to the German armed forces both by your own efforts and by the information which you gave of German disposition and movements.

Many Special Air Service troops are still behind enemy lines; others are being reformed for new tasks. To all of them I say 'Well done, and good luck.'

Amidst the freezing fog in the hills somewhere to the east of Moussey, Franks and his men were in need of all the luck they could get.

On 9 October 1944 the SAS colonel bowed to the inevitable. With little ammo, explosives, food or shelter available to his men, he ordered that Operation Loyton to be brought to a close. A mission originally scheduled to last from two to three weeks – the time it was expected in which US forces would reach the Vosges – had morphed into an eight-week epic.

'I decided to end the operation,' Franks noted in the war diary, 'and instructed parties to make their way to the American lines as best they could.'

Franks split his men into four- and six-man units. Each was to leave at different times and via different routes, to try to maximize their chances of making it through alive. Franks would remain with a headquarters element – consisting of Major Power, Captains Sykes and Hislop, plus two others – at an RV sited in the Celles Valley. There they would wait for forty-eight hours, hoping to link up with David Dill's rearguard, Captain Henry Druce and others.

Of course, Lieutenant Dill and his men had been taken captive, and Druce was headed back towards the lines, but in the chaotic and hunted situation that Franks found himself in he knew none of that. The SAS colonel also wanted to make one last attempt to bring Major Dennis Reynolds and Captain Whately-Smith in from the cold, and to get those two officers on their way back to friendly lines.

Wishing each other *bonne chance*, the remaining Op Loyton warriors split up. Some forty men turned westwards, slipping into the dank and dripping forest and heading towards enemy and, hopefully in due course, friendly, lines. Franks' party of six turned north, making for the Celles Valley. It had been raining solidly for days now, the downpour turning to sleet and snow on the high ground. The conditions were the most miserable and soul-destroying yet.

On arrival at their RV grid, Franks' party took shelter in a deserted sawmill. It was safer to billet themselves in the forest, but even the hardiest of souls couldn't sleep out in such conditions – not for days on end. That evening they helped themselves to some apples stored in a barn owned by some villagers who had helped the SAS in the past.

Sykes went to speak to the family, but he found them utterly terrified. The Gestapo had discovered their sympathies and they had come to arrest the man of the house. Not finding him, they had delivered an ultimatum: either he gave himself up, or they would return and burn down the family home. His wife was distraught; with an elderly mother and a baby, what was she to do?

Franks' force slept the night in the sawmill. The following morning they paid a last visit to the forester who had been acting as their go-between with the two SAS officers hidden in the Pierre-Percée cave. The forester was adamant: with the Celles Valley crawling with Germans, if Major Reynolds and

Captain Whately-Smith broke cover, it would probably prove the death of them.

Franks asked the forester to pass them a final message. They were to lie low in their cave and await the arrival of the Americans. It couldn't be long now. The forester gave what little food he could to the SAS men as sustenance for their onward journey, and each party bade the other farewell. By the time Franks and his men made it back to the sawmill, the Gestapo had arrived in the neighbourhood.

It was late in the afternoon, and the six Special Forces men were forced to watch from their place of hiding as the Gestapo interrogated the French family. Their questions were all about the whereabouts of the missing husband and the 'British parachutists'. The woman of the house answered, but she clearly didn't satisfy Isselhorst's men; they proceeded to round up her livestock and throw it into their military truck, after which they smashed up her home and set it ablaze.

Franks and his men were itching to gun down the five Gestapo bully boys. They could so easily have killed Isselhorst's Nazi thugs. But what then? They could hardly take an old woman, a mother and a baby with them to cross the front lines. Alternatively, if they left them here surrounded by Gestapo corpses, the family's fate would be sealed. It seemed that the only way to at least save their lives was to do the most difficult thing of all and to not intervene.

Burning up with rage and anger, Franks ordered his men to hold their fire. It would have been so easy for the woman of the house to slip the Gestapo a quiet word: *the men you seek are hiding in the sawmill*. But not a word was said. Instead, she watched in silence as her home and all her worldly possessions were destroyed before her eyes. The last the SAS men saw were two tearful, forlorn figures carrying a baby, walking north into the pouring rain.

With Druce departed, and scattered SAS teams making their way across the lines, John Hislop was the last remaining member of those 'originals' who had dropped with Druce onto the 12 August DZ. Chilled to the bone and with a dull hunger gnawing at his guts, Hislop's nerves were on edge. To make matters worse, the sole surviving Jed Set was most definitely on the blink.

The morning of 12 October dawned blissfully fine and clear – perfect conditions for making radio contact with London. Hislop managed to raise SFHQ to ask if there was any final task required of the rump of Op Loyton, before they too departed for the lines. The reply was the one that all had hoped for: the last men on the ground were to return forthwith.

Message received, Hislop smashed up and buried the Jed Set and burned the code books. There was an air of finality about doing so, one replete with promise and menace in equal measure. Promise, because they were finally homeward bound; menace, because of what lay between these men and safety: several thousand German troops resorting to ever more desperate measures to stem the tide of the Allied advance.

The SAS parties that had gone ahead of Franks' force had run the gauntlet of that menace. Extraordinarily, in some cases they had continued to battle alone, surrounded and running short of everything needed to sustain life and to wage war.

In one case, Lieutenant Swayne – the man who had destroyed the eleventh German staff car – had discovered that the enemy was running ammunition supplies to the front using 'ambulances' marked with a Red Cross. This was against all the rules of war. Vehicles marked with that universally respected symbol were granted unhindered access to the battlefield, for they were presumed to be carrying wounded.

Swayne had three men under his command. Two couldn't swim, so they needed to find an unguarded bridge to cross the Meurthe. There were none. Trapped on the wrong side of the river, they were forced to go to ground. But upon rumbling the enemy's 'ambulance deception', they decided to have one last strike and blow up an ambulance-cum-ammo-truck. The massive explosion tore apart two other 'ambulances' travelling in convoy and likewise packed full of war materiel.

Swayne's men were also confronted by thirty Tiger and Panther tanks moving through the forest, many of which were likewise marked with the Red Cross symbol. This time, there was little the SAS men could do to stop them. Indeed, they would only make it through to safety with the help of the locals, who dressed them in women's clothing and make-up to hide them from the rampaging enemy troops.

Driven to ever more desperate extremes of brutality, the local SS officer ordered the 'evacuation' of the village in which Lieutenant Swayne's men were hiding. Once the villagers had taken to the road, the SS proceeded to machine-gun the evacuees. Scores of innocents were mown down on the streets.

Into such bloody mayhem headed Colonel Franks and his force of six. They reached the Meurthe at nightfall, only to find that the railway bridge they had intended to cross was guarded by hyper-alert sentries. Franks, Hislop, Sykes, Power and their two fellows were chased away by a salvo of grenades. Franks' party also had a man who couldn't swim – Squadron Sergeant Major (SSM) White – and they encountered similar trouble in finding an unguarded bridge.

Eventually, Colonel Franks and Major Power decided they would have to risk swimming the Meurthe with White held between them. They reached the far bank, to discover that the forest thinned noticeably. As day broke the six men found themselves moving through sparse cover, compared to the dense forests they had grown used to in the Vosges.

They had to move with extreme caution now, skirting around enemy positions and diving flat in the bush at the approach of any vehicle. By dusk they'd reached a position where they figured the German front line had to lie. They paused in a patch of woodland to do a map check. Gathered closely around a shaded torch, they tried to work out exactly where they were. Suddenly, an arm emerged from the darkness, a finger jabbing at a spot on the map.

'*Du bist hier.*' You are here.

Unnoticed, some German soldiers had approached to help what they presumed was a friendly patrol unsure of its location. For a split second Franks and his men were frozen to the spot, before they took to their heels. They thundered out of the wood and into a ploughed field. Major Power promptly tripped on a telephone wire and went flying, but being a seasoned rugby player he was up and running again in a flash.

Shots rang out of the darkness, which spurred the six to run even faster. They'd put 500 yards between themselves and the enemy gunners when finally they paused to catch their breath. The firing had ceased now, but on all sides they could detect signs of an enemy presence, including what sounded like a ration truck doing the rounds.

They pressed onwards through the freezing night, pausing just before dawn to grab a few of hours' desperate rest. By now Chris Sykes was hallucinating with the cold and the hunger, and imagining Germans at every turn. At first light the party was on the move again, brushing off the thick crust of frost that had settled onto their torn, blood-and-mud-spattered uniforms.

It was past midday when Colonel Franks, in the lead, whipped around and started running back the way he had come, his eyes staring wildly, cheeks cadaverous and jaw jutting bonily from his skin.

The familiar cry rang out from behind him: '*Achtung!*'

It was followed by a volley of shots, one of which tore into the wooden stock of SSM White's M1 carbine. The six men ran, losing each other in the bullet-riven chaos. Hislop, Major Power and one other – SAS man Joe Owens – headed in one direction, with Colonel Franks leading Chris Sykes and SSM White in the other. Hislop, Power and Owens went to ground in the thick undergrowth, as the sound of search parties drew ever closer.

They lay still as death, pistols cocked, as bayonets jabbed into bushes to either side of their hiding place. Just when it seemed that the enemy must discover them, a massive barrage of incoming fire slammed into what had to be the German's front-line trenches. American forces had unleashed an attack. Those forming the search party dashed back to their posts, saving Hislop et al. from almost certain discovery.

SAS board a Bristol Bombay aircraft.
In August 1944 some sixty men would parachute 500 miles behind enemy lines into the Vosges Mountains of northeastern France, on the fateful Operation Loyton, in what would become known as 'the SAS's Arnhem'.

Members of 2 SAS muster.
The censor has blacked out the SAS cap badge in the photo, to prevent identification. The inclement weather of June and July 1944 would delay their mission for several weeks, with fatal consequences for many.

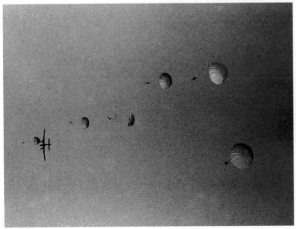

In the Summer of 1944 Winston Churchill and American President Roosevelt ordered a series of massive operations to drop weapons to the French Resistance, alongside Special Forces to train and fight with them. In Operation Cadillac alone some 300 American Liberator bombers parachuted 400 tonnes of arms to the Resistance forces ranged across the Dordogne.

Hauptsturmführer Karl Buck, Camp Commandant at Schirmek's security camp, where those SAS and SOE agents captured during the Vosges mission were taken for processing.

Josef Kramer, formerly of Auschwitz and Belsen, and then Commandant of Naztweiler Concentration Camp, where those Special Forces members taken prisoner in the Vosges were sent for extermination.

Reinhard Gehlen, Hitler's powerful commander of intelligence on the Eastern Front, who would become a foremost CIA asset, like so many Nazi war criminals, including some of the chief architects of the Vosges atrocities.

Oberwachtmeister Heinrich 'Stuka' Neuschwanger – named Stuka after the hated German dive-bomber. A brutal sadist, he led the torture and murder of Special Forces captured in the Vosges.

Captain Victor Gough commanded a three-man SOE 'Jedburgh' unit, tasked to link up with the Resistance and raise bloody insurrection in the Vosges. Taken captive, he was one of those who would never return.

Major Peter Lancelot John le Poer Power MC, a former tea-planter from Ceylon, who would prove himself an SAS raider par excellence, taking out the enemy's top commanders.

Captain John Hislop (pictured after the war), a champion horseracing jockey, was accused by the regular army of having a 'regrettable lack of military aptitude'. His actions with the SAS in the Vosges would prove otherwise.

Captain Henry Carey Druce, of the SAS and SOE, who earned renown for heading into battle in a black silk top hat. He escaped from the Gestapo's clutches, and specialized in sneaking through enemy lines dressed as a French peasant.

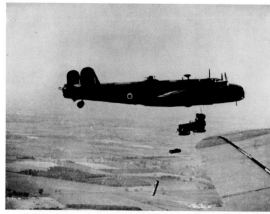

Hit-and-run jeep-mounted operations were the SAS's speciality. Amazingly, the RAF air-dropped jeeps into the rugged Vosges mountains, so the SAS could wreak havoc on the German lines, so enabling Allied forces to break through into Germany itself.

Jeeps parachuted into the Vosges often had to be retrieved from trees. 'Even worse was getting rid of the parachutes, so the Germans wouldn't know we'd been there', remarked Canadian airman and honorary SAS man Lou Fiddick.

The jeeps' Vickers machine guns were perfect for shooting up staff cars, to terrorise the enemy's high ranks – a key aim of Colonel Brian Franks' force in the Vosges. With heavier armour the SAS men scattered explosive charges disguised as rocks to blow apart passing vehicles, as with these captured half-tracked rocket launchers.

CAPTAIN JONES REPORTING FROM SCHIRMECK S/R!

WHAT—NO CABBAGE SOUP?

The unbreakable spirit of SOE officer Victor Gough. Captured, beaten and tortured horrifically, he found the strength to draw these cartoons while incarcerated in Schirmek's *Sicherunglager* (security camp) and held in underground cells. They served to bolster his fellow SOE and SAS captives' morale.

The usual suspects. Concentration Camp Natzweiler's *Lager Wache* – the camp guard – those who oversaw the murder of hundreds of French Resistance fighters, as well as the SAS and SOE who had fought alongside them in the Vosges.

Last stand. SAS Lieutenant Black and seven others were surrounded in this building, and fought to their last bullet. They were taken captive by those who were under orders from Hitler to exterminate all captured Allied Special Forces, 'without mercy wherever they find them.'

A French Resistance fighter, more commonly know as 'the Maquis'. In the Vosges, thousands joined forces with the SAS to rise up against the hated enemy, only for the Gestapo and SS to inflict terrible vengeance.

Captured SOE agents Diana Rowden and Vera Leigh (pictured) – together with Sonya Olschanezky and Andrée Borrel – were sent to Natzweiler for termination. Their cases would become a key focus of the SAS Nazi hunters, in particular tracking down the SS camp doctor who had injected each woman with a supposedly lethal toxin.

The furnace at Natzweiler. When the four female SOE agents were fed into the ovens by the camp's chief executioner, *Hauptscharführer* Peter Straub, one at least was still alive. Resisting to the last, she reached up and raked his face with her nails, the scars from which enabled the SAS Nazi hunters to track down and identify her killer.

The Natzweiler gas generator. Inmates were used as live human guinea pigs on which to test the Nazi's fearsome chemical weapons, plus the antidotes to them.

In the summer of 1945 SAS Major Bill Barkworth's Nazi-hunters exhumed this mass grave, in the Erlich Forest, on the outskirts of the German city of Gaggenau, unearthing the bodies of their former SAS and SOE comrades. In doing so they solved the fate of some of the thirty-one missing SAS and SOE operators captured in the Vosges.

SOE Captain and Russian Prince Yuri 'Yurka' Galitzine, whose discovery of the horrors at Natzweiler would transform him into a Nazi hunter without equal. Captain Galitzine was the driving force behind the secret SAS man-hunting teams.

Lest we forget. SAS Sergeant Fitzpatrick and Troopers Conway and Elliott, three of the ten buried in the graveyard at Moussey, a village that has become part of the SAS legend, due to its unwavering loyalty during the war.

The fighting lasted until nightfall, which gave the three men the perfect opportunity to slip away. The night was pitch dark, but Major Power set a compass bearing for where he figured the nearest US positions had to be. The three men set out, with Hislop holding onto Major Power's belt and Owens holding onto Hislop's in turn. Thanks to the SAS major's sterling skills at navigation they reached a road that he was certain lay in friendly hands, and they took cover in some bushes.

Come daybreak, they saw a patrol of US troops marching down the road. The three men rose from the undergrowth and, waving and shouting for joy, they announced their arrival and their deliverance from all but certain death.

It was the morning of 15 October 1944. For Captain John Hislop, a man once accused of having a 'regrettable lack of military aptitude', Op Loyton had turned into a two-month ordeal. Colonel Franks, Captain Chris Sykes and SSM White also made it that morning, though the colonel was shot in the arm when the Americans mistook him for one of the enemy.

In dribs and drabs, other Op Loyton teams also made it through to US forces, although after his repeated raids against the enemy – including the one, dramatic strike onto German soil – Lieutenant Karl Marx was so ill that he practically had to crawl through the lines. So sick was he as a result of his travails in the Vosges that he would be invalided out of the army.

There were others who were even less fortunate. Lieutenant Johnsen's Phantom party was shot to pieces, only a badly wounded Johnsen managing to drag himself across the lines. The others lay where they had fallen, gunned down by the enemy in no-man's-land.

And in a cave in the woods at Pierre-Percée, two SAS officers were readying themselves to make their own foray towards the Allied lines. Major Dennis Reynolds was much recovered from his wounds, and he, like Captain Whately-Smith, was impatient to join the war and to fight.

But their efforts to do so would end in darkness and bloody ruin.

Chapter Sixteen

Barely two weeks after being shot and injured while crossing the lines, the indefatigable Colonel Franks issued a 'SECRET' memo on the fate of the eighty-two men deployed on Op Loyton – Phantoms, Jedburghs and SAS alike. Just a handful were recorded as 'killed in action'. They included Sergeant Lodge, Troopers Davis and Hall and Corporal Kasperovitch.

By contrast, thirty-one were listed as 'MISSING, BELIEVED PW' (PW standing for prisoner of war) or simply as 'MISSING'. The 'missing' included Captain Gough, Lieutenant Dill and his 'rearguard' party, as well as Major Reynolds and Captain Whately-Smith – the last of the Op Loyton force to try to effect an escape. None had made it through to Allied lines.

In short, little or nothing was known about the fate of more than one-third of Colonel Franks' force. The 2 SAS commander had failed to bring them home, but he lived in hope that some at least might have been taken as prisoners of war. Which raised the question: what might the future hold for those captives?

Against seemingly impossible odds, Operation Loyton had delivered; chaos and havoc had been spread across the Vosges. The war diary listed the impact the long weeks of raiding had had upon the main supply routes that ran through the valleys:

'SAS attacks and demolitions have reduced enemy use of this road by estimated 50% plus . . . Due to SAS attacks and demolitions this road is no longer available to enemy traffic . . .' Two major railways were listed as 'knocked out by SAS; not in use'.

As Captain Hislop commented, it was only after the end of the mission that the true extent of Loyton's impact could be gauged, including the extent of disruption and alarm to which the SAS presence gave rise amongst the Germans. 'Troops in the area were kept in a state of permanent tension, never knowing when they were likely to be ambushed, or blown up by a mine laid on a road.'

Nothing struck fear into the hearts of the enemy foot soldiers more than witnessing their high command being targeted and killed. On Op Loyton, the SAS plan of hitting staff cars above all else had paid massive dividends. With an entire German division having been diverted to the hunt, Loyton also scored a major victory simply by pinning down thousands of German troops who would have been better deployed fighting on the front.

Viewed from this standpoint, *Standartenführer* Isselhorst's Waldfest had proved something of a failure. Across the Vosges thousands of villagers had been rounded up, beaten, tortured, killed or shipped off to the concentration camps, but that had not put a stop to Op Loyton. And with the withdrawal of the majority of Franks' men, Isselhorst and his cronies were left with only one target for their retribution: a few dozen Special Forces captives.

Colonel Franks and his fellow commanders suspected that the future for those men might well be bleak, but they had no clear idea of the fate of the 'missing'. The first clues as to what the enemy intended for them would come from the most unlikely of quarters.

In the final days of October 1944 the Americans made their long-awaited advance into the Vosges. It happened against all expectations. In the terrible conditions of that storm-swept autumn, Patton's army was unable to rely upon Allied air power to provide the decisive advantage. Likewise, the US General's armour was rendered largely impotent by the freezing, snow-bound conditions.

Patton's 7th Army broke through by the sheer force of ballsy, courageous soldiering, as American infantry fought a series of savage, uphill battles, advancing through snowdrifts and dark, frozen woodlands, and often closing at close quarters with the enemy. Indeed, the 7th Army's victory represented the first time in recorded history that an attacker had succeeded in vanquishing a defender entrenched in the Vosges, by force of arms alone.

One man within the 7th Army had a somewhat different agenda, one that wasn't limited purely to waging war. Prince Yuri 'Yurka' Galitzine, a 21-year-old Russian royal born to an English mother, was attached to the 7th Army as part of the Political Warfare Executive (PWE), an SOE spin-off tasked with propaganda operations. The aim of the PWE was to win the information war by placing positive stories about the Allies and negative ones about the enemy in the press.

Two months earlier, Captain Galitzine had landed on a beach at St. Tropez, then a quiet and little-known village on

France's Mediterranean coast. He was part of a three-man PWE team – consisting of himself, an American and a Frenchman – charged by Allied high command with gathering intelligence on whatever secrets the retreating German forces might have left behind.

Born in Japan, Galitzine had lived in Austria and France, before moving to Britain with his mother. He'd led a privileged youth, moving in high society, and prior to the war he'd even flirted with the Right Club – a right-wing London group that had included Nazi sympathizers. But the young, aristocratic and decidedly dashing Russian-English prince, who wore his dark hair fashionably long, was about to come face to face with the appalling reality of Nazism.

In Nice, his team was one of the first to enter the city's recently vacated Gestapo headquarters. As he surveyed the scene before him Galitzine's deep brown eyes were full of an honest determination coupled with an instinctive empathy. What he would witness in the Gestapo's cellar-cum-torture-chamber would sicken and revolt this innately humane man.

There were eleven bodies in the cellar, Galitzine recalled. 'One of them was the daughter of the mayor, Eliane Valiano, and I was horrified.' The young woman was six months pregnant and she had been raped after death. 'I couldn't believe it. I just couldn't believe that people could behave like that.'

Sadly, by Nazi Germany's standards Prince Galitzine hadn't seen anything yet. As the 7th Army had pushed eastwards of the Vosges and taken Strasbourg, the entire records of the local Gestapo – *Standartenführer* Isselhorst's command – had been captured. They in turn led Prince Galitzine to Schirmek, and to a discovery that would change his life for ever: the concentration camp at Natzweiler.

'I was briefed to go,' recalled Galitzine, 'because I was told there was a "concentration camp".' At the time few amongst the Allies had any idea what a concentration camp might be, but as Galiztine drove into the hills above Schirmek he was about to find out.

At first, he was struck by the majestic beauty of the Vosges Mountains in winter, which were carpeted with thick and verdant forests right up to the snow line. It was a long and winding climb, Natzweiler itself lying at 9,000 feet of altitude. Even as he drew closer, Galitzine still imagined the concentration camp to be some kind of tented affair.

'The first thing that really struck one was the smell; the most ghastly sickly-sweet smell,' he remarked. Ominously, it hit him from a considerable distance before he reached the camp. He didn't realise until he saw the evidence with his own eyes, but it was the smell of bodies; of human flesh burned in the crematorium.

At Natzweiler there were scattered urns lying about full of human ashes, coffins stacked high and piles upon piles of filthy, stinking clothing. Galitzine saw a 'few rather dazed chaps in striped suits wandering around – not very many of them'. The more healthy and active prisoners had wandered off to the nearby villages to try to find help.

Sickened and uncomprehending – *what in God's name had happened here?* – the former right-wing bon vivant struggled to come to terms with what he had stumbled into. Galitzine found those survivors who were compos mentis and able to talk. They explained to him what a 'concentration camp' was, and as they did so the scales fell from the young SOE captain's eyes.

Provoked to a cold fury, Galitzine was determined to document every horror and inhumanity. He set about compiling a briefing on the camp, entitled 'Special Report on German concentration camp (KZ NATZWEILER)'. Directed to his boss, the 'Chief, Liberated Areas Section, PWD SHAEF' (the Political Warfare Directorate of Supreme Headquarters Allied Expeditionary Force), it began: 'This report is based upon personal investigations and observations made during operations . . .'.

What Galitzine discovered was this. In 1941 someone – Hitler? Himmler? – had decided that the Nazi Party buildings in Nuremberg needed to be faced with the finest red Alsatian granite. The best source of the stone was a quarry adjacent to Natzweiler, and so the former ski resort was transformed into a labour camp, from which inmates would be worked to their deaths in the nearby stone quarry.

'This camp was to be a distributing and restocking centre for slave labour,' Galitzine reported, 'with the idea of "working the prisoners to death".'

By the spring of 1943 there were fifteen barracks huts in three rows, built on a 'terrace' hewn out of the mountainside. The surrounding area was cleared of its few civilian inhabitants and made a no-go zone. The camp was ringed by a double row of razor wire, with guard posts set at intervals. The fence was electrified with a high voltage current, and Natzweiler came complete with its own crematorium – the ovens in which the dead and the near-dead would be burned.

A Junkers aircraft factory was also built on the 'terrace' as an alternative work site for the slave labour force. When enough red granite had been mined, Natzweiler became a holding camp. From there, 'inmates' were shipped out in work parties to whatever enterprise might require such slave labour – including several underground armament factories and the nearby Mercedes-Benz plant, which manufactured trucks for the *Wehrmacht*. When a contingent was deemed too exhausted or sick to serve a 'useful purpose' any more, they were shipped back to Natzweiler, for termination.

The earliest inmates were German political prisoners – mostly communists and anti-Nazis. Then came the Polish, Dutch, Norwegian, Czech, Greek, Italian and Russian enemies of the Reich. And, finally, suspected members of the French Resistance were shipped through Natzweiler's dark gates. Prisoners were classified according to their 'crimes': political opponents, homosexuals, forced-labour dodgers, Jews.

But the worst classification of all was reserved for the least fortunate of inmates. 'Those prisoners who were considered more dangerous or who had attempted to escape were designated 'N.N.' – the NN standing for Nacht und Nebel (Night and Fog),' Galitzine reported. 'These prisoners wore a yellow patch with three black circles over the heart. They could be shot for the slightest misdemeanour and were not allowed any mail or communication with other persons.'

Captured Maquis were invariably classed as *Nacht und Nebel*.

The labourers worked eleven hours a day, on a starvation diet of a thrice-daily crust of bread and bowl of thin 'soup'. Prisoners resorted to eating grass, dung and even digging up worms in the muddy floor of the quarry. Disease was rife. In addition to its crematorium, Natzweiler had a highly experimental form of a gas chamber, perhaps the most chilling of Galitzine's discoveries.

In the ultimate irony, the gas chamber was sited in a converted block of the former 'Alpine style' ski resort. Its purpose was to test out nerve gases and other chemical weapons, using the prisoners as human guinea pigs. A slot in the door to the 12-foot-by-12-foot chamber enabled the insertion of a gas cartridge containing whatever agent was being tested. A glass panel could be slid back to enable the 'scientists' to observe the effects of the gassing.

'Each prisoner was fed well a week before being gassed,' Galitzine reported. 'Some even got out alive when the gas failed to work, but they always died in some other way later. The doctors tried to "revive" patients by injections of antidotes to the gas. Most of the victims in the gas chamber were women . . .' They were stripped naked, then crammed into the chamber.

Incredibly, the Natzweiler camp commandant's house – a seemingly quaint Hansel-and-Gretel building set over three floors – lay just a few dozen yards from the camp perimeter. Josef Kramer, who had served as commandant at both Auschwitz and Belsen during his time, had lived there with his family, as had Heinrich Schwarz, another former Auschwitz commandant. The house had an open-air swimming pool set to one side, and the other offered a view through the razor wire towards the massed ranks of huts. A track ran by the house and pool: this was the route the condemned took to the gas chamber.

Natzweiler, Galitzine discovered, had been a tool of what was later to become known as Hitler's 'Final Solution'. Medical experiments were carried out on Jewish inmates, to 'prove' the 'inferiority' of the Jewish race – *Untermensch* (subhumans) in Nazi-speak. 'The prisoners were used unhesitatingly as human guinea pigs,' Galitzine wrote, with barely disguised revulsion. 'Bodies were found preserved in alcohol in jars, some being already cut up. The prison numbers of all bodies are available which will permit identification.'

Serendipitously perhaps, four of the survivors that Galitzine managed to speak to were members of the Resistance. They were to describe to Galitzine one horrifying incident that would reveal the fate of some of those who had disappeared in the valleys of the Vosges, when the SAS had been waging war there.

'By hangings and shooting in the neck, 92 women and approximately 300 men were killed during the night of the 1st to 2nd Sept 1944,' Galitzine wrote. 'The corpses were stacked up in a cellar, in which the blood was 20 cm. high . . . They are alleged to be a group of partisans who had been captured in the vicinity.'

Natzweiler lies approximately 10 miles due east of Moussey. The timing of this mass killing, plus the geography and the numbers, tie up with the first of the Waldfest deportations from the Rabodeau Valley of those alleged to be Maquis ('partisans').

But of even more relevance to Operation Loyton were Galitzine's final discoveries at Natzweiler. He heard rumours that fellow soldiers – Allied elite operators, like him – had lost their lives in this place of hell. He unearthed the first concrete evidence in some pencil drawings made of Natzweiler inmates, which bore the signature 'B.J. Stonehouse'. Stonehouse was a British officer held at Natzweiler, along with a supposedly fellow British elite forces operator, called Patrick O'Leary.

Galitzine presumed that both Stonehouse and O'Leary had been 'terminated', and he reported them as dead. The deeper he dug, the more evidence he uncovered. There were suggestions that American airmen had been incarcerated at Natzweiler. An eyewitness spoke of four British women being executed at the camp, and there were suggestions they may have been fellow SOE agents. Plus there were reports that an officer of the Special Air Service had been held at the camp – fate unknown.

Galitzine's report was rushed direct to SHAEF in Paris. In the winter of 1944 the world was still a long way from uncovering the horrors of the concentration camps. Belsen and Auschwitz would not be liberated for another five months. The terrible aberrations that Prince Galitzine had so painstakingly documented at Natzweiler were utterly unknown to the world right then.

Galitzine expected his report to provoke a storm of outrage at SHAEF. He anticipated a major press conference would be called, at which his findings would be presented to a horrified world press corps. Instead, his report was quietly and efficiently buried. The truth about Natzweiler was suppressed, and Galitzine himself was ordered to keep quiet about whatever he may have discovered there.

A freethinker by nature, Galitzine was beside himself with anger. 'I got a rude signal from headquarters saying that I wasn't to discuss this with anyone,' Galitzine recalled. His report into Natzweiler was to be buried.

He was shocked and appalled. This was the first concentration camp that the Allies had ever run into. His report was the first official document to catalogue the existence of such a place, and to detail its horrific excesses. Why then had it been suppressed? Typically, Prince Galitzine demanded answers.

The only explanation he was ever offered was that if the true horrors of the concentration camps were exposed, it 'might make the Germans resist all the more and . . . they would feel there was no hope'. If the Allies branded the whole of the German nation as being responsible for such evil, the German people might never give up. In short, it might prolong the war.

But such arguments made little sense to Galitzine. Hitler had ordered that there would be 'no surrender' anyway, so how could exposing a place like Natzweiler make it any worse? Galitzine was left bitterly disappointed and troubled; doubly so, as some of those held at Natzweiler appeared to have been fellow Allied soldiers.

As it happened, Galitzine was a personal friend of Captain Henry Carey Druce, the two men having been at officer training corps together. He was also an acquaintance of SAS Major Dennis Reynolds and Captain Whately-Smith, two of the Op Loyton 'missing'. It was only natural that Galitzine would take his report – rejected and silenced by Allied High Command – to a group of fellow mavericks at SAS headquarters.

Attached to Galitzine's document was an appendix, containing a list of twenty-two 'German War Criminals in the STRUTHOF affair' (Struthof being an alternative name for

Natzweiler). It detailed those key figures at the camp – predominantly SS – who had brutalized and terminated thousands of prisoners, including very possibly some of the Op Loyton 'missing'. These were also the mass killers who had tortured and executed so many of the suspected Maquis from Moussey and the wider Rabodeau Valley.

Galitzine listed the killers in Annex A in his report. The following pages – Annex B – were titled 'Witnesses for Crimes committed at Struthof Camp'. First on the list was Ernst Krenzer, a civil engineer forced to work in the quarry, and a Maquis intelligence agent. Next came M. Nicole, a stonemason and another Maquis, also forced to work in the quarry. Further down the page was Pastor Herring, a local priest who had helped pass food parcels to the starving prisoners.

There were eighteen witnesses in all, and their statements cataloguing Natzweiler's horrors ran to many pages. Clearly, Galitzine had expected more from his report than simply a storm of media coverage and a howl of global outrage; he'd expected justice. Sadly, all three seemed to have eluded him.

Yet as Colonel Franks cast his eye down Galitzine's list, he had the first inklings that, come hell or high water, the killers must be hunted down.

Chapter Seventeen

In late November 1944 the British government was finally forced to initiate action over Nazi war crimes. The catalyst for this was the horrific execution of the Stalag Luft escapees – those whose story was immortalized in the *The Great Escape*.

In the spring of 1944, seventy-three POWs from the German prison camp Stalag Luft III had escaped by tunnelling under the wire. Within days all but three had been recaptured. Dozens of the would-be escapees were subsequently executed, as a result of which a statement was made in British parliament condemning the killings as 'an odious crime against the laws and conventions of war'.

The press blew the story of these cold-blooded murders wide open, a horrified British public pressurizing their government to act. Military courts were established to try Nazi war criminals for 'violations of the laws and usages of war committed . . . since 2 September 1939'. But the Foreign Office – authors and executors of British foreign policy – exerted pressure at the very highest level to try to bring an end to such trials before they could even get started.

Why? The truth was that, in the closing stages of the Second World War, Nazi Germany was no longer the West's foremost enemy. The powers that be were already turning their attention towards Stalin's Russia and Communism, and what would become known as the Cold War. As an – almost unbelievable – testament to how seriously this shift in policy was being treated, consider Winston Churchill's Operation Unthinkable. Drafted in the latter stages of the war, this was his plan for Western military forces to roll east of Berlin, and to take Russia.

Unthinkable had a start date of 1 July 1945. On that day, British, Polish, American, Australian, Canadian and other troops operating alongside their former enemies, the soldiers of the *Wehrmacht*, were to invade Russia. It made 'sense' to fight alongside the *Wehrmacht*. After all, the German military had waged war against the Soviet Red Army, and the German intelligence community had carried out espionage against the Russians. On the Eastern Front they had gained invaluable know-how that would be essential for any force that might wish to march on Moscow, and they were the only military-intelligence apparatus with such experience.

Operation Unthinkable was vetoed by US President Roosevelt, but it reflected the view held at the highest level: the Russians were the new enemy. In this light, it is perhaps easier to understand why Prince Galitzine's November 1944 discoveries at Natzweiler were so rapidly and comprehensively quashed. They were 'inconvenient' to the pervading realpolitik, as would be any hunt for the Nazi war criminals who had orchestrated and executed such mass murder.

But, thankfully, there were those who refused to let pragmatism triumph over what was just and right. First and foremost amongst them was Colonel Brian Franks.

* * *

In early December 1944 a letter landed on Colonel Franks' desk with concrete news of the missing. Of course, the commander of 2 SAS had many things on his mind right then, in addition to the fate of those lost on Op Loyton. He had units in action from Norway through to Italy and at all points in between. But the letter was nonetheless electrifying.

It was from the American Red Cross, and it listed the names of some of the British and American POWs who had been detained in Schirmek's *Sicherungslager* – the 'security camp' that had served as the processing facility for all Waldfest captives. It included the following, with military service numbers:

Lieut. Garis P. Jacoby, ASN 0556376 (American)
Sgt. Michael Pipcock, ASN 16176838 (American)
Captain Whately-Smith, SAS 113612 (British)
Major Dennis B. Reynolds, 2 SAS Regt 130856 (British)
Captain Victor Gough, 148884, Somerset Light Infantry,
    Attached HQ Special Forces (British)
Lieutenant David Dill, 2 SAS 265704 (British).

The author of the letter, one Henry W. Dunning, concluded: 'On the 8th November 1944 these soldiers were still alive. I was able to talk with them personally several times and promised to advise their families . . .'

As a result of Dunning's surprise revelations, the War Office wrote to the relatives of those British soldiers named. To Gough's family they stated: 'It would appear that this officer was seen in the hands of the Gestapo on the 8th November,

1944 . . . We cannot accept this as an official prisoner of war report, but we think we ought to pass this information on to the next-of-kin . . .'

For Colonel Franks, this was tantalizing evidence that some at least of the Op Loyton missing might well be alive. In January 1945 Captain Gough, Lieutenant Dill, Major Reynolds and Captain Whately-Smith were officially listed as 'missing, believed prisoner of war'. But by then Colonel Franks had taken his own, unilateral action to launch the search for those operators he had lost in the Vosges.

The two individuals he chose to lead that search were both intimates of Op Loyton. One, Chris Sykes, had been amongst the last to cross the German lines at the mission's bloody end. The other, Major Bill Barkworth, was the chief of 2 SAS's intelligence cell, and the man who had given Captain Henry Carey Druce his eleventh-hour briefing when he had taken over command of the initial insertion into the Vosges.

In December 1944, Sykes and Barkworth returned to the Rabodeau Valley – the Vale of Tears – charged to leave no stone unturned in the quest for the missing. Perhaps unwittingly, Colonel Franks had just dispatched to the field an individual who would go on to earn a fearsome reputation as a manhunter without equal.

Within days, the first bodies would be found.

Major Eric 'Bill' Barkworth was a brilliant, maverick-spirited individualist, a man with little time for regulations or red tape. Slim, wiry and with dark eyes betraying a razor-sharp intellect, plus an unshakeable calm incorruptibility, Barkworth's defining feature was his resolute lack of respect for dumb rank or privilege.

A core value of the SAS was to value 'merit above rank'; those who led did so by dint of their innate skill and regardless of their rank. Likewise, in Barkworth's book, respect had to be earned. He also had little truck with mindless rules and regulations or for traditions steeped in prejudice and privilege. He broke the rules when the rules needed to be broken. That is what had made him such a fine SAS officer, and it would make him a war-criminal hunter without compare.

Barkworth's other major quality as a Nazi-hunter was his gift for languages; he spoke German like a native and was almost as well versed in French. Brought up in the post-card-perfect seaside town of Sidmouth, Devon, Barkworth had served in the Somerset Light Infantry before joining the SAS, as had the missing Jedburgh operator, Victor Gough.

With Major Barkworth at his side, Captain Sykes returned to the Vosges. It was a very different place from the one that he had left some two months earlier. As General Patton's forces had streamed across the Meurthe, the Germans had been driven out of the valleys. For four long years they had held the Vosges in a vice of grey-uniformed and jackbooted steel. Now the hills and their people were free again, and Sykes found the experience almost overwhelming.

'It was wonderful simply to stand in a street in broad daylight,' Sykes wrote of his return. 'I must confess that it was with a feeling of some trepidation that I returned to our town [Moussey]: so much had been suffered, and so much of it for our unworthy sakes. But their loyalty was without stint. I was acclaimed as if I had saved the world. We had become a legend.'

In returning to the Vosges, Sykes came face to face with what had been hidden from the Op Loyton party when immersed in the fight of their lives: how successful their mission had proved.

'It has not yet been explained why the Germans did not remain to fight in those easily defendable valleys. Is it possible that they *still* felt too uncertain of their position, *still* believed in a vast hidden host waiting for the sign to rise in all their thousands?'

By that 'host' Sykes meant the Vosges Maquis, armed and directed by a few dozen Op Loyton fighters. In the Vosges the SAS had 'caused panic to the enemies of France in a whole province . . . dislocated German military dispositions in a whole sector of the front line . . . raised an army in defence of all that makes human life honourable and endurable, and . . . inspired a loyalty and love . . .'

Sykes revisited those locals who had played such a vital role in the SAS's fortunes, including the indomitable Mme Rossi. After the Op Loyton force had been withdrawn, she had had her final confrontation with her oppressors.

'The Boche were always around the house,' she told Sykes. 'They guessed all right. So one day I called out to their Sergeant: "Hi, you! Are you looking for billets for your men? Come in here. I have plenty of room and plenty of hay!" They went.'

Sykes could well imagine in what spirit Mme Rossi had made such an offer. He'd brought with him a form to complete, so she could be put forward for the King's Medal. Mme Rossi cut

Sykes short as he tried to get her to fill out the form, placing a firm but gentle hand on his shoulder.

'But no,' she told him. 'Look – this is not for me. This – it's for the soldiers, the military.'

Sykes met again with the many with whom friendship had been forged in dark adversity: Albert Freine, the long-suffering gamekeeper and Maquis intelligence chief; Simone, the legendary sylph-like Maquis guide, who had led Major Power and his men across the war-ravaged mountains; plus the Celles Valley forester who had served as Colonel Franks' go-between.

From those and others he would hear the first intimations of what horrors had befallen the missing. But it was to be Abbé Gassman, the Moussey village priest, who would lead Sykes and Barkworth to the first indisputable evidence – the human remains.

Abbé Gassman was one of the only leaders of the Moussey Maquis who had remained at large. In one of *Standartenführer* Isselhorst's final round-ups, Moussey's redoubtable mayor had joined the many hundreds already incarcerated in the concentration camps. The mayor had argued that if all the men of Moussey were being shipped to the camps, then he had to join them. That was his responsibility as mayor.

Under Gassman's guidance, Sykes and Barkworth headed to a farm called La Fosse, set several miles to the north-west of Moussey. They steeled themselves for what they feared they would find there.

'In the outhouse, which had been demolished and burnt, a complete vertebral column was found,' recorded Barkworth. 'The destruction by fire was so complete that very little remained, but it was possible to trace deeper in the ashes the positions of at least two bodies.

'In each case the knee bones and the powdered mass of bone which represented the skull were easily distinguishable. Amongst those remains the following articles were found . . . which are part of an SAS parachutist's clothing and equipment . . .' Barkworth listed the identifiable artefacts discovered in the ashes.

Labels from parachute pack.
Buckles from braces (stamped 'Police and Firemen').
Zip fastener clasp.
Steel from jumping jacket clip.
Hook and eye from battledress.
Part of suspender.
Two buckles from battledress blouse.
One buckle from rucksack.
Nine parts of parachute harness.

That was all that remained of three murdered SAS men. Sergeant Fitzpatrick, and Troopers John Conway and John Elliot had gone missing during the airdrop of the first week of September in the hills above Pierre-Percée. The parachutists had drifted into the fog-bound trees, one breaking his leg upon landing, and they had gone into hiding in a farmhouse on the outskirts of the village of Pexonne.

In his post-operation memo, Colonel Franks had listed all three men as 'Missing – believed PW'. Now the truth had been revealed beyond all doubt.

Showing his early flair for such detective work, Barkworth interviewed several local witnesses. Leon Muller was a neighbour of the farm at La Fosse. He told Barkworth: 'On Tuesday 19th September 1944, at or about 10.00 hours, I saw a saloon car and lorry approach from Pexonne. The car was blue-grey. The truck, army colour. They asked my wife the way to La Fosse . . . There was one man in the lorry sitting between two Germans.'

Barkworth had brought with him mugshots of the thirty-one missing men. He showed Monsieur Muller a photograph of Sergeant Fitzpatrick. Muller confirmed that this was the figure he had seen in the truck cab. 'I recognise him from the photograph as Sgt. Fitzpatrick. I heard three bursts of a light machinegun from La Fosse, in all about ten shots, and then I saw the shed burning. The truck then left.'

In light of such testimony – corroborated by several witnesses – Barkworth was able to write conclusively of Fitzpatrick, Conway and Elliot: 'Murdered by Germans at a farm, La Fosse, near Pexonne, on 17.9.44.'

There was worse to come.

At Le Harcholet, a tiny hamlet lying just to the south-east of Moussey, more SAS had perished. They had lost their lives in the most horrifying of ways. Three men dressed in khaki uniform had been herded inside a barn adjoining a house called the Maison Quiren. Eyewitnesses spoke of two sporting 'red berets' and one a peaked mountain cap. That latter figure was handcuffed and wearing wire-rimmed glasses, and the others had their hands tied.

The barn was set on fire. 'The victims were hung up before the burning, as I could see human forms through the flames,' recounted Madame Beneit, a neighbour and witness to the murders.

Victor Launay, another Le Harcholet neighbour who had sheltered one of the SAS victims, identified that man as being Lieutenant Silly. Before leaving, the German soldiers had shot up the barn and thrown in grenades. 'As they left they were laughing,' remarked Madame Beneit.

Little had survived the intense heat of the conflagration, but Barkworth and Sykes did find what appeared to be SAS officer Silly's smashed glasses lying in the burnt-out ruins of the barn, plus a British military dog tag. That ID disk had belonged to SAS trooper Brown, a man who had been burned to death alongside Lieutenant Silly.

Lieutenant Silly had been one of Colonel Franks' most resourceful raiders. The last that Franks had seen of him had been when he'd ordered his men to split up and make for the Allied lines. Silly had been one of a party of ten who'd tried to cross the River Meurthe. They'd been split up, Silly getting captured by the enemy on 10 October. And, somehow, the SAS lieutenant had ended up getting burned to death in a barn in Le Harcholet six days later.

As Barkworth and Sykes discovered, Silly, Brown and a third, as yet unidentified soldier, had been taken by the Gestapo to be killed where they had once been sheltered. The SAS men had come to rely upon one Le Harcholet household during those dire days when they had been on the verge of starvation. In the home of the Feys, Madeleine Fey – then just seventeen years old – had prepared a daily tureen of soup for the British raiders.

The famished SAS men had come at dusk in threes and fours to eat. At the rear of the Feys' garden a small bridge led across a stream, a faint path snaking into the thickly wooded high ground. If it was too dangerous for the soldiers to come to the house, Madeleine would carry the soup tureen up to their hidden camp and feed them there.

One October night the four SAS men had been in the Feys' kitchen when there was a harsh rapping at the door. Madeleine had bundled them out of the rear and thrust them into the pigsty, a rough wooden and stone lean-to tacked onto one end of the house. Meanwhile her father, Auguste, had made a show of throwing open the shutters at the front, so as to check who was visiting at this late hour.

Then he encountered 'problems' getting the key to turn in the lock to let the Gestapo in. Finally he got it open, declaring: '*Voila! On ouvre!*' (There! It's open!) By then the British soldiers had been hidden where they would never be discovered, although in the rush for the pigsty one had managed to drop his weapon down the Feys' well.

While the Feys hadn't witnessed Lieutenant Silly and his fellows being murdered, a near neighbour, Mme Renée Haouy, had. Mme Haouy's husband was one of those seized during the 24 September mass arrests in Moussey. He would never return from the concentration camps. On the day that Lieutenant Silly and his fellows were murdered, Mme Haouy was ordered by the Gestapo to stay inside her house and to close all the shutters.

She had acted as if complying, but had kept one open a crack so she could spy on what was happening. She saw the three men being thrown into the burning building, and the shots fired into it to finish them off.

By now, Barkworth and Sykes had discovered beyond doubt the fates of five of the missing, but what they thirsted for more than anything were the names of their killers. A final eyewitness was to provide that crucial lead.

A doctor living in the nearby village of Senones had seen three British soldiers – Lieutenant Silly amongst them – driven to Le Harcholete. When none had returned, he'd asked a Gestapo officer billeted locally what had been done with those men.

'Paratroopers captured in battle are treated normally,' he had replied. 'But *Nachtschirmfalljäger* dropped behind the lines in small parties are shot as spies and saboteurs. '*Ils n'existent plus,*' he continued. '*Nous leur rendons la politesse.* They do the same to our paratroopers.'

The German word *Nachtschirmfalljäger* means 'night-parachutist-fighters'. The French translates as: 'They no longer exist . . . We return to them the favour done to us.'

That officer was identified as *Oberscharführer* (Company Sergeant Major) Max Kessler.

Kessler had just leapt to the top of Major Bill Barkworth's most-wanted list.

Barkworth and Sykes' report was delivered to Colonel Franks in early January 1945. Marked 'TOP SECRET', it contained some hugely perceptive conclusions. 'A definite policy lies behind German treatment of paratroopers. None of the atrocities discovered indicate murders committed in the heat of combat.'

Of the cases concerning Sergeant Fitzpatrick's and Lieutenant Silly's groups – where the burned remains had been discovered, confirming who had died – they wrote: '[They] follow a similar technique of planned murder carried out several days after capture.'

Barkworth and Sykes had scored one further breakthrough in the Vosges. All witnesses had spoken of SAS captives being held and interrogated by the Gestapo. Moreover, some papers belonging to an SAS Lieutenant Black and his group had been discovered at the former Gestapo headquarters. Whatever was happening to the SAS captives, the Gestapo was clearly at the centre of it all.

In their report Barkworth and Sykes listed two dozen Op Loyton men as either 'missing', 'prisoner of war', or 'probably prisoner of war'. If those twenty-four individuals were still alive, then it seemed there was still real cause for hope. But Barkworth and Sykes' unpalatable conclusion was that the fate of each man taken captive lay in the hands of the Gestapo.

'All SAS prisoners remain in permanent Gestapo custody, and no complacent view can be taken of them.'

Chapter Eighteen

On 15 January 1945, just days after receiving the Sykes-Barkworth report, Colonel Franks penned a letter to Brigadier General Roderick McLeod, the outgoing SAS brigade commander. In it he pointed out that Sykes and Barkworth had proved 'beyond all doubt that six men were murdered, of whom five have been identified . . . The possibility of further atrocities cannot be ruled out.'

Referencing the reported words of SD officer Max Kessler, Franks surmised: 'some order at some time has been issued to the effect that SAS Troops should be shot, whether or not they are in uniform. This is, I believe, contrary to the statement made by the German Commanding Officer who is at present a prisoner in our hands, but in his present position he is hardly likely to say that British Parachutists would be shot.'

Who exactly that captured German officer was remains unclear. But for months there had been persistent rumours about what amounted to a blanket Nazi 'execution order' for any captured SAS men. Those rumours had started with the spring 1944 escape of SAS Lieutenant Quentin Hughes from a German train then steaming across Italy, having learned that the Gestapo planned to execute him as a 'saboteur'.

Hughes' report represented the first evidence secured by the SAS that such an execution order might exist. The six murders uncovered by Sykes and Barkworth, plus Max Kessler's reported testimony, gave credence to Hughes' claims. And, as luck would have it, absolute proof positive of Hitler's kill order was about to fall into Allied hands.

On 25 January 1945 four copies of what was to become known as Hitler's 'Commando Order' were delivered to 2 SAS headquarters, under the heading 'German Order to Kill Captured Allied Commandos and Parachutists'. Two copies of the order were sent direct to Captain Sykes, one of which was to be passed to Major Barkworth.

The soon-to-be-infamous document had been captured by the French intelligence services, who had in turn handed it over to the Paris headquarters of the American OSS, and from there it had made its way into the possession of the SAS. The Commando Order, issued by Adolf Hitler himself, was supposedly a reaction to one of the very first British Special Forces operations.

On 3 October 1942 a tiny raiding party had launched Operation Basalt, a mission commanded by Captain Brian Appleyard and Lieutenant Anders Lassen. Their tiny force had sped across the Channel in a diminutive motor launch known as the 'Little Pisser', scaled the cliffs of the Channel Island of Sark, and taken some of the occupying German garrison captive.

But while trying to spirit their prisoners off the island and into the waiting boat, all but one of the Germans had broken free. In the ensuing melee some had been shot. They'd had their hands tied upon being taken captive, which led to screaming headlines in the German-controlled press that German prisoners had been tied up and executed: 'British Attack and Bind German Troops in Sark. Immediate Reprisals for Disgraceful Episode'.

Upon hearing of the attack, Hitler flew into a towering rage. Two weeks after the Sark raid, his response was ready: the Commando Order. Issued on 18 October 1942, Hitler must have known he was decreeing that war crimes be committed. The efforts to hide the order's existence from the Allies were extraordinary. It was classified 'MOST SECRET', was issued to high-ranking officers only and was to be committed to memory, after which all printed copies were to be destroyed.

Such extreme levels of secrecy seemed to have worked; it had taken more than two years for a copy to fall into Allied hands. Those sent to Franks, Sykes and Barkworth included a commentary from the OSS. 'The first of the following two orders was issued by Führer Headquarters on 18 October 1942, and re-issued, with a supplementary order . . . following the [D-Day] invasion of France.'

The original order, citing the previous British 'commando' raids such as that on Sark as justification, stated: 'In future, Germany will resort to the same methods in regards to these groups of British saboteurs and their accomplices – that is to say, German troops will exterminate them without mercy wherever they find them.

'Henceforth all enemy troops encountered by German troops during so-called commando operations . . . though they appear to be soldiers in uniform or demolition groups, armed or unarmed, are to be exterminated to the last man, either in combat or pursuit . . . If such men appear to be about to surrender, no quarter should be given to them – on general principle.'

Hitler's order ends with a chilling warning to any who might have the temerity to oppose it. 'I will summon before the tribunal of war, all leaders and officers who fail to carry out these instructions – either by failure to inform their men or by their disobedience of this order in action.'

The supplementary order, issued following the Normandy landings, was even more extreme: 'In spite of the Anglo-American landings in France, the Führer's order of 18 October 1942, regarding the destruction of saboteurs and terrorists, remains fully valid . . . All members of terrorist and saboteur bands, including (on general principle) all parachutists encountered outside the immediate combat zone, are to be executed.'

German commanders were ordered to: 'Report daily the numbers of saboteurs thus liquidated . . . The number of executions must appear in the daily communiqué of the Wehrmacht to serve as a warning to potential terrorists.' The measures to maintain 'secrecy' regarding the order were laid out in black and white. 'The copies going to Regts and Gen Staff are to be destroyed by the latter when its contents have been noted. A certificate of destruction should be returned to this HQ.'

One can imagine Franks, Sykes and Barkworth's feelings upon reading these captured documents. In light of the Commando Order, the horrific killings that Barkworth and Sykes had uncovered in the valleys of the Vosges made every sense. Doubtless, the other Op Loyton captives would have faced a similar fate, and all seemed lost for the two dozen men still listed as 'missing, believed PW'. Lesser men might well have let matters lie there, but not these.

The fallout from the revelations of the Commando Order continued. Top secret communiqués flew back and forth between British Airborne Corps – the unit then in command of the SAS – and the War Office, raising extreme concerns about the fate of captured Special Forces operators. The general consensus seemed to be that they were being held for interrogation by the Gestapo, after which they were being killed.

The issues raised were legion, not least of which was how to deploy the SAS in light of the order. 'It will be appreciated that the whole policy regarding employment of SAS troops is affected by the treatment of any personnel captured. The enemy realizes this and obviously, as part of their propaganda to stop SAS activities, have issued orders that these parachutists are "saboteurs" and will be shot.'

There was also the pressing issue of how much to tell the men on the ground. In the late winter of 1944–45 there were dozens of SAS units serving as the vanguard of forces thrusting into Germany itself. For example, Captain Henry Carey Druce was about to lead a daring SAS mission from the Dutch city of Arnhem to penetrate German lines. It was a tasking that he would complete with 'devastating effect' – but what if any of his men were taken captive?

By late February 1945, some form of decision seemed to have been taken on that point. A 'SECRET & CONFIDENTIAL' memo issued from high command to SFHQ stated the following regarding French members of the SAS: 'After consideration of this problem it has been decided not to inform the troops.' The reasons cited are: '(a) They expect to be shot already. (b) It would only provide a good excuse for any delinquents that might wish to retire from the struggle.'

There was a war still to be fought, and it seemed that the SAS troopers were to be kept in the dark about Hitler's infamous order.

One other aspect of this whole affair was being pursued at the very highest levels: the hunting down of the war criminals who were carrying out Hitler's kill order. In the spring of 1945 Brigadier 'Mad' Mike Calvert took over command of the SAS from McLeod. Calvert stressed how 'every effort should be made to apprehend these criminals, to seek out the evidence and bring them to trial'.

Brigadier Calvert and Colonel Franks were of a like mind. Under their influence, lobbying took place of the most influential friends of the Regiment within the political establishment to get backing for such action. But Franks – the one senior SAS commander with the most invested in this issue personally – could already sense the way the wind was blowing, as could Calvert.

'SHAEF and most organizations in Europe have an end of term feeling, and do not want to be bothered with anything that gives extra work,' Brigadier Calvert wrote to Colonel Franks. 'As this is accentuated by the fact that the British are not themselves of a nature which seeks revenge, it is difficult to convince . . . people that this is not a case of revenge, but of bringing criminals to trial for very serious offences.'

One other member of this amorphous grouping – Prince Yurka Galitzine – was raising his voice in support of war crimes investigations. He became particularly vocal following the Allies' 15 April 1945 'discovery' of the concentration camps. Galitzine had been forced to keep quiet five months earlier, when he had documented Natzweiler and tried so hard to raise the alarm. But with newsreel of the horrors of Belsen playing out in British cinemas, the wall of silence had finally been broken.

Galitzine had been thwarted over Natzweiler, but he sensed that now was his time. His own personal experiences made him acutely aware of the war crimes issue, and the need to pursue and prosecute the Nazi war criminals. Yet he was worried how much would actually be done.

'I had a feeling that even by VE Day the impetus was beginning to . . . slacken,' Galitzine recalled. 'The senior people in the War Office – they seemed to be all for a quiet life, and so did the politicians.'

Galitzine's understanding of the horrors perpetrated by the Nazis was extraordinarily perceptive and way ahead of its time. As the war drew to a close, he drafted a proposal for what he called the International Bureau of Information (IBI). It aimed to combat the use of propaganda and brainwashing – which had been used to such effect in Nazi Germany – to enable despots, dictators and mass killers to seize control of entire nations.

'Few people realize the part propaganda has played in this war,' Galitzine wrote. 'It might well be said that Germany declared war on the world in 1933 when Hitler launched his propaganda offensive against civilization, and it is certain that the measure of success he achieved was in the main due to the influencing of public opinion, especially in undermining the unity of his victims by propaganda.'

Unsurprisingly, Galitzine's IBI didn't get taken up by the world powers. In the spring of 1945 their priorities lay elsewhere. But he was about to land himself a posting that would place the Nazi war criminals very much more firmly within his grasp. The War Office – under pressure owing to the Belsen and Auschwitz revelations – belatedly established a war crimes investigation team, working out of their Eaton Square office, in London's exclusive Belgravia district.

Just a stone's throw from Buckingham Palace, the War Office's number 20 Eaton Square facility was set within a grand, white-fronted, Georgian building some six storeys high. There was nothing in particular to set it apart from the neighbouring properties, which were mostly inhabited by the London well-to-do. Officially, Galitzine was now working for the Adjutant-General's Branch 3 – Violation of the Laws and Usages of War – or 'AG3-VW', for short.

At AG3-VW he would truly find his calling.

But when it came to tracing the Op Loyton missing, all trails seemed to have gone cold. Barkworth and Sykes had done all they could on the ground in the Vosges. The bodies – the remains – of six men had been found, and five had been identified. Five families had been written to, the news of their son's or husband's deaths providing some degree of closure. But for the majority there was nothing; as Hitler had decreed, their loved ones had been swallowed up into the Night and the Fog.

Requests for news of the missing were coming in thick and fast. A Mr J.R.H. Pinckney wrote to SAS headquarters, requesting news of his missing son, Philip Pinckney. 'We should be very anxious for any personal items of news or belongings which may be available, or may be found with the Authorities . . . Very little has been said about the work of these SAS Regiments, and perhaps something may be forthcoming to the relatives in due course.'

Colonel Franks promised to do everything in his power to discover what had happened, but desperate requests for information were being received from all quarters. Alsace Maquis leader Colonel Grandval wrote from the Vosges, seeking news on behalf of M. de Bouvier, whose son, Henry, had been a Maquis fighter.

Henry de Bouvier 'is supposed to have exfiltrated on around the 15th of October, with Captain V.A. Gough, of the Jedburgh Team JACOB,' wrote the French colonel. However, M. de Bouvier, 'is without any news of his son, Henry, since the middle of October.'

Since Captain Victor Gough was one of those listed as 'missing – presumed PW', there was little that Colonel Franks could tell the worried French father, although he hungered for the truth. It was the same with all of the 'missing': friends, relatives, loved ones and former comrades had been left in a terrible limbo, wondering what may have happened.

But all of that was about to change with one letter sent from France.

On 8 May 1945, VE Day, the war in Europe ended. But neither Franks, Barkworth, nor any of their men were much in the mood to celebrate. Their minds were turned to darker matters:

the fate of the missing, and catching those who had tortured and murdered them.

Just a week after VE Day, Franks issued instructions to Barkworth: he was to lead a force to investigate 'the murder of personnel of this Regiment taken prisoner in Eastern France during the months of August, September and October 1944'.

Colonel Brian Franks' initiative was inspired in part by the bombshell news that he had just received regarding the Op Loyton missing. By now a vanquished Germany was being split into zones of occupation, each overseen by one of the main Allied powers. There were four: a British zone, an American zone, a Russian zone and a French one. The French zone was by far the smallest, but it did encompass those areas of Germany immediately east of the Vosges.

The French had written to the War Office regarding several bodies that had been found buried in some woodland close to the Gaggenau concentration camp, which lay in the French occupation zone. Gaggenau was itself a sub-camp of Natzweiler, and had thus been part of *Standartenführer* Isselhorst's area of command. One of those corpses had been tentatively identified as a former Op Loyton operative.

So it was that Colonel Franks was alerted to the next place to search for the missing. Franks ordered Barkworth to lead an SAS team to Gaggenau. Along with Sykes, Barkworth chose to take with him Sergeant Fred 'Dusty' Rhodes, one of his most trusted lieutenants. Rhodes was another of those who'd briefed Captain Henry Carey Druce, prior to his last-minute departure on Op Loyton. He'd also opted to fly on several of the Loyton re-supply drops, to help dispatch parachutists and to kick containers out of the bomb bays.

A tough and unyielding Yorkshireman, Rhodes – like Barkworth, Sykes and Franks – felt a powerful personal connection to Op Loyton and the missing. As they set out for Dover riding in one of the original SAS jeeps, plus a 15-hundred-weight Bedford truck laden with supplies, they little knew their quest would take them four years to complete and encompass so many disparate countries.

Three years earlier, Barkworth had recruited Rhodes into the SAS, and the two men were close. Rhodes had been serving with the Coldstream Guards, fighting in North Africa. Pulled back from the front line for a rest period, Rhodes and a pal had come across a notice about a 'special unit' seeking applicants. Having zero idea what the 'SAS' might be, both men went for an interview with the then Captain Barkworth.

'After a lot of questions that delved really, really deep into your background . . . we were given twenty-four hours to pack all our gear,' Rhodes remarked of his selection by Barkworth. Training commenced immediately. 'There was a mountain we used to call The Jebel. You used to put your pack on and to prove your physical fitness you had to run up this mountain, and time it in different stages from the bottom to the top and from the top to the bottom. If you failed in any way you were finished with the Regiment.'

Rhodes was recruited into Barkworth's newly formed intelligence section. At first he worried if this was 'real soldiering', especially as the men of the cell weren't allowed to deploy on operations, in case of capture. 'The intelligence unit held so much information. When one knows that there are seven or eight operations going on somewhere behind the enemy lines . . .' If a man from the intelligence cell were taken captive, he might break under torture and blow all those missions.

But when Rhodes saw how successful missions based upon intelligence had proved, he understood how crucial was his role. Later, he and his fellow intel people were allowed to go on purely 'hit-and-run' type operations, where the chances of getting captured were less than on a mission behind enemy lines. 'We would either go by submarine or go by destroyer, and . . . hit a certain building or a certain bridge or hit a certain airport.'

In many ways the sandy-haired, blue-eyed Rhodes and his commanding officer, Barkworth, were birds of a feather: unconventional, risk-taking nonconformists. One story from the closing stages of the war illustrates this most powerfully. Barkworth's intelligence section had deployed into Germany to help take the surrender of enemy units. A group of elite troops was holed up in a thick-walled castle. Major Barkworth went there to negotiate with their commander.

'They said they would surrender to nobody but a member of the Brigadier Guards,' Rhodes recalled, the Brigadier Guards being another name for the Coldstream Guards. Barkworth's response to the German officer's request was this: 'That's all right, I've got one here for you.' He turned to Rhodes. 'Right then, come on – here goes: show them what the Brigadier Guards can do!'

'The whole bloody lot surrendered!' Rhodes recalled. 'The officer surrendered, and he surrendered the whole garrison to one former member of the Brigadier Guards, but he would not surrender to anybody else, because the Brigadier Guards [stood] in very high esteem . . . with the German Army at that time.'

Rhodes described Barkworth as, 'a very eccentric person. He could be arrogant, he could be amusing, he could be the most awkward person that one could ever wish to meet. But at the same time he was a very loyal person . . . to the people who worked for him.'

Rhodes and Barkworth would form the cornerstones of the SAS unit tasked to hunt down the Nazi killers.

'We aimed to make Gaggenau our headquarters,' remarked Rhodes, 'possibly because one wouldn't think it was central to the area we were working in. We had a . . . good working relationship with the French and the Americans – only being possibly 10 miles from the American zone. We were able to use the Americans' specialists – pathologists and so on, to do autopsies on the bodies we found . . .'

There were corpses in the forests around Gaggenau awaiting exhumation, so they might yield up their dark secrets. Rhodes believed in an eye for an eye. He and his fellow SAS operators had been briefed that if ever they were captured and threatened with execution, they should throw the threat right back in their captor's faces. Any would-be executioners of SAS men were to be told that they would be hunted down in turn.

'We already knew the end product of a person being caught,' remarked Rhodes. '[We] were told to tell people the Regiment would investigate the causes of the death and I always think that was the intention of the Regiment anyway. I don't think it was something just thought up . . . We had two priorities: one was to find all our SAS comrades; the second was to make sure no one who'd killed any SAS soldiers escaped justice.'

The Regiment would hunt them down; that had always been the plan. And as far as these men were concerned, such promises of retribution had to be kept.

Chapter Nineteen

In the aftermath of defeat, Germany – the nation that Barkworth, Rhodes, Sykes et al were heading into – was in utter chaos. So much so that in late May 1945 the Allies felt they had far more pressing priorities than hunting for war criminals. The entire country was at risk of starvation. In response, the Allied powers had launched Operation Barleycorn, in which every able-bodied German – the hundreds and thousands of POWs first and foremost – was being sent into the fields, to reap and to sow.

The entire nation seemed to be in flux. Refugees were fleeing from the east – from Stalin's Russia – into the Western zones of control. German civilians had been hiding in the countryside to escape the devastating effect of Allied bombing; now they were trying to return to their homes in the nation's bombed-out and dysfunctional towns and cities.

More than anything, the Allied powers feared a mass famine in Germany, for with it would come pestilence and disease. At every turn there was hunger, suffering and misery. When Barkworth and team stopped en route to eat their rations, from out of nowhere they found themselves surrounded by a silent horde of children. The urchins stood, transfixed, their eyes unnaturally enlarged by the withering effects of hunger, watching every crumb of food as it disappeared.

It was abundantly clear that the German children bore no responsibility for the horrors visited on the world by the Nazi regime. They, too, were the victims of the dark evil and mega-lomania that had gripped this land. The SAS men understood this instinctively; they ended up throwing their food to the children and moving rapidly on.

To some, Barkworth's present quest might perhaps seem an obtuse and unjustifiable one. The fate of a few dozen missing SAS was being prioritized above that of an entire nation in the throes of near collapse. Moreover, what made the Op Loyton missing so *special*? At every turn, the Allies were being confronted by the horrors that Nazi Germany had perpetrated; in the British zone alone there were some eighty concentration camps, slave-labour centres and extermination facilities.

What made the Op Loyton killers – arguably minor war criminals, when compared to those who had murdered hundreds of thousands – so worthy of retribution? Surely those who had orchestrated the mass extermination of millions – at Belsen, Auschwitz, Buchenwald and Dachau, to name but a few of the camps – should form the primary focus of any manhunt?

Well indeed, they should and they would. The headline camps would attract the lion's share of Allied efforts to seek justice and retribution. It was for that very reason that Colonel Franks had taken the unilateral action of sending this tiny SAS force on its present mission. *Lest we forget.*

Gaggenau straddles the Murg River, a tributary of the Rhine, lying just a few dozen kilometres to east of the Vosges. During the war the main employer in the area had been the

Mercedes-Benz vehicle factory, which had drawn the inevitable Allied bombing raids to it. In September and October 1944 hundreds of US Air Force B-17s had rained down destruction on the automobile complex, and as a result around 70 per cent of the city had been destroyed.

In the Bad Rotenfels district a camp had been built housing 1,500 forced labourers who slaved away in the Daimler-Benz plant. To the rear of the automobile factory sat a patch of woodland known as the Erlich Forest. In summer a place of grand deciduous woodland, in the spring of 1945 the trees were just coming back into leafy bloom. But the thrusting sap of life contrasted starkly with what lay buried beneath the forest floor.

Before heading for that forest, Barkworth needed to find himself a base of operations. He chose to requisition a 1930s modernist, angular, Bauhaus-style residence called the Villa Degler, which until very recently had been the home of a prominent local Nazi. When the French had taken control of the city they had arrested Herr Degler, and in a neat role reversal Barkworth moved his team into his recently vacated home.

Herr Degler's wife and two teenage daughters were commanded by Barkworth to do the cooking and the cleaning for his newly installed Nazi-hunting team. Stark and blocky on the outside, the Villa Degler was all golden candelabras, polished wooden shutters and tasteful decor on the inside. More importantly, it had a large and secure cellar that would make a perfect holding cell for what Barkworth intended to corral here: his prisoners.

From the roof of the Villa Degler Barkworth set up his all-important radio communications, manned by a Phantom team, so he could speak direct to SAS headquarters. Very few, if any, British troops were based in the French zone of occupation, so all supplies – human and materiel – would either have to be shipped out from the UK, or from the British zone, situated 60 miles to their north. Direct and efficient communication would be key.

The only other English-speaking forces in the vicinity were an American war crimes investigation team, who had been drafted in because the mass grave that had drawn Barkworth was also said to contain Americans. The US team was led by a Colonel David Chavez Jr, and he and his group of experts would prove to be one of Barkworth's greatest allies in the hunt for the missing and their killers.

Early on the morning of 10 June, Barkworth's men and those of Colonel Chavez gathered in the eerie dawn quiet of the Erlich Forest. The task before them would consume their every waking moment for the next ten days. This was not going to be the first exhumation; the French had made one – somewhat chaotic – effort to dig up the bodies and identify them, which had prompted the original letter that Colonel Franks had received about SAS men being buried here.

Shortly after French troops had seized Gaggenau, the locals had warned them about a mass grave in the forest. A number of prisoners from the Rotenfels labour camp had been taken into the cover of the trees and shot. The corpses were tipped into two bomb craters lying side by side, and buried there.

The French had gone to investigate. When they were first exhumed, the twenty-seven bodies had been in a fine state of preservation. The dead had been buried almost immediately after their executions, and had barely begun to decompose. But unfortunately, after the French had dug them up, the pile of corpses had been left to cook in the spring sunshine for eight days.

When Barkworth, Sykes and Rhodes – plus Chavez and his American team – arrived to carry out the second dig, they would be met by a far less palatable set of circumstances. Chavez's team included a pair of expert pathologists. As the digging commenced and the smell began to permeate the atmosphere, they explained to Major Barkworth and their colonel – a British and an American officer, seeking a reckoning for their dead comrades – what they might expect to find.

Buried within minutes of their deaths and under a good depth of heavy soil, the corpses – although some six months old by the time of their first exhumation – had been almost mummified. The conditions underground were dry and cool – a foot or more below ground the temperature only ever varies marginally – and the skin had gone through a 'tanning' process, becoming brown and leathery. Body tissue had turned to a fatty wax called adipocere, which is the consistency of moist clay.

But once the air and the heat and the spring insect life had been allowed to get to the bodies, real decomposition would have set in. Flies would have laid their eggs, which in turn would result in maggot infestations. Soft tissues would have started to discolour, disintegrate and putrefy, leaving only solid body parts – the tendons and ligaments – attached to the skeletons. It was at this stage of decay that the bodies were now likely to be found.

Barkworth and his men rounded up some German prisoners to do the digging. They were the former managers of the nearby

Mercedes-Benz factory, which had used the prisoners from the Rotenfels camp to build the cars and trucks that they had supplied to the *Wehrmacht*. Most of the forced labourers had been processed through Natzweiler – Rotenfels being a substation of the 'mother camp' – and they were kept in the same kind of terrible state as all Natzweiler victims.

In spite of their protestations, the factory managers would have known full well the savagery visited upon their labourers and that they were quite simply starving, not to mention being worked until they dropped dead, or were ripe for termination.

'We felt that they had been responsible for the people being shot and killed,' Rhodes remarked of the Daimler-Benz factory managers. 'We thought that nobody could shed that responsibility. So many of them said they didn't know anything about it. Well, I don't believe that.'

With thick rags wrapped around their faces to try to filter out the stench, the former factory managers were forced to dig. Retching and wretched, they began to uncover the first of the remains. Colonel Chavez's pathologists had set up a temporary 'morgue' in a chapel of rest at a cemetery in the forest. The first of the gruesome remains were carried into the makeshift morgue so the pathologists could get to work.

A few weeks before, Barkworth and Sykes had uncovered the burned remains of their six comrades in the Vosges. That had been bad enough. But the most they had discovered there were the charred remnants of human skeletons. This exhumation in the Erlich Forest would prove infinitely worse.

As Barkworth, Sykes and Rhodes watched the former factory managers shovelling out the dirt, they felt certain that here lay the bodies of men that they had known personally and fought alongside in the most testing theatres of war. Operating under such extreme conditions as they had experienced on Op Loyton, friendships had been forged on a deeper and more heartfelt level that was ever possible in normal life.

The tension and the emotions were running high.

'Sometimes, there was just the faint resemblance . . .' reflected Rhodes, of the bodies. 'You could pick out the features of certain people you knew so well. You could say: Yes, this is Captain So-and-So. But you couldn't always do that, and identification like that wasn't sufficient for the authorities. You had to have formal identification.'

It was by comparing the teeth in the victims' skulls with known dental records that several of the victims were named. Some of the corpses were dressed in what was still recognizable as civilian clothing, but one was found to be wearing British Army-pattern shirt and pants. His teeth were found to match exactly the dental card of SAS Trooper Griffin. Number six on the list of the Op Loyton missing had been found and identified.

A body dressed in a British Army pullover was found to be wearing blue swimming trunks. His teeth seemed to correspond to the dental records of SAS Parachutist Ashe, another of the Op Loyton missing, but it was only a partial match. The clincher proved to be the blue trunks.

In his report on the exhumation Barkworth noted: 'Examination by the American war crimes team revealed that the swimming trunks had the following markings: 'Nicol Brown & Coyle Ltd. Halifax' and 'UMBRO' on separate tags.'

An SAS colleague remembered that Ashe had deployed on Op Loyton wearing just such a pair of blue trunks.

The corpse of Victor Gough was the next to be identified. All that remained of his clothing was one grey Army-pattern sock, but the teeth did seem to match the Jedburgh Captain's dental records. The clincher was the post-mortem carried out by the Americans; the body had had its appendix removed, which matched Gough's medical records perfectly.

Captain Victor Gough, the leader of Jedburgh team Jacob – who alone had soldiered on with the Alsace Maquis heroically, having lost his fellow Jedburghs to death and to capture – had survived so much, only to be murdered in a forest on the outskirts of Gaggenau, and disposed of in a mass grave.

The fourth Op Loyton victim was a particularly poignant one. A body was unearthed wearing an airborne-pattern jump smock of the type that fastened between the legs, to prevent it billowing up during a parachute jump. In the chapel-cum-morgue the teeth were examined, but they didn't seem to match any available dental card. Another means of identifying the body would have to be found.

Barkworth noticed that on the left wrist there was an Army-issue watch. All such watches had a dedicated number and had to be signed for. Barkworth decided to check. He found that the number of the watch corresponded to that signed out by Lieutenant David Dill – the baby-faced SAS officer who'd proved himself so astonishingly tough and calm under pressure during Op Loyton.

Lieutenant Dill had commanded the rearguard left at the SAS's final Moussey base. Dill and his force of six had been surrounded by the massive German force and they had fought to the last bullet. 'You are my prisoner,' the German officer had told Lieutenant Dill. 'You are a soldier and so am I.'

From one patch of war-ravaged woodland Lieutenant Dill had somehow found his way to another, but in far darker circumstances. His identification was confirmed beyond all doubt when the American pathologists discovered that the right elbow had been previously broken, matching Dill's medical records. They also recovered two metal stars – the 'pips' of a Lieutenant – on one shoulder of his shirt, and some English chocolate in one of his pockets.

Other identifications proved more straightforward; in the cases of Major Dennis Reynolds and Captain Andy Whately-Smith, the partially decomposed bodies were found to be still wearing their dog tags. At some stage after Colonel Franks' force had made for Allied lines, the SAS major who was recovering from being shot in the arm, and the captain who had stuck loyally by his side, must have abandoned their cave at Pierre-Percée. But whatever journey they had intended to take, it had ended here in this dark woodland.

Two other corpses were similarly identified via their tags. They were Curtis E. Hodges and Michael Pipcock, two of the American airmen that Colonel Chavez and his team had come here hoping to find.

Five of these men – Dill, Gough, Reynolds, Whately-Smith, and the American, Pipcock – had been listed in the Red Cross letter send to Colonel Franks, in November 1944. On 8 November 1944 they had been present and alive, held as prisoners at Schirmek's *Sicherungslager*. Somehow, from there they had ended up being thrown into a mass grave here in the Erlich Forest.

By 20 June 1945 the exhumations were complete. Two more corpses had been tentatively identified as American. The remainder were dressed in civilian clothing, and were mostly members of the French Resistance. Their details, such as the teams had been able to establish, were passed to the French authorities.

As a result of the Erlich Forest exhumations six more of the Op Loyton missing had been found. The list of the unsolved cases was shrinking; eighteen remained. The challenge now for Barkworth was to discover just how those six Op Loyton men had been killed and who was responsible, and then to track down the perpetrators.

Piecing together the history of the killings proved less problematic than Barkworth had feared. Witnesses – mostly former prisoners of the Rotenfels camp, but also some of the former camp staff – stepped forward to tell Barkworth the harrowing tale.

On 25 November 1944 the chief of the Rotenfels camp, Commandant Wunsch, had received orders to execute all British and American POWs held there. Those orders had originated from *Standartenführer* Isselhorst, and this was the first concrete mention that Barkworth had come across of his part in orchestrating such killings. Isselhorst's name and role were duly noted.

Abbé Alphonse Hett, a French priest held at Rotenfels as a suspected Maquis, related to Barkworth what he had witnessed on that fateful day. Fourteen prisoners had been ordered to parade outside their huts; they included ten men wearing British or American military uniforms, plus four dressed as civilians (including two fellow priests, Abbé Roth and Abbé Claude).

The commander of the camp guards, a Lieutenant Nussberger, ordered the fourteen prisoners to climb aboard a closed truck. As they tried to mount up clutching their meagre bundles of possessions, Nussberger's men – Ostertag, Ullrich, Zimmermann and Neuschwanger – wrestled their baggage away from them. Everything was to be left behind. On seeing this, Abbé Hett knew instinctively that these men were being taken away to be murdered.

The truck pulled out. It was the last Abbé Hett was to see of the prisoners. The story was then taken up by Albert Arnold, a French POW forced to work at Rotenfels as a driver. He was at the wheel of the truck that day. He was told to drive to the edge of the Erlich Forest. He drew to a halt where instructed, and the first group of three prisoners was marched away. The driver heard shots ring out, as did all aboard the truck.

The remaining prisoners were taken away in groups of three. Those about to be killed were forced to stand on the lip of the bomb crater, where they could clearly see their dead comrades. The corpses were partially undressed and their clothes and boots either looted or piled up and burned, presumably to hide the evidence of their identities. At the last moment one of the priests had tried to break away. He made it 100 yards into the woods before being gunned down.

Once the fourteen had been killed, a group of Russian POWs was marched into the forest and made to shovel earth on top of the corpses, filling in the bomb craters. One of those POWs managed to remove a crumpled photograph from the pocket of one of the victims. It showed what had to be his loved ones.

On the liberation of the Rotenfels camp that photo had been handed over to a Swiss consul living locally, who subsequently got it into Allied hands. It was passed to Barkworth, and those who knew SAS Trooper Griffin confirmed that it was his.

Abbé Hett related to Barkworth the kind of treatment meted out to the captured men during their dark weeks of captivity. They had been held longest at Schirmek's *Sicherungslager*, only being transferred to Gaggenau when US forces overran the Vosges. At Schirmek one man in particular, *Oberwachtmeister* (Lieutenant) Heinrich Neuschwanger, had unleashed savagery on the British prisoners. They were dragged to the camp washroom, strung up by their hands and beaten so severely that their bones showed through their skin.

Neuschwanger was a particularly bloodthirsty individual, who was never happier than when he had beatings or killings with which to 'amuse' himself. According to what the priest told Barkworth, Major Reynolds had remarked 'that he would not have thought it possible for the body to withstand such pain without death occurring'. In other words, he could not understand why he was still alive.

Amongst the prisoners Neuschwanger had earned the nickname 'Stuka', which resulted from his predilection for stamping on the prostrate forms of his captives, like the pouncing dive-bomber of the same name. Major Reynolds, Captains Whately-Smith and Gough, plus Lieutenant Dill had been beaten to within an inch of their lives while in captivity, which would explain why none had tried to escape when they were driven to their deaths in the Erlich Forest.

According to witnesses, *Oberwachtmeister* Neuschwanger had argued that all British and American POWs needed to be shot, 'since when the Allies came camp staff would be killed'. Neuschwanger was supposedly the foremost triggerman who had gunned down the captives as they stood on the edge of their mass grave.

Oberwachtmeister Heinrich Neuschwanger had just leapt to the top of Barkworth's list of the most wanted, ahead even of Max Kessler, the Gestapo officer who had overseen the murders and the burning of the bodies in the Vosges.

Following his Gaggenau investigations, Barkworth understood more fully the roles played by Schirmek's *Sicherungslager* and its relationship to Natzweiler. Writing of Natzweiler, he noted: 'Here was the full machinery for the elimination and destruction of prisoners, and it was hither from Schirmek that these were sent for execution.' Generally, prisoners were held, interrogated and tortured at Schirmek; but they were sent on to Natzweiler for termination.

Other names were added to Barkworth's most-wanted list, including more key figures from the camps. At the top of a Barkworth report entitled 'War Criminals – Wanted reports have been made out against the following', was *Hauptsturmführer* Karl Buck, Schirmek's one-legged, morphine-addicted camp commandant. Barkworth listed Buck as being responsible for 'giving, transmitting or carrying out orders to shoot ten British and American victims'.

Amongst those listed as responsible for 'impromptu atrocities in the Vosges area' was *Sturmbannführer* Hans Dietrich Ernst, the SS officer who had sent eight hundred French Jews to their deaths at Auschwitz, and whose *Einsatzkommando* Ernst had perpetrated the worst predations of Waldfest. There was also a Julius Gehrum, the former head of the border guard force, and one of Isselhorst's most brutal enforcers. And of course, there was *Standartenführer* Dr Erich Isselhorst himself, the grandmaster of it all.

Somewhere out there in the fluid chaos of Germany, these men – these guilty men – were hiding. The hunt was about to begin in earnest. 'All details known including Rank, Christian name and home address are shown where available on the Wanted Reports,' Barkworth noted. Those wanted reports were to be circulated via London to all Allied authorities.

Barkworth's full report on the Gaggenau atrocities was completed by 15 July 1945. It concluded: 'Those who have had the patience to read this . . . will realize the urgency of bringing the German criminals to justice.'

As luck would have it, Barkworth was about to seize the first of his most wanted.

Chapter Twenty

By the summer of 1945 the survivors of the Waldfest deportations had returned. Of the 231 who had been taken from Moussey, 178 did not come back. Of those who did, some were so weakened and sickly from the effects of what they had suffered that they too would die. Across the Rabodeau Valley a thousand-odd villagers had been taken, most of whom never returned to their homes.

The valley of a thousand tears had become the vale of the widows.

As the dark and bitter truth began to emerge about Hitler's Commando Order and its impact upon Allied victims, the news hit the world press. On 7 June Reuters released a front-page story entitled 'The 168 Steps of Torture'. It revealed that the remains of forty-eight parachutists murdered by the SS had been discovered at the Mauthausen concentration camp in Austria.

The Reuters story read: 'According to liberated prisoners, they were made to carry rocks up 168 steps leading to the top of a quarry, while guards lashed them with whips and threatened to shoot if the rocks fell.' They were then made to throw the rocks off and repeat the entire process all over again. The torture ended on 6 September 1944, when, 'on the orders of

Himmler, the half-dead men were shot as they struggled up the steps'.

Elsewhere it was reported how the private effects of men missing from 1 SAS had been recovered from Belsen, leaving little doubt as to the soldiers' fate. But the sheer scale of the atrocities and the numbers of Nazis involved remained mind-numbing. It was as if an avalanche of atrocities had thundered across Western Europe, burying it in horror, and in spite of Barkworth's 'Wanted' reports many war criminals were escaping the Allied dragnet.

On 12 June 1945, just as Barkworth was about to issue his report on the Gaggenau atrocities, *Standartenführer* Dr Erich Isselhorst was captured – or, rather, he handed himself in. Ironically, it was to the soldiers of the US 7th Army – those who had helped drive his forces out of the Vosges – that Isselhorst had chosen to give himself up.

Together with his wife, Isselhorst had spent weeks lying low in a remote lumberjack cabin in Sachenbach, a mountainous area of southern Germany close to the Austrian border. Until recently, he had remained an unreconstructed Nazi and apparently unrepentant. He'd written a letter to his wife, boasting of how he'd shown himself to be a true disciple of the Führer, unlike those just 'paying lip service'. Isselhorst had described his 'unshakeable faith in the good and pure nature of National Socialism [Nazism], the spirit of the Reich and its people, and the invulnerability of our leader'.

Dressed in civilian clothing and holding false papers in the name of Georg Horst, at first Isselhorst had tried to ride out the storm of the Allies' arrival by remaining in hiding. But by June

1945, he had clearly made the decision that his fortunes would be best served if he could ingratiate himself with the most powerful of Germany's occupying forces: the Americans.

From the records of his subsequent interrogations, it seems clear that the Americans were torn about Isselhorst. On the one hand, the US 7th Army's War Crimes Branch suspected the SS and Gestapo commander of being involved with atrocities. On the other, its counter-intelligence staff realized that Isselhorst had fought on the Eastern Front, and that could make him useful.

'The following leads on Counter Intelligence personalities have been provided by SS *Standartenführer* Dr. Erich Isselhorst, now in custody,' notes a 'CONFIDENTIAL' letter from Headquarters, United States Forces, European Theatre. Those leads concern Isselhorst's SS and Gestapo colleagues who had either fought against the Russian Red Army, or spied upon Stalin's regime.

Isselhorst quickly made his intentions clear to his captors. 'Isselhorst has offered to work for us in the capacity of an informer,' concluded one typewritten US memo. A handwritten note in the margin stated: 'IC not sure of him yet' – IC stood for the 7th Army's 'Interrogation Centre'. The US Army's interests in Isselhorst were listed as: 'A. Organisation and personalities of Amt IV RSHA. B. The Sipo in Russia.'

'Amt IV' was the Gestapo, and the 'SIPO' was the Reich's security police, but the focus of the American's interest was clearly Isselhorst's Russian experiences and expertise. Commenting on Isselhorst's time serving on the Eastern Front, the interrogation report stated: 'Political police; anti-Maquis measures in close collaboration with local anti-communists, making use of the age-old hatred between Ukrainians and White Russians.'

For an American military contemplating a new war – the Cold War – such experiences might well prove invaluable. As to Isselhorst's personality, the interrogation officer stated that while he 'tried to make a good impression . . . He has an unpleasant personality and a character that seems cowardly. He is worried about his wife and mother and obviously concerned about his own fate.'

At the same time the Americans were liaising with the British over Isselhorst. A 'SECRET' July 1945 cable from London advised caution over Isselhorst. 'STILL CONVINCED NAZI,' it warned. Yet in spite of this, the Americans were clearly tempted to work with him.

'Greying hair, light blue eyes . . . very intelligent, hard worker, good appearance,' concluded a US 7th Army assessment of Isselhorst's professional abilities. 'Suggest Isselhorst be used as lead present locations,' concluded a 'SECRET' 7th Army cable, urging that he be employed to help round up valuable Gestapo officers, and to further the 7th Army's intelligence outreach into the Soviet zone and Stalin's Russia: the new enemy.

So far, Isselhorst's detention and his ingratiating behaviour towards the Americans had escaped Barkworth's notice. But as luck would have it, another of the most wanted had already fallen into the SAS commander's hands: *Hauptsturmführer* Karl Buck, Schirmek's former commandant, was safely ensconced in the Villa Degler's cellar-cum-prison-cell, and singing like a canary.

At this early stage of proceedings, word had yet to get out that the hunt for the Nazi war criminals was on. Incredibly, many of the 'wanted' didn't appear to think that they had done anything particularly wrong. Karl Buck was one of those. Returning to his family home, he'd planned to slip back quietly into the life that he had led as a civilian before the war. That was until Barkworth had arrived on his doorstep to take him to the Villa Degler's interrogation cell.

With his level, unshakeable gaze and fluent German, Barkworth would prove an interrogator almost without equal, although his means and his methods would surprise some. He had already stressed 'the urgency of bringing the German criminals to justice'. He felt that urgency most personally. He was utterly driven and unrelenting, and he fuelled his murderously long hours with both drink and drugs.

Barkworth's team had now been boosted to thirteen to help cope with the punishing workload. In a letter to Colonel Franks, one of his men explained just how intensive was their schedule – in part to excuse his terrible handwritten scrawl.

'It is now about two in the morning and I've been working the last two days on the Barkworth system,' SAS Captain Henry Parker wrote, '. . . a mixture of whisky, Benzedrine and no sleep – also I'm not good at typing at the best of times.'

Old habits died hard.

Barkworth and his team's relentless, Benzedrine-fuelled work routine meant that an interrogation visit to the Villa Degler cellar could happen at any time of the day or night. But other than that, Barkworth treated his captives with a remarkable politeness and decency, almost as if by doing so they might be convinced that he empathized with them. Yet he never offered them more than these two stark choices: either they confess and turn evidence against their superiors, or they should expect zero clemency in the forthcoming war crimes trials.

'Few Germans interrogated by him, even the many who had signed confessions of guilt and even the most hardened of Gestapo men have failed to comment on his courtesy and consideration,' noted Captain Prince Galitzine, in a handwritten assessment of Barkworth's interrogation methods. 'Some have even mistaken him for the ex-Gestapo chief of that area whose physical likeness and even the German accent is so like Bill that it startles the prisoners.'

One of the Rotenfels staff, Siegmund Weber, had recently faced a Barkworth interrogation. Weber had played a minor role compared to 'Stuka' Neuschwanger or Camp Commandant Buck. He had served as the Rotenfels camp quartermaster – a glorified storeman. His value was that he was a witness to Neuschwanger's beatings and his savagery.

But shortly after Barkworth had interrogated him, Weber had attempted suicide – testimony to the steel that the SAS officer could put into his questioning. Barkworth's methods likewise worked wonders with Karl Buck.

'During the summer of 1944 a number of camps were constructed east of the Rhine, which came under my command,' Buck recounted to Barkworth, regarding the Gaggenau atrocities. One of those was the Rotenfels camp. 'These were in connection with . . . the Daimler Benz Company, in order to provide labour for their factories.'

Buck tried to paint himself as whiter than white, while laying the blame at Isselhorst's door. 'I wish to place on the record that during the whole time that I was commandant of this camp no prisoner was killed by my orders.' One of Isselhorst's deputies had come to him that summer, Buck explained, with orders that 'any bailed-out airmen or parachutists who might be taken prisoner and brought to my camp, were to be killed. He suggested this might be done in the surrounding woods.'

Buck claimed that he had refused Isselhorst's orders. The most that he had been willing to do was send such airmen and parachutists to Natzweiler, where the camp executioner, *Hauptscharführer* Peter Straub, might deal with them. He described Straub as having, 'extremely small eyes, pale face, reddish hair and an impediment in his speech which caused him to pull the corners of his mouth'.

Buck spoke about one of Straub's final mass executions. 'On 18 October [1944], a party which I estimate at 125 strong, which had arrived at Schirmek from Strasbourg was sent to Natzweiler.' This group was summarily killed, confirming Natzweiler's role as a liquidation centre for those no longer deemed 'useful' to the Reich, and Straub's role as the mass executioner.

As US forces had advanced into the Vosges, Buck had driven to Gaggenau and 'arranged with the Mercedes Benz firm for a supply of sufficient trucks to evacuate the prisoners across the Rhine. This was in accordance with a secret order that I had received from Dr. Isselhorst. This order was accompanied by verbal instructions to shoot certain prisoners, including the British and American POWs.'

Buck had disobeyed his orders, because 'I did not consider that it would be wise to leave fresh mass graves behind.' Instead, he took all the prisoners direct to the Rotenfels camp. But Buck professed to Barkworth that 'I stood in fear of Dr. Isselhorst, who I know would not only have had me executed, but also would attack my family should I act contrary to his orders.'

So it was that Buck had passed the buck; he'd ordered Wunsch, the Rotenfels commandant, to shoot the British and American prisoners, thus carrying out Isselhorst's command. 'I told him to destroy any evidence which might lead to the discovery of this crime, and take such precautions as would be normal – such as destruction of papers bearing their names, and any uniforms or any other aids of identification that might be on their bodies.'

By anyone's reckoning, this was an explosive confession. It bore the signature of 'Karl Gustaf Wilhelm Buck', and had a typewritten note beside it, signed off by Barkworth: 'I certify that the above statement was read to the witness, in his own language, prior to his signature . . .'

With Buck's testimony secured, the case of the Gaggenau atrocities had been largely solved. Barkworth now knew how the British Special Forces and their US airmen comrades had ended up in Gaggenau, and why. He knew on whose orders those men had been executed, and who had done the killing. And with Buck firmly in custody, one of the key architects of their demise was ready to face trial.

More suspects would doubtless be tracked down. But Barkworth was keen to stress the need for secrecy if they were to succeed in getting those they most sought into the Villa

Degler cell. In a telephone call to London he urged: 'Extreme care should be taken to ensure that no news that the SAS are searching for [X suspect] should reach the wanted man's ears.'

Colonel Franks' subsequent letter to Brigadier Calvert, the overall SAS Commander, reflected how well Barkworth and his team had done. 'I had a long talk with Col. Chavez [the American war crimes investigator] and was much impressed by his desire to help us. He expressed amazement that the British investigation . . . should be left in the hands of one single officer. He showed great gratitude for the assistance he had received from Barkworth . . .'

Chavez's surprise at the size and scope of the British team reflected his own, impressive set-up. His Gaggenau unit included two pathologists, several professional interrogators, two legal experts, plus shorthand typists and photographers to help document the crime scenes and to take witness statements. By contrast, Barkworth's unit consisted of no specialists whatsoever; it was the 2 SAS intelligence cell reconstituted as a DIY manhunting unit, which only made it all the more impressive that they were doing so well.

Having secured Buck's testimony, Barkworth's intention now was to search far and wide for the suspects: the trigger-man, 'Stuka' Neuschwanger; *Hauptscharführer* Peter Straub, the Natzweiler executioner; Max Kessler, the Gestapo officer and Vosges killer; *Sturmbannführer* Hans Dietrich Ernst, the SS officer and Vosges murder squad commander; Julius Gehrum, Isselhorst's brutal enforcer; and chiefly, of course, Isselhorst himself.

He would need to search scores of private addresses and scour the POW camps across four zones of occupation, each with its own set of rules and regulations. War criminals had even sought to hide themselves amongst the ranks of the 'liberated armies', claiming to be French, Czech or Polish soldiers. Where necessary, their numbers would need to be checked. Barkworth's refusal to be daunted by red tape would yield swift results, but it would also earn him any number of enemies.

The coming search would take his men into some of the most horrific places on earth – ones that few could ever have imagined possible. One of the first, and perhaps the worst, was a building set beneath the prison in nearby Strasbourg. The place needed to be crossed off Barkworth's list, so Sergeant Dusty Rhodes was sent to check that none of the Op Loyton missing were there.

'A lot of experiments had been carried out on human bodies,' Rhodes recalled. 'There was . . . an enormous room that was absolutely full of human body parts, all preserved in formalin, in tanks. Now . . . it was our job to go around and look at each one . . . There were heads and faces and arms and legs; if one saw possibly a tattoo on an arm which one knew from regimental badges or English sayings . . . There was a possibility that some of our people could have been there.'

Thankfully, as far as Rhodes could tell, none of the Op Loyton missing had been chopped up by the Nazis and preserved in vats of formaldehyde.

Amongst other excursions that Barkworth had planned was a return visit to Moussey. New leads from the Gaggenau investigation needed to be pursued in the Rabodeau Valley and surroundings. Moreover, he and Sykes were keen to deliver in person a formal letter of thanks from the SAS Regiment.

Entitled 'Letter . . . to the citizens of Moussey as a form of thank you for their help', it read:

I wish to express to you something of the gratitude which all the officers and men of the Special Air Service Brigade . . . feel towards you for the selfless devotion and memorable courage with which you aided them in the accomplishment of their tasks. The help you gave contributed in a large measure to any success we achieved, and we are full of admiration for the disregard of danger and generosity of spirit with which that help was given.

All men who were involved in the bitter conflict of 1939–1945 grew to recognize the importance to victory of civilian loyalty, steadfastness and determination. We realize that in no country and at no time did the practice of those virtues demand greater firmness than in France under German occupation, and that nowhere was that firmness more abundantly forthcoming.

It continued in a similar vein. Signed by Brigadier Calvert, it wished 'all good fortune' to the Moussey villagers and to France and offered the Regiment's 'most sincere thanks'. It was a fitting tribute to the villagers, and one that Barkworth and Sykes wished to deliver in person to several of their most valued Moussey friends.

But even as they prepared to head west into the Vosges, the work of this barely nascent manhunting unit was about to be brought to a premature and dramatic end.

Increasingly that summer, the SAS Regiment had been forced to wage an unanticipated war – a battle for its very survival. As the Second World War had drawn to a close, so Winston Churchill had been voted out of power, the weary minds of the British public turning away from the grim years of conflict. Two months after VE Day the first election since the start of the war was held, for democracy itself had been put on hold during the conflict. It resulted in a shock defeat for Churchill, and a landslide victory bringing Labour's Clement Attlee to power.

Churchill had been the earliest and most outspoken advocate of Special Forces operations and irregular warfare. In the earliest stages of the war he'd challenged his military commanders to think the unthinkable, using guerrilla warfare, hit-and-run tactics and sabotage as a means to take the fight to the enemy in the most unexpected of ways. He'd challenged his military to 'prepare hunter troops for a butcher-and-bolt reign of terror', calling for 'volunteers for special duties' to man the ranks of the raiders.

Churchill had promised these men little more than a short but glorious career and almost certain death, and he had backed to the hilt those who had answered his call. He had once been asked in Parliament by Simon Wingfield-Digby, the MP for West Dorset, a question about British Special Forces fighting in southern Europe.

'Is it true, Mr Prime Minister, that there is a body of men out in the Aegean Islands, fighting under the Union Flag, that are nothing short of being a band of murderous, renegade cut-throats?'

Churchill had had an entirely apposite answer: 'If you do not take your seat and keep quiet, I will send you out to join them.'

But in the late summer of 1945 Churchill was no longer the man in power, and it was looking as if the days of this private army of maverick rule-breakers were numbered. The SAS had been warned that it was in imminent danger of being disbanded. The wheels had been set in motion by a military establishment that had never truly warmed to the gentleman warriors, eccentrics, desperadoes and buccaneers who made up the Regiment, and which was anxious to be rid of them once and for all.

It was in full knowledge of this that Colonel Franks wrote to his commanding officer, Brigadier Calvert, in late July 1945, expressing his frustration about the war crimes issue. 'I am sure you will understand my feelings in this matter. At present, I very much doubt whether even a small percentage of the perpetrators of these crimes will be brought to justice. I feel personally responsible, not only to the families of these officers and men, but also to the men themselves.'

Franks signed off his letter with this: 'There are no lengths to which I would not go to ensure that action is taken.'

There are no lengths to which I would not go to ensure that action is taken: for the man then commanding 2 SAS these were strong words indeed.

Chapter Twenty-one

Colonel Franks' quest for justice was not simply on behalf of his own SAS men. On the same day that he had written to Brigadier Calvert, promising that there were *no lengths to which he would not go to ensure action was taken,* he'd also penned a letter to the SOE's Baker Street headquarters, regarding their missing men.

'I enclose copy of Major Barkworth's [Gaggenau] report, since it contains a good deal of information regarding the fate of Captain V. Gough who was with me in the Vosges, and whose death is now proved . . . Unfortunately I do not know the address of his next of kin, and am therefore unable to write to them.'

Franks felt every loss, and every war crime, most personally. Yet how could justice be achieved for any of the victims and their families, if the SAS was about to be shut down? The issue troubled Franks mightily, but there seemed little that he or anyone else could do to stop the seemingly inevitable, much though they might try.

Colonel Franks, Brigadier Calvert and others had plenty of ideas about how the SAS could be used, now that the war was won. Franks had earned the reputation of being one of the Regiment's most original thinkers. He had proved himself an inspirational leader and a man of courage, understanding and initiative. He was also intensely loyal, as his dogged pursuit of the war crimes issue was proving. He commanded great respect within elite forces circles.

Franks and Calvert argued that post-war Special Forces roles might include behind-the-lines deployments in any Third World War with Russia, putting down rebellions in various parts of the empire, as well as hunting down the Nazi war criminals. As Brigadier Calvert was about to be posted to the Indian Army, it would fall to Colonel Franks to try to ensure that the SAS survived in some shape or form. He was absolutely determined to see that it would.

But the British military chiefs were equally determined to see the unit go. They had been reticent about creating Special Forces in the first place, and argued there was certainly no place for them now, in peacetime. Criticism of the SAS ranged from accusations of elitism and the dangers of private armies inculcating 'unacceptable attitudes' amongst the rank and file, to charges that they were impossible to control or to fit into operational plans. The fact that the ranks of the Regiment were made up of so many foreigners and even the odd civilian was doubly troubling.

The top brass argued that Special Forces took up an inordinate amount of senior commanders' time, both in terms of fitting them into operational plans and dealing with the fallout from 'undisciplined behaviour' and 'unsanctioned operations' – in other words, the men on the ground deciding to go off and do their own thing. The SAS was also accused of 'skimming' the regular military of its best officers and men, and likewise sucking up a disproportionate amount of resources.

In short, the SAS had made powerful enemies who in the summer of 1945 they were determined to win the day. But equally, Colonel Franks was determined to thwart them. If the SAS had to be seen to fall on its sword, so be it. Publicly, it would do so. But privately, Franks was working at every level to ensure that the Regiment would survive, albeit in a wholly secretive and stealthy way.

The SAS colonel held several cards in his hand. Firstly, he enjoyed the absolute backing of Winston Churchill. So chary had the former prime minister been of the military establishment that he had created many of his earliest butcher-and-bolt raiding units outside the military apparatus entirely. The SOE was part of the Ministry for Economic Warfare, and many of Churchill's raiding forces were made up of SOE agents.

Secondly, Colonel Franks had as fine an ally as one could wish for within the ranks of 2 SAS: Randolph Churchill. The former prime minister's son had served with the SAS in North Africa and in the Balkans, and was an SAS aficionado without equal. With both the father and son so intimately involved, Colonel Franks prepared to play the long game, rallying political friends to his cause and lobbying the higher echelons of the Whitehall establishment.

In the meantime, the scene was set for the SAS to go underground, and foremost amongst its clandestine units would be Barkworth's Nazi hunters.

*   *   *

While Franks was fighting his high-level battles in London, Barkworth, Sykes, Rhodes et al. were busy at the coalface. Amidst the burning quest for vengeance, none of them had forgotten the one place that had suffered more than any: the village of Moussey.

In early August 1945, Barkworth led his team back to the Rabodeau Valley. They came seeking evidence, but equally they came to answer a call from the villagers to honour the fallen. They were holding a memorial service for all who had perished in the concentration camps, and to consecrate a military cemetery for those who had perished in battle.

The remembrance service was staged at the very spot where the SS had rounded up the men of the village on 24 September 1944, and where Captain Druce had shot up the SS parade the same day. As Barkworth and his men observed the solemn gathering, the true extent of the tragedy that had struck this place became clear. The last flames of hope were flickering into darkness as villagers realized that the missing were never going to return.

Not a family had escaped loss, and the neighbouring villages were likewise bereaved and bereft. Widows and orphans thronged the streets. But nowhere had suffered to the same extent as Moussey, and the villagers would not have been hit as hard had they not harboured the Operation Loyton force so actively and for such a long time.

Yet the men of the Regiment – those who had been killed in the battles in the woods, or murdered locally by the Gestapo – were buried side by side with the French victims, in Moussey's main graveyard. There was no ill feeling here; quite the reverse.

The villagers asked for a set of the SAS colours to hang in their church, and they wanted to know the names of those who had died so they could be inscribed on the Moussey war memorials and for ever remembered.

The streets were clogged with stooped, black-clad figures – women and children, burdened with their sadness and their loss. There was one surprising splash of colour. For the remembrance service the priest of Moussey, Abbé Gassman, had donned a red SAS beret, one that had been sent to him by the commander of the mission that had cost his flock so dear – Colonel Brian Franks.

Abbé Gassman knew that he had a busy time ahead of him. In Catholic tradition, a requiem mass would need to be held for each and every household that had lost someone. He figured it would take him the best part of a year to complete all those he needed to perform for the bereaved in Moussey.

One villager who had returned from Rotenfels had been locked up there along with Lieutenant David Dill. Barkworth carried with him everywhere the photos of the 'missing'. He showed Lieutenant Dill's photo to the villager who had shared his cell.

'Yes, that's him. That's certainly him,' the villager confirmed. 'That's definitely his charming smile.'

Throughout the long and terrible weeks of captivity – from 7 October to 25 November 1944 – Lieutenant Dill had refused to salute even one of his Gestapo captors. This had served to infuriate them. It was the SAS lieutenant's sole form of resistance, but it had attracted savage beatings on a daily basis – though even those weren't sufficient to break his spirit. On one occasion Dill was lying on a straw mattress, following an agony of torture, when a woman prisoner was thrust into his cell. Dill had levered himself to his feet and offered her his bed, taking for himself the cold stone of the floor.

The villager had last seen Lieutenant Dill shortly before he was driven out to the Erlich Forest, to face Stuka Neuschwanger. In spite of everything, even then his charming smile had still been with him.

Barkworth and his team left Moussey laden down with an even greater sense of responsibility, and with further evidence to drive their investigations. Yet even as they headed back to Gaggenau, the proverbial sword of Damocles was hanging over their operations. The planned disbandment date for the SAS Brigade had been set for late September 1945 – less than a month away.

Barkworth and his team were painfully aware that the sands of time were running out, but short of forgoing all sleep there was little they could do to up their pace of operations. And so it was fortunate that their single greatest ally in the fight for survival would shortly be arriving at their Villa Degler headquarters.

Captain Prince Yuri 'Yurka' Galitzine, war crimes investigator at the War Office's 20 Eaton Square branch was Gaggenau-bound. He carried with him 200 copies of Barkworth's wanted lists to distribute around the Allied authorities. As Galitzine had penned the first ever report into Natzweiler, he commanded more than a little respect from Barkworth's Gallic hosts.

Of particular interest to the French was Josef Kramer, who was scheduled to stand trial over the Belsen atrocities. As the French pointed out to Galitzine, Kramer has commanded Natzweiler for three and a half years, living in the Hansel-and-Gretel house that stood beside the camp fence. By contrast, he had been at Belsen for barely a matter of months before that camp was liberated, but Belsen had grabbed all the headlines.

Understandably, the French wanted Kramer to stand trial for the crimes that he had committed at Natzweiler against the French Resistance. They stressed how vital it was for the people of the Vosges to see Kramer tried – as a morale booster and to see justice being done. The French authorities had tried approaching the British Army of the Rhine (BAOR), to ask for Kramer to be handed into French custody following the forth-coming Belsen trials, but they had enjoyed little success.

Galitzine wasn't overly surprised. Barkworth's team had received even less help from the BAOR – the force garrisoning the British zone of occupation. In fact, the BAOR had been actively obstructive, especially concerning some of Barkworth's less orthodox methods of tracking down war criminals. Galitzine was in entire agreement with his French hosts: Kramer needed to be tried by the French. It didn't particularly matter who hanged him – French or British – as long as the sadist and mass murderer swung for his crimes.

At the Villa Degler, Galitzine rendezvoused with Barkworth, plus his twelve-man team. It was immediately obvious how under-staffed and ill-equipped they were. Their only transport with which to search across Germany and France – and very possibly nations further afield – were four jeeps that had been airdropped into France on several operations during the war. They were held together with wire, string and a good few prayers.

Despite this, Galitzine found morale at the Villa Degler to be amazingly high, and Barkworth bullish about his chances of success, if only he were given the time and the resources to properly finish the job.

'He has managed to account for the murder and torture of all except 18,' Galitzine noted of the Op Loyton missing. Galitzine wrote of the 'very fine work being done by the present team', stressing how 'the chances of . . . solving the last cases quickly are good'.

Galitzine also noticed that in contrast to what their detractors might claim, the SAS team was seeking justice on behalf of many more than simply their own. 'Major Barkworth had followed up all War Crimes against other British or American personnel uncovered in the area . . . he has about fourteen additional non-SAS cases on his hands.'

What Barkworth needed now was more personnel and more time, and not to face the threat of imminent closure. To help Galitzine understand how pressing his needs were, the SAS major listed the key priorities for his ongoing investigations:

Obtain photographs of Strasbourg Gestapo for possible identification by . . . witnesses.
See MALZOF re the unknown American alleged to be buried at Schutterwald.
Establish evidence of beatings prior to death.
Outstanding . . . bodies not yet found or accounted for . . .
This is split into

(a) a party of 8 (BLACK'S stick, provisionally traced from Schirmek to Strasbourg).

(b) a party of 8 (DILL's stick, provisionally traced . . . to Schirmek . . .)

Evidence regarding perpetrators should be obtainable from members of Gestapo column active Moussey area period 20 Aug 1944 (at least one prisoner held).

The list went on and on.

The one thing that Galitzine figured the Barkworth team wasn't doing – and it certainly wasn't their area of expertise – was using the media. He contacted the press and radio team that he had commanded while attached to the US 7th Army. They were still in existence and in theatre.

'Their assistance was enlisted in the launching of a campaign advertising for witnesses who might be of value,' Galitzine noted. That press campaign was fired up even before he prepared to leave the area en route to London.

But prior to departure, there was one pressing issue that needed to be aired. While Galitzine knew how Barkworth's team was 'all 100% keen and doing a very fine job', he was equally aware that the days of this extraordinary enterprise were seemingly numbered. 'In the near future the team will be faced with many . . . difficulties,' he noted, 'and will require all the help that can be given.'

In the Villa Degler's sumptuous drawing room, and with a bottle of spirits placed on the round wooden table between them, they ruminated over the future. That table was one upon which the men more normally played cards during their rare evenings off. A US carbine was propped casually against the side of the table. A lighted candle lay in the middle, shadows flickering conspiratorially across the walls.

One of Barkworth's men used his Fairbairn-Sykes fighting knife to slice off a hunk of bread, feeding it into his mouth as he talked. Nearly everyone was smoking, and a somewhat agreeable smog thickened the intense and febrile atmosphere.

Galitzine confirmed the men's worst fears. Right now, 2 SAS stood to be disbanded by the end of September at the latest. The HQ of 2 SAS, at Glebe House in Colchester, would be closed down shortly thereafter. Glebe House presently provided all the communications and logistical backup for Barkworth and his men.

As Barkworth pointed out, losing the Glebe House set-up would 'seriously dislocate' his entire operation – not that, strictly speaking, they should still even be operating by then, for the SAS itself would have been terminated. Barkworth outlined the minimum requirements that would enable him to continue with his present mission, if somehow that could be sorted.

He needed to keep his twelve-man team. Ideally, he wanted more. He needed a headquarters and liaison unit somewhere in the UK – London, ideally – without which very little would be possible in the field. And above all else he needed to retain his Phantom signallers, providing a direct radio link to whatever might be his headquarters. As Barkworth pointed out, there existed 'no other means of contact with the outside world. Postal communications non-existent'.

Over their time together in the Villa Degler, Galitzine and Barkworth had gelled. Though from somewhat different backgrounds, they shared a number of qualities: a rigorous and unshakeable sense of right and wrong; a can-do, maverick attitude; a fine intellect; a healthy disregard for unnecessary rules and red tape. And born of this was a solution to the problem that they then faced – one as breathtaking as it was unorthodox.

Barkworth's unit would 'go dark'. It would slip beneath the radar. These thirteen men who wore the SAS beret and winged dagger as they hunted the Nazi war criminals would officially cease to exist. In effect, Galitzine's 20 Eaton Square outfit would take control of their activities, massaging budgets, equipment and personnel out of a War Office that was still in something of a post-war meltdown.

Galitzine would 'hide' the SAS manhunters amidst all the chaos and confusion of the War Office system. Even as the SAS was formally disbanded, so Barkworth's team would become a hidden and deniable adjunct to AG3-VW. In Germany, they would continue to operate as if they had every right to do so – they would be hiding in plain sight.

Barkworth and Galitzine's conviction that they must continue with this vital work, come what may, was strengthened by their recent experiences. In early August a team of 'official' war crimes investigators had been sent from the BAOR to 'assist' Barkworth's efforts. Having just completed their Belsen investigations, their offer of help may well have been genuine. The results proved desultory.

Galitzine and Barkworth had talked through the debacle. 'Investigation was not recognized as a job of the team,' they concluded. 'No attempt was made to find bodies or to dig about for evidence, but they purely went over ground already covered, or went after witnesses already known to exist.'

The BAOR team's commander, a Lieutenant Colonel Genn, had even confided to Barkworth: 'The difficulties of organization are so great that I am only marking time.'

When Genn suggested that it might be better if he and his team left the Villa Degler, Barkworth readily agreed. They'd spent less than a month there. As just one illustration of how lacklustre was their approach, Barkworth cited the actions of the team's so-called 'pathologist'. He was in truth an Army medical officer who'd been held as a POW, and who'd completed a very short course in pathology following the war.

One case brought to him by Barkworth involved a body whose identification was proving difficult. The BAOR pathologist suggested that the corpse should be 'left to weather for a year', after which identification might somehow prove easier. Barkworth had taken the case to Colonel Chavez's man. He had managed to identify the body after three days' work. He pointed out that the British 'pathologist's' proposal would have rendered the task almost impossible.

More to the point, Barkworth did not have a year to spare.

Lieutenant Colonel Genn had penned a report on his work in Gaggenau. It concluded that Barkworth's efforts to trace the eighteen missing, 'have now reached a dead end . . . The . . . missing members of 2 SAS still remain untraced, and it is considered that as far as this Team is concerned no avenue remains which can be usefully followed up.'

Inexplicably, Genn concluded of those who had been held at Natzweiler: 'It may be assumed that possible extermination of Allied personnel occurred. The case is considered too vague to follow up. It is noted that of the Allied personnel known to have been in [Natzweiler] . . . all are believed to be safe and well in England.'

Safe and well in England. The mind boggled.

Genn's recommendation was for the 'final discarding of any further investigations' of the Op Loyton missing.

Barkworth countered the colonel's criticisms with a pithy one-liner: 'It is not agreed that no avenue remains; it is however agreed that [Genn's team] is perhaps most usefully employed elsewhere.'

Towards the end of September 1945, the BAOR upped their rhetoric still further. In terms of the eighteen missing men, 'only a miracle' would provide evidence to solve their cases. Even more damningly, the BAOR stated: 'Barkworth's material conforms to no known legal standards of proof and is very often based on pure hearsay . . . and could not possibly be used for our purposes.' In other words, Barkworth's evidence would not stand up in a court of law.

Galitzine begged to differ, as did the legal experts under his purview. The BAOR's objections seemed driven by a fear that Barkworth was not only treading on their toes, but that his work was in danger of showing up their own lack of zeal, not to mention their commitment to getting results.

'The SAS team are all personal friends of the missing men whose cases they are investigating and also of their families,' Galitzine noted. 'In addition they are inspired by the esprit de corps of their Regiment.' To his mind this was one of their greatest strengths and the source of their tireless motivation. Captain Galitzine wasn't about to let that be thwarted by either a jealous BAOR or the War Office's top brass.

As Barkworth and Galitzine discussed plans for their future covert operation, a new phrase tripped off the tongue to describe this fresh phase of operations.

Barkworth's team would become 'the Secret Hunters'.

Chapter Twenty-two

'Officially' the Secret Hunters took on the name of 'The SAS War Crimes Investigation Team' – the SAS WCIT. Whether the name referred to the fact that the war crimes had been perpetrated against an SAS unit, or that the investigators were SAS, remains unclear. Perhaps it was left deliberately ambiguous. Either way, their 'official' identity – 'SAS WCIT' – should further their attempt to hide in plain sight.

With the SAS's closure pending, Barkworth faced further antagonism from his chief detractors; within the BAOR's ranks he was making few friends.

'They regarded him as very unorthodox,' Galitzine reflected. 'Not prepared to give the proper respect due either to rank or system, so that wherever possible obstacles were put in his way. So you had tremendous cooperation with the French zone and the American zone, but in the British zone you had absolute antipathy. At one stage he was actually forbidden to operate in the British zone, which made life very difficult indeed.'

A large part of Barkworth's problems stemmed from his insistence on behaving as an SAS man would, while surrounded by the regular British military establishment in peacetime. Following his sojourn with the Villa Degler team, Galitzine had gone to visit one of the key people in charge of the British zone of occupation. That man, while aware of Barkworth's unique qualities, had largely washed his hands of him.

'Frankly, there are times when I just cannot help him, because he's his own worst enemy. He will in fact insult generals or brigadiers or he will do things which he knows you're not allowed to do in the army. He'll walk into a mess improperly dressed or he'll bring a sergeant-major into the officers' mess – that sort of thing.'

A sergeant – like Dusty Rhodes – was not permitted in a British Army officers' mess, because by definition it was reserved for officers only. Rarely had the SAS had a mess of any sort. More often than not they had made use of the local North African, Italian or French bars or brothels in the areas where they operated: locations in which they were fond of drinking, and where officers and men could rub shoulders with little distinction between ranks.

In Barkworth's book, men like Rhodes were absolutely his equal, regardless of their rank, and should be treated as such. Indeed, Sergeant Fred 'Dusty' Rhodes was about to prove his worth to the chief Nazi hunter one hundred times over.

The trail to *Hauptscharführer* Straub – Natzweiler's chief executioner – had been a long and convoluted one, even by Barkworth's standards. It had started in London, at the Eaton Square office of Prince Galitzine. Though he had been ordered to bury it, Galitzine's December 1944 Natzweiler report had very much done the rounds. One of the desks it had landed upon was that of Vera Atkins, one of the SOE's chief spymasters.

With Churchill's fall from power, the SOE was also scheduled for closure. But like Colonel Franks and Major Barkworth, Vera Atkins – who had worked within the SOE's French 'F' Section, recruiting and dispatching female agents to France – felt a burning sense of responsibility to 'her people', those that she had sent into harm's way.

Of the hundred or so F Section agents who were taken prisoner by the enemy, only twenty-six had returned. For an SOE agent parachuted into occupied France dressed in civilian clothing, capture had spelled almost certain torture and death.

'You owe people something, after all, who have fought for you and risked their life for you,' Atkins averred. She, like Barkworth, believed the missing had to be traced, and their killers hunted down.

That summer, Atkins had read in Galitzine's Natzweiler report of a British prisoner called Brian Stonehouse – the man who had made the pencil drawings of his fellow Natzweiler inmates. Atkins recognized Stonehouse as an SOE agent serving with her own F Section. More to the point, she knew that he had survived. Galitzine had also written of a group of British women allegedly executed at Natzweiler, who may have been fellow SOE agents.

Acting on a hunch, Atkins had shown the returned Stonehouse photos of four of her missing agents: Andrée Borrel, Diana Rowden, Sonya Olschanezky and Vera Leigh. As far as Stonehouse could remember, in the summer of 1944 it was those very women who had been brought to Natzweiler by their SS captors, whereupon they were taken to the crematorium to be killed.

Atkins felt the loss of the four acutely, especially as Andrée Borrel was the first ever female agent that the SOE had parachuted into occupied France. She paid a visit to Galitzine's Eaton Square office to follow up the case. It was there that Galitzine was able to reveal to her who the real expert on Natzweiler and its victims now was: Major Barkworth of the SAS.

Galitzine's opinion of the man was striking. 'This officer – known as "Bill" to his friends – was a man of enterprise and resource, who knew Germany well, talked the language like a native and was endowed with a complete disregard for higher authority. He started with the scantiest of evidence, persisted when others would have given up, and finally succeeded in such an uncanny way that British, French and Americans alike christened him "the Lawrence of Occupied Germany".'

Learning of Barkworth and his work, Atkins decided to travel out to Gaggenau to meet him. The two Nazi hunters hit it off immediately. From Barkworth, Atkins secured the leads that she needed – the survivors from Natzweiler who could testify to what had happened to her four missing agents.

The story that emerged was a particularly horrifying one. Injected with what they were told was a typhoid vaccine, the four women had in truth been given some kind of a knockout dose – most likely carbolic acid (Phenol), one of the Nazi's favourite killer drugs. The camp doctor who had administered the injections was an SS man called Werner Rohde. The women were fed one by one into the Natzweiler crematoria – the ovens in which the camp staff burned the bodies of the dead.

But Doctor Rohde must have got his doses wrong. One of the women had come back to consciousness, even as she was slid towards the flames, and she had managed to rake the face of her killer with her long fingernails. The man who had proceeded to thrust her into the furnace and burn her alive was Natzweiler's chief executioner, *Hauptscharführer* Peter Straub.

As luck would have it, Barkworth had recently been given details of what might be *Hauptscharführer* Straub's home address. After meeting Atkins, the Natzweiler executioner's arrest had become a high priority, for obvious reasons. There was no evidence that Straub would be 'at home', but Barkworth figured it was worth sending a team to the address that he had for him, just to be certain.

That team was led by his redoubtable right-hand man and long-time Villa Degler enforcer, Sergeant Dusty Rhodes. Travelling in the ageing, war-worn jeeps, Rhodes and company set out driving north-east, towards where the French zone of occupation ended. The home address that Barkworth had for Straub lay in the city of Mannheim, which was across the border in the American zone.

One of the major criticisms levelled at Barkworth by the BAOR and other detractors was that he and his men zoomed about in their jeeps willy-nilly, never bothering to secure the proper papers to pass through the various zones of occupation. They were right. Frankly, Barkworth couldn't be bothered. He did not have the time to do the paperwork. More to the point, he did not want to flag up to anyone outside of the Villa Degler where he was going, or why.

All systems were leaky. If word got out to the man he was hunting that a Barkworth team was on its way, his prey would fast disappear. It was best to arrive unannounced, and to circumvent or blag their way through any troublesome checkpoints. But the BAOR in particular hated it. They never knew where Barkworth was going to pop up next, which was why they had tried to ban him from operating in the British zone.

Likewise, Rhodes would be blagging his way through to Mannheim.

During the war, some 2,000 of the city's Jews had been dispatched to the extermination camps. But in time Mannheim's heavy industries had attracted the Allied bombers, and during several night raids the city centre had been flattened. It was through that kind of war-ravaged landscape that Rhodes found himself driving, dodging around piles of blasted rubble and bomb craters – not to mention several tiresome French and American checkpoints – as he sought out the Natzweiler executioner's home.

As Rhodes climbed the steps that led to what he hoped was Straub's door, he reminded himself how the Nazis had issued many of their people with false identity papers at war's end, with the intention that they should continue the fight after the Allies had seized Germany, forming an underground army called 'The Werewolves'. Straub might well have such false documents. There was also a booming black market in occupied Germany, so he could also have purchased himself a new identity.

It was around one o'clock in the morning when a heavily armed Rhodes rapped on the door. A young woman came and answered. She looked shocked at the SAS's team's surprise arrival. There was a figure seated behind her in the living room, smoking a cigar. He appeared decidedly less perturbed. That man denied that he was Peter Straub. But upon studying his features closely, Rhodes realized that he held a trump card.

Rhodes knew well the horrific story of how the four SOE agents had met their end. 'Straub . . . was putting the women into the cremator after they'd been injected and were supposed to be dead,' Rhodes recalled. 'One of the women, on being pushed into the furnace, regained consciousness and at that instant she clawed Straub down one side of his face. He still had the marks of that woman's fingernails as scars . . .'

False papers or not, Rhodes was certain that this was their man. Straub was arrested and taken back to the Villa Degler at gunpoint, where his interrogators – Barkworth and Vera Atkins – awaited. So significant was Straub's arrest that a third interrogator, Lieutenant Colonel Gerald Draper, a legal eagle with extensive war crimes experience, was also present.

At first Straub tried to deny everything. He claimed he had been away on leave when the four SOE agents had been killed. He blamed the entire thing on camp doctor and fellow SS officer Rohde, who had administered the injections. 'I never lifted a finger against a single prisoner and never saw any in uniform,' Straub tried to argue. But none of that could explain away the livid scars on his cheek.

Over time, his interrogators broke him down. Finally, Straub began to talk. Bit by bit he revealed the truth of what had happened, but he tried to excuse it all by professing that he was 'only following orders'. Once the story of the four female agents had been clarified – it had indeed happened in the horrifying way that Atkins had been told – they moved on to other executions at Natzweiler.

Straub spoke about the main means of killing: hanging. His interrogators went to great lengths to establish the height of the stool upon which the condemned were made to stand, before it was kicked away. Straub did not prove clever enough – or maybe he just didn't care – to realize the thrust of the questioning. By the end his interrogators had established that the stool was not high enough to achieve a 'proper' hanging.

Straub's victims had died of a slow strangulation, as opposed to a long drop that would break the neck, causing death pretty much instantaneously. Straub hadn't even proved a very efficient executioner. Or maybe this had all been deliberate. Perhaps the victims had been left to writhe and to struggle at the end of the noose as a gruesome warning.

As the interrogation drew to a close, Straub mentioned, almost boastfully, the number of 'pieces' that he had killed in a day. At that stage the former Natzweiler executioner was told the following: 'You leave this room on your hands and knees like an animal. You are not fit to stand and talk to human beings on your legs.'

The four female SOE agents had been executed on orders direct from Berlin. They had been classified as *Nacht und Nebel* – night and fog – prisoners, which was why they had been sent to Natzweiler. Being *Nacht und Nebel*, the Berlin orders stated that they were to be 'destroyed without trace'. Well, their physical remains had indeed been reduced to a heap of ashes. But, against all odds, the truth of their murder and who was responsible had been uncovered by the Nazi hunters.

All the more worrying, therefore, that Barkworth's unit was about to face the hangman's noose itself.

*   *   *

By the end of September 1945, the SAS had already started destroying sensitive files in preparation for its disbandment. At the same time, questions were being raised about the legitimacy of Barkworth's Villa Degler operations.

'The question has arisen as to the authorization and accreditation of various investigating officers or teams operating in France,' stated a 29 September letter from the War Office. 'We are anxious that no misunderstanding . . . should exist in regard to officers and their teams . . . Will you please say in the case of Major Barkworth and his team what was the originating authority for dispatch and to what headquarters or unit are they accredited.'

One wonders who was supposed to answer such a query, when the SAS itself was in the midst of being shut down.

On 4 October 1945 orders were issued for the formal disbandment of the SAS. The 'Urgent Memorandum' stated: 'It has been decided to disband the Special Air Services Regt . . . Disbandment will commence on 5 Oct 45 and will be completed by 16 Nov 45 . . . The attention . . . is directed to the instructions contained in pamphlet "Disbandment of units . . . 1945", copies of which are being forwarded . . . Complete disbandment will be reported to the War Office . . .'

On 5 October passing-out parades took place at the 1 and 2 SAS headquarters, as the men prepared either to return to their 'home' regiments, to volunteer for other airborne units or to leave the military altogether. On the face of it the SAS headquarters staff had been left to tie up any loose ends – paperwork, remaining stores and the like – before the final shutdown.

That left Barkworth's Villa Degler unit as the single largest group of SAS anywhere in the world that was still somehow 'operational'. Colonel Franks was determined to keep Barkworth's unit going, come hell or high water.

Just days after the 5 October formal disbandment, Franks put into place stage one of his 'SAS survival plan'. The Special Air Service Regimental Association was founded, holding its first meeting on 12 October at Colonel Franks' Wyvenhoe Park headquarters. Franks was appointed its chairman, with Lieutenant Colonel David Stirling, the original founder of the SAS, as president.

In the face of War Office apathy and fudge, Franks took further decisive action. Having founded the SAS Association, he recruited Winston Churchill as its patron. Churchill – one of the most prescient politicians of his time – was acutely aware of the Soviet threat to Europe. In 1946 he would popularize the phrase the 'Iron Curtain'. He understood how keeping alive a force like the SAS – one of the few units primed to cause havoc behind enemy lines – was vital to Britain's ability to combat such a threat.

Working closely with the former prime minister, plus his son, Randolph Churchill, Franks put in place the second part of his SAS survival plan – the formation of a 'shadow headquarters'. There was little doubt that Colonel Franks was the prime mover in preserving the SAS. The Regiment was on life support, but via Franks' efforts it was at least still breathing.

Even David Stirling would go on to remark: 'Had it not been for Brian Franks we would have been consigned to oblivion.'

During the war years, Stirling's determination to do what was right, no matter what 'the fossilized layers of shit' at high command determined, had been a defining feature of the SAS.

He'd orchestrated several 'private enterprise jobs' in defiance of high command, leading to the accusations of the SAS being a 'private army'.

Now Colonel Franks, with Stirling's help, was about to embark upon the single greatest 'private enterprise job' of all. Prior to the war, Franks had worked in senior management at the palatial Hyde Park Hotel in Kensington, west London. It was there that he now established the SAS's shadow headquarters, 'requisitioning' a couple of rooms as an HQ of operations. The bar of the hotel became the unofficial SAS briefing room, and the place where Colonel Franks would meet his Villa Degler commander, on Barkworth's rare visits to London.

On one thing Franks was absolutely adamant. In spite of their deniable status, Barkworth's team would continue to wear the trademark Regimental insignia that so defined the unit. They would continue to wear the distinctive SAS beret, and they would proudly sport the winged-dagger insignia bearing the timeless motto: 'Who Dares Wins.'

Determined to see the Op Loyton war criminals face justice, the Barkworth team fulfilled another vital function: it would serve to keep the SAS functioning in the shadows until the winds of fortune blew more favourably and the Regiment could be reformed, as Franks was determined it would be. Of course, certain individuals within the War Office bureaucracy were already primed to quietly assist such covert operations.

When the order was issued to disband the SAS, Colonel Franks went to speak to Prince Galitzine. 'I'm going to ask you a very big favour,' he told him. 'Is there any means by which you can keep this team going?' By 'this team' Franks meant the all-imporant Villa Degler operation. Galitzine told Franks that he'd see what he could do.

Without any formal permission or clearance, Galitzine managed to take advantage of the post-war confusion at the War Office, and massage budgets, rations, supplies and more out of the chaos. He even managed to ensure that wages would continue to be paid to Barkworth and his men.

'They weren't mercenaries,' Galitzine remarked. 'They were being paid by the War Office; we were paying them all right . . .'

Officially, Barkworth, Rhodes and all on the Villa Degler operation were listed as having returned to their parent regiments. This would serve as a cover in case of any difficult questions being raised by inquisitive Whitehall mandarins, politicians or the press. Barkworth's Villa Degler team had always been semi-official.

Now, they had slipped completely into the shadows.

Chapter Twenty-three

In October 1945, shortly after Barkworth's team had 'gone dark', Galitzine authored a paper entitled 'War Crimes "Man Hunting" Teams'. Its intention appears to have been to trumpet the successes of the Barkworth unit at the highest level, without revealing that they were still very much in operation.

In his paper Galitzine advocated the expansion of such efforts, based upon the SAS model. On the 'question of manhunting . . . they have proven particularly successful', he declared. He called for the formation of several 'Man Hunting teams', each of 100 or more operators. Those teams should contain a 'high percentage of officers trained in intelligence and signals work'. They should have 'great mobility' and 'good signals communications over very long distances', and such efforts should be considered as an 'Operation of War'.

In essence, what Galitzine was describing was the Villa Degler unit. His paper seems to have been an attempt to bring Barkworth's team in from the cold. Basically, he was saying: *we need these kinds of units – oh, and here's one I made earlier, so let's start here. And let's build on this model and expand it massively.*

Unsurprisingly, Galitzine's paper attracted attention. The BAOR in particular was furious. In a 'Confidential' 24 November letter, one A.G. Somerhough, of the BAOR's legal staff, wrote: 'It is difficult to criticize this paper as it is so obviously based on a complete misconception'. Of the work by the Villa Degler team, Somerhough commented: 'If this is Major Barkworth's unit, I understood its purpose was to discover the bodies of murdered SAS personnel, not to track down the criminals and that they had been there months and that up to a short time ago they had not arrested anybody.'

Somerhough was a powerful adversary. A highly experienced military legal officer, he had earned three Mentions in Dispatches during the war. His increasingly negative comments carried weight. Even so, the criticism implicit in Galitzine's paper – that not enough was being done by the existing bodies – seems to have hit home. At the end of November Prime Minister Clement Attlee authored a personal note addressed to the Secretary of State for War.

'I am concerned at the delays which have occurred in dealing with these matters . . . It is essential that . . . the persons on whom rests the responsibility for the investigation of War Crimes and bringing to trial of their authors should be officers with drive and energy, and that the high priority to be accorded to War Crimes should be fully understood.'

In the winter of 1945 there seems to have been division at the heart of the British government: on the one hand, the doves wanted to disband the military machine as swiftly as possible and to deliver to a weary British public a long-anticipated peace dividend. On the other, the hawks wanted a resolute and robust war crimes machinery to be put in place to ensure that justice was done.

As there was no concrete response to Galitzine's 'Man Hunting' paper, it seems that the doves won out. Or, rather, it may simply have been a triumph of sheer pragmatism. Britain immediately post-war was close to ruin. The cost of fighting had bled the country dry, the Treasury was facing bankruptcy and to many minds the priorities of rebuilding the shattered economy trumped those of hunting down war criminals, no matter how egregious their crimes.

Either way, Barkworth's manhunting unit was left out in the cold.

Simply because it was the best and most secretive location, Galitzine's Eaton Square office became the clandestine resupply and communications back-up for Barkworth's team. From there direct radio links would be maintained between London and Gaggenau. A 30 November memo entitled 'War Crimes Investigation, SAS' – penned almost two months *after* the Regiment's official disbandment – sets out the means of maintaining such communications.

'Two ORs [other ranks – men who weren't officers] are being accommodated for duty in Room 404 as W/T Signal Rear Link to the SAS . . . This will entail the working of a small W/T transmitting and receiving set from the roof of . . . Eaton Square. The transmitting set will be worked off batteries . . . and it is intended that the receiver be worked off the house circuit.'

The two men manning this radio 'rear link' were SAS operators Freddie Oakes and John Sumnall, veteran members of the Villa Degler manhunting unit.

At the very highest level, strings were being pulled to keep the Secret Hunters in business. 'Colonel Franks . . . was extremely well connected and knew an awful lot of people . . .',

Galitzine remarked. Franks used such connections to keep the Villa Degler unit in operation. Galitzine didn't feel inclined to ask him who exactly were these high-level supporters, 'because we felt the whole thing was so unofficial the less it was talked about the better'.

By the late autumn of 1945 the Villa Degler team was still in business, but it was clinging on by its fingertips. Barkworth had no formal authority to operate; no specific background or training in his task; no official budget; and the SAS Regiment had been formally disbanded, which meant his unit didn't in theory exist. He was answerable only to Galitzine's Eaton Square set-up, and to Colonel Franks' shadow HQ at the Hyde Park Hotel. In other words, he was answerable to no one.

A lesser man might have baulked at the hand that fate had dealt him, but as far as Barkworth was concerned it freed him up to do as he pleased. Released at last from the chains that had bound him – red tape and bureaucracy is hard to apply to an off-the-books unit that simply doesn't exist – Barkworth believed that anything was possible.

Barkworth was a truly remarkable man, according to Galitzine. He was 'a mystic . . . a thinker; absolutely dedicated to the job he had of looking for his missing people'. No measure was too extreme for Barkworth, if it might further the cause of the hunt.

By now, the case of the Natzweiler murders – the four SOE women burned to death in the ovens – had been well and truly solved. Having nailed Straub, Barkworth's team had proceeded to round up the chief architects of the evil. The camp medical orderly had been tracked down in hiding in southern France. The camp doctor – Werner Rohde – had been traced to the American zone of occupation, just as Straub had been.

But where Barkworth and his team had reached a seeming dead end was in tracing the eighteen remaining Op Loyton 'missing'. Galitzine received a radio call in his Eaton Square office, bemoaning how all their leads seemed to have come to naught. He packed his bags and headed out to Gaggenau, flying into Frankfurt, where Barkworth met him with a jeep and a firm handshake.

Together they drove to the Villa Degler. En route Barkworth made a passing remark, one that shocked the largely imper-turbable Galitzine. 'You know, we tried planchette last night – you know, the Ouija board.'

For a brief moment Galitzine became the pompous War Office official that he most certainly was not. 'You can't mean you did this! I mean, it's ridiculous—'

'Why not?' Barkworth cut in. If people were murdered during the war, surely they'd want to communicate what had happened to them, and by whatever means possible.

Galitzine lapsed into silence.

He couldn't argue with Barkworth's logic.

That evening, he joined Barkworth and four other members of his team at the round wooden table in the Villa Degler's drawing room. A candle burned dimly; there was little electric-ity yet in bombed-out Gaggenau. The room struck Galitzine as being no longer simply conspiratorial; there was some-thing . . . otherworldly lurking just out of vision amongst the shadows. He felt his heart thumping as Barkworth arranged the 'tools' of the Ouija board, and they readied themselves to commune with the dead.

Numbered playing cards were laid on the table, plus all the letters of the alphabet and the words 'yes' and 'no'. An upturned glass was placed in the middle. Suddenly, an English name came up. 'The glass spelled out 'F-o-r-d-h-a-m, Flight Sergeant RCAF,' remarked Galitzine. 'And then – "Killed at Cirey, in the Vosges."'

The glass revealed that the crew had been flying a Lancaster bomber.

The Ouija board continued to 'talk' to those assembled around the table long into the night. Everyone was exhausted, but they were in a high state of feverish excitement and couldn't tear themselves away.

The Ouija board revealed that three of the Lancaster crew had been killed on crash-landing, but two had survived. Apparently, Fordham and one other ariman had been marched out to a grove of lime trees, just outside of Cirey village, where they were made to dig their own graves, before being shot in the back of the head.

As dawn was almost upon them, the Villa Degler men asked a final question of the Ouija board: 'Do you know the names of any of the Germans involved?' The glass spelled out a name.

The gathering broke up. Some rushed to prepare the jeeps for the journey to Cirey, a village that lies some 15 kilometres to the north of Moussey. Others powered up the radio set and sent an urgent message to Eaton Square, asking if the RAF missing persons bureau could trace the Lancaster bomber that had supposedly gone down.

They asked for: 'Details of aircraft and crews all planes reported missing, either (a) over Vosges area, (b) en route to or from raids which would take them over Vosges area and which are not known to have crashed elsewhere. Consider Stuttgart raids the most fruitful. Period required 20 July until 31 Aug 44. Attach great importance to early production of these details so hope it will be possible.'

A second message was sent to CROWCASS – the Paris-based central registry of the wanted; formally the 'Central Registry of War Crimes and Security Suspects' – asking if they held a German prisoner of war bearing the name thrown up by the Ouija board. That done, Barkworth, Galitzine et al downed some Benzedrine and jumped in the jeeps, tearing off with the rising sun to their backs.

'We . . . roared off in a high state of fever to Cirey,' Galitzine recalled, which was set about eighty miles away, on the far side of the Rhine – in France. It was early on a winter's morning by the time the Secret Hunters reached the village, and the locals were just heading out to go and till their fields.

A pair of flying boots was recovered from one of the Cirey villager's houses. Three unmarked graves – those of the Lancaster crew that had died upon crash-landing – were discovered in the churchyard. Finally, they found some villagers who knew of the shootings. They were led into the woodland, which was thick with lime trees, and shown the location of the killings. Sure enough, when they dug they turned up two bodies.

Upon their return to Gaggenau, a radio message was waiting. CROWCASS had discovered that the French were holding a German prisoner of the name thrown up by the Ouija board.

He claimed to be a private in the *Wehrmacht*, but once Barkworth drove over to interrogate him, the man soon cracked. He had actually served in the Gestapo, and he became the chief suspect in the Cirey killings.

When Galitzine returned to London, he passed the scribbles that he'd made recording the question-and-answer session around the Ouija board to his elderly War Office secretary. She was used to taking down interrogation notes, and she began to type away. But all of a sudden this prim and proper lady reached the moment where the Ouija board spelled out, 'I was killed at Cirey in the Vosges'.

Galitzine's secretary let out a scream and rushed out of the room. Shortly thereafter Galitzine was called before three senior-ranking War Office officials to explain himself.

'How dare you do anything like this?' they demanded of Galitzine. He was accused of conduct unbecoming in an officer and a gentleman, in 'dealing with Ouija boards'.

Galitzine held his ground. He pointed out that despite the unorthodox means, they'd unearthed two bodies in the woods and arrested a German suspect.

The War Office mandarins glanced at each other. There were raised eyebrows. 'Well, if you *hadn't* got two bodies and a prisoner you'd be court martialled.'

The two men murdered at Cirey had nothing to do with the SAS. They had served with the Royal Canadian Air Force. Yet Barkworth had pursued their killers as avidly as if they had been two of the remaining Op Loyton missing.

Of *their* fate and whereabouts all leads seemed to have gone cold. In desperation, Barkworth turned again to checking through some of the key documents seized in the earliest days of his operations – the papers that he'd found in Isselhorst's Strasbourg headquarters, detailing the names and roles of his units and their men.

One name jumped out at him: Georg Zahringer. Zahringer had served on *Einsatzkommando* Ernst – the unit commanded by *Sturmbannführer* Hans Dietrich Ernst. Barkworth knew of the *Einsatzkommando*'s unsavoury reputation. Working on the presumption that a leopard never changes its spots – a death squad is a death squad, no matter where it is deployed – Barkworth figured Zahringer would be well worth talking to.

As it happened, a man with that name had just been arrested. When Barkworth went to interrogate him, he quickly realized that here was his long-awaited breakthrough. It was the winter of 1945, and Zahringer's testimony would prove to be a game-changer. What Zahringer described to Barkworth would enable one of the final pieces of the jigsaw puzzle to fall into place.

Lieutenant David Dill's murder had already been solved; he had been killed with the other Special Forces officers at the Erlich Forest massacre. But the fate of the rest of his rearguard party – those left to keep watch over the SAS's final Basse de Lieumont base – remained a mystery. Now Zahringer would solve that mystery, painting a terrible picture of the final hours of Dill's command.

After Dill and his men had been captured, their Panzer division captors had held them for forty-eight hours. But then they were delivered into the evil embrace of *Sturmbannführer* Hans Dietrich Ernst. At his Saales headquarters, situated some 6 miles to the south-east of Moussey, Ernst separated the SAS officer from his men. While Lieutenant Dill was Schirmek-bound, the eight other ranks were destined for a far more immediate and gruesome reckoning.

On 15 October – nine days after their capture – they were loaded aboard a truck, which Zahringer happened to be driving. He was ordered to head for La Grande Fosse, a farmstead that lay just to the west of Saales.

'We came to a spot where there was a thick fir wood on the left hand side,' Zahringer related to Barkworth. 'I noticed no one until I saw Opelt . . . standing by the turn-off of a track to the left . . . He waved to me to back my truck up this track, which I did . . .

'Opelt ordered me to open the back of the truck and the first prisoner was made to get down,' Zahringer continued. 'They were all hand-cuffed . . . Schossig, who spoke English, told him to take his clothes off. This the prisoner did. He was then taken, held by the arms by Wuttke and Gaede into the wood . . . Wuttke was carrying a . . . pistol, and Gaede also had a weapon with him. Practically immediately I heard a shot.

'The remaining English prisoners in the truck did not say anything, but remained silent,' Zahringer recalled. One of the two priests must have told the men to kneel, and he began to administer the last rites. The prisoners were heard praying in a language that Zahringer presumed had to be English. One by one they were led away, as further shots rang out through the trees.

It came to the last man. 'Just before he was taken away, he said something to Schossig, in English,' Zahringer told Barkworth. 'I asked Schossig what he said, and he told me that the Englishman had said: "We were good men." I followed this last prisoner and saw how he was made to stand near the edge of an open grave which contained the naked dead bodies of his comrades . . . He was not trembling.'

That last prisoner was shot, and pushed into the open grave. The discarded clothes were gathered up and burned.

After confessing to so much, Zahringer seemed to get cold feet, at least when it came to leading Barkworth and his men to the site of the mass grave. Perhaps he feared he would end up joining the corpses. He feigned forgetfulness. It had been a wet and foggy autumn day, Zahringer argued, and he couldn't remember exactly which turn-off he had taken into the forest. Barkworth and his men knew the rough location, but that was pretty much all.

Barkworth sent Dusty Rhodes to Saales, with the seemingly impossible task of scouring several square kilometres of woodland. It was the first week of November 1945, over a year after the killings had happened. No matter how large the clearing for the grave had been, the forest would have reclaimed it by now.

On a bitter November morning Rhodes and three others set out driving west from Saales. He had a rough idea of the kind of location he was looking for, based upon Zahringer's testimony.

'They were driven through the forest, down this lane to the side of a small embankment,' Rhodes recalled. 'A very shallow grave had been dug . . . One by one they were ordered out of the vehicle, moved to the top of this small embankment and shot through the back of the head.'

Rhodes needed to find a lane leading into the forest large enough to take a German Army truck, and with a small embankment lying to one side. But the terrain here was extremely challenging. The road climbed steeply as it neared La Grande Fosse, switch-backing around precipitous bends and snaking through the dark pinewood. The ground was cut with ancient First World War trench systems – the Vosges had also formed the front line of battle in that war – which made the task of finding the grave doubly challenging.

There was one apparent upside. The forest bisected by the road stretched for a quarter of a mile, no more. Though it was exceptionally dense, it was within this relatively small area that the bodies had to lie. Here and there, to either side, rutted forestry tracks sliced into the gloom. Zahringer had been certain of one thing during his interrogation: he'd taken a left-hand turn off the road.

Rhodes and his fellows looked closely as they drove along the road. At each track they stopped the jeep, but neither that day's search nor the next yielded any results. Fortunately Rhodes was as doggedly determined as his boss. 'It seemed to us to be an impossible task, but at the end of the day we weren't going to give in until we'd searched every square inch if it came to that.'

Rhodes set out for a further try. He was a horticulturist by training, and he'd worked as a municipal park gardener prior to the war. He knew his vegetation well. At one point he halted, realizing that a patch of undergrowth was noticeably younger than that surrounding it. He pulled out a shovel from the jeep and began to dig. He'd little more than scratched the surface when he unearthed a big toe.

'I knew then that we'd found the eight missing SAS personnel,' Rhodes remarked. 'The big toe which came out I put into a matchbox and took back to Gaggenau with me.' He presented it to Barkworth. '[I] gave it to him, with my compliments, because he was concerned we were not moving fast enough on that one.'

On 6 November 1945 Rhodes returned to the site, together with one of the American pathologists, plus a work party of German prisoners. They were made to dig up the bodies of their fellow countrymen's victims. The rapid burial of the corpses meant that they emerged remarkably well preserved. For those who had served with them, most would be recognized by sight alone.

They were Sergeants Hay and Neville, Lance Corporals Robinson and Austin, and Troopers Bennet, Weaver, Church and McGovern. Sergeant 'Jock' Hay was of course Captain Henry Druce's redoubtable troop sergeant, the man Druce had insisted on taking with him when given his eleventh-hour orders to take command of the Op Loyton advance party.

A bullet the same calibre as used in a German Luger pistol was found embedded in the head of Trooper Church, whose body was the first to have tumbled into the grave. Spent rifle shell cases were found scattered amongst the bodies, suggesting that more than one 'shooter' had been engaged in the killing.

Barely a month previously the BAOR's war crimes investigator, Lieutenant Colonel Genn, had stated that 'only a miracle' would provide the evidence to solve the outstanding cases of the missing Op Loyton eighteen. Well, Barkworth had had his (partial) miracle. Eight more had been found, and the eighteen had become ten.

A crucial aspect regarding these murders was picked up by Barkworth. Ernst had sent a radio message to his superior, Isselhorst, claiming that the eight 'parachutists' had been shot 'whilst trying to escape'. This was clearly not the case; they had been murdered in cold blood. It looked as if Ernst had acted upon his own initiative in deciding to shoot the men, for Isselhorst had wanted them brought to Schirmek, for 'processing'.

Following the discovery of the La Grande Fosse killings, *Standartenführer* Isselhorst remained at the top of Barkworth's wanted list. But a new name was vying with him for pole position: *Sturmbannführer* Hans Dietrich Ernst, the man who had disregarded orders from a superior officer so that he might have eight SAS murdered in the woods of the Vosges.

By now 1945 was almost at an end, and the more horrors Barkworth uncovered the more he hungered for justice. As the year blew through to 1946, he would find that his hunger would finally be sated.

Chapter Twenty-four

In spite of the stunning results that they had achieved, sending Barkworth's team 'dark' had its problems. They could hardly hide their activities from one of their greatest detractors – the BAOR. In the winter of 1945, the BAOR knew full well that Barkworth's unit was still in operation.

The BAOR's reaction was to try to draw the Villa Degler operators into their own clutches. If they couldn't discredit and shut down Barkworth and his team, they would trap and take control of them. A wireless message from the BAOR's legal unit summed up the kind of pressure that the Villa Degler mission was being subjected to.

'Message to Barkworth. Quote one. Your team for ADM is part of this unit. Your ADM controlled only by this unit, not, repeat not by . . . London. Two. Fwd all requests, complaints or ADM to this unit as instructed. Three. FWD immediate nominal roll and arrange exchange views this HQ. Unquote.'

'ADM' stood for administration. 'Nominal roll' meant all the names of those in Barkworth's Villa Degler operation.

The BAOR legal team was doing its damnedest to drag Barkworth's outfit out of the shadows. That would sound the death knell, burying the Villa Degler team under an avalanche of mindless bureaucracy and toady protocol. More importantly, it would sever Barkworth's direct command and control via London, which in turn would threaten to blow wide open the Secret Hunters' deniability.

By now – and in spite of the SAS Regiment being 'no more' – Barkworth had working under him three officers and twenty-one men. In the search for the wanted, he had his 'SAS' scouring the POW camps, where they had already discovered war crimes suspects hiding amongst the prisoners. But trawling through dozens of camps set hundreds of miles apart was a massive undertaking.

Galitzine summed up the enormity of the task: 'All vehicles of the unit average over 200 miles a day when they are on the road. Trips are being made the whole time throughout the French and American zones, from the Czech border to Saar, from Hanover to Lake Constance – and now trips to Holland . . . Schleswig-Holstein and the Ruhr . . . Next month visits are scheduled to S.W. France, Paris and Austria. These journeys have nearly all resulted in the capture of at least one accused – the total now being "under arrest" is 51.'

At the same time, Barkworth was overseeing a separate investigation to the far south, in Italy. Captain Henry Parker – the aficionado of the Barkworth whisky, Benzedrine and no sleep system – had been sent to investigate the disappearance of several Special Forces operators captured during a sabotage mission behind enemy lines. Barkworth's tentacles were also reaching as far north as Norway, where he was seeking the arrest of the entire personnel of *Einsatzkommando* Tanzmann, a unit that appeared to have played a key role in Operation Waldfest.

Allowing all of that to fall into the labyrinth of BAOR officialdom would render such operations next to impossible. There is little evidence that Barkworth responded to any of the BAOR communiqués seeking to reel him in, or at least not in writing.

Instead, on 6 December 1945 a missive went out from the Eaton Square AG3-VW office, stating that 'Major Barkworth will be winding up the investigation during December [1945].' The suggestion – which appears to have been little more than a smokescreen – was that the Villa Degler outfit was being disbanded. In truth, it was being strengthened.

On 8 December, on orders from Eaton Square, an SAS Trooper Ratcliffe – a soldier from a non-existent unit – was dispatched from the London port of Tilbury on a ferry bound for Antwerp, to rendezvous there with Barkworth. He was driving a truck laden with the following supplies destined for the Villa Degler operation:

2 Charging engines for W/T sets.
1 Amplifier.
9 Tannoy speakers for amplifier.
1 Jeep type outer cover.
1 Motor Gasket Kit (Ford).
34 – gall. Jerricans (petrol)

. . . And so the list continued.

The truck driven by Trooper Ratcliffe also carried: '1 Tin Box containing Secret Documents, Stationary . . . Several rolls of maps', for the attention of Major Barkworth.

On the one hand, AG3-VW was sending out radio messages and telegrams suggesting that the Villa Degler operation was being shut down: 'Confirmed we agree disbandment Major Barkworth's team . . .' 'Confirm that agree to withdrawal to UK for disbandment personnel, transport and equipment of MAJOR BARKWORTH'S Team.'

Yet at the same time, Galitzine was writing to all and sundry – those whom he counted as close and influential friends – seeking to bolster Barkworth's cloak-and-dagger operation. 'They are a little isolated band and any further help you can give them will be most appreciated.'

In the closing days of 1945 there was a sense of driving urgency about the Villa Degler set-up, one underpinned by an extraordinary Benzedrine-fuelled energy. While Galitzine, Franks et al were struggling to buy enough time for the completion of their under-the-radar manhunting operations, Barkworth was about to unleash his single greatest broadside.

The 'SAS' major was burning the midnight oil as never before, preparing a mammoth, ninety-page report that would demonstrate to Colonel Franks that his mission was very much accomplished. In May 1945 Franks had charged Barkworth with solving the cases of the Op Loyton missing. Barkworth's end of year 'Missing Parachutists' report was to be the proof that this – and so much more – had been achieved.

That report would be printed on 2nd Special Air Service 'official' paper, with the winged-dagger SAS badge emblazoned across the front – some three months after the Regiment had been disbanded. It would be addressed to 'The Commanding

Officer, Special Air Service Regiment' – a position that officially did not exist any more. And Barkworth would include a telling quote from Shakespeare on its opening page.

> But in these cases
> We still have judgment here; that we but teach
> Bloody instructions, which being taught return
> To plague the inventor.
>
> *Macbeth*, Act 1 Scene VII.

In other words, the SAS would sit in judgment over the Op Loyton killers; and those who had indulged in torture and mass murder would reap what they had sown.

In a sense, Barkworth's report was the ultimate cry of defiance. It screamed out two seminal points. One: you cannot so easily kill off the SAS Regiment. Two: no matter what, justice will be done. It laid out the arguments for fourteen separate war crimes cases to be brought to trial, covering some *thirty-nine* victims – the extras being the downed American and Canadian airmen and other Allied servicemen and women killed alongside the SAS.

Three months previously, the BAOR legal team had declared that 'only a miracle' would solve the cases of the Op Loyton missing. *Now this.* Barkworth's report would prove an extraordinary testament to the sheer tenacity and brilliance of the Villa Degler team, who had achieved the seemingly unachievable within a timescale that few would have imagined possible.

Radio traffic from Barkworth to Franks reflected the frenetic pace of activity, as the two men raced towards a finish line of sorts. Or rather, as matters turned out, it would be a race towards a new beginning.

'One. Printed report complete Saturday night. Two. A few witnesses remain from whom sworn statements will be taken. Three. Request Oxford at Frankfurt or Strasbourg to fly me back Sunday 18th onwards. Shall bring copies printed report with me . . . Six. If Black's stick found and time short will not dig up.'

The 'Oxford' reference was to a light aircraft – an Airspeed AS.10 Oxford training aeroplane – one that Barkworth needed to fly him back to London with his 'Missing Parachutists' reports in hand. 'Black's stick' referred to a further group of eight SAS men who had been murdered on the orders of SS *Sturmbannführer* Hans Dietrich Ernst. Time was clearly so tight that Barkworth feared he couldn't afford to 'dig up' the 'Black stick' bodies, even if they were found.

A further radio message reported a slight slippage in the proposed time schedule: 'Work continuing top pressure. Hope be ready by Sunday if printing continues night shift. Monday would make things easier.'

The fate of Black's stick had been revealed by one of the *Einzatskommando* Tanzmann suspects. Shortly before the Vosges fell to US forces, the men of *Einzatskommando Tanzmann* had been posted to Norway in an effort to bolster the Reich's defences in the north. In due course much of the unit had been arrested, posing under false names as the crew of a surrendered U-boat.

As Barkworth made clear, he wanted to get his hands on as many of the *Einzatskommando* Tanzmann men as possible.

'Those who are not wanted for War Crimes against British should be detained as wanted by French, as Kdo. Tanzmann was responsible for atrocities.' Amongst their ranks would be many of the Moussey villagers' oppressors.

When *Einzatskommando* Tanzmann veteran Walter Janzen had been handed over to Barkworth, his interrogation solved the case of eight of the remaining ten Op Loyton 'missing'. On 14 September 1944 eight SAS had been captured in the firefight at the sawmill in the Celles Valley. Three were those who'd become separated from Lieutenant Karl Marx's party, as they were chased across the hills by German search dogs. The other five were a sabotage party commanded by Lieutenant James Black.

Janzen had been one of those in the *Einzatskommando* Tanzmann force sent out to seize Black and his men. The SAS unit had run out of ammo and been captured, whereupon all eight had been handed over to a local *Wehrmacht* unit. But when Janzen returned to his headquarters, *Sturmbannführer* Hans Dietrich Ernst – their overall commander – had taken the news very badly indeed.

'Ernst was in a great fury, and cursed us all,' Janzen told Barkworth. 'Orders had already been issued by Ernst to have the eight prisoners fetched back to our unit . . . Ernst told both me and Albrecht that a secret Reich order existed that parachutists should be shot. He further told us that we both ought to know this.'

Janzen went on to relate how the eight men were driven into the woods outside of St. Dié, stripped naked and shot in the head – in scenes remarkably reminiscent of those in which the previous eight SAS men had been murdered. Janzen denied any role in the killings, but described how he had approached the mass grave at the end, 'to shovel the earth in'. The SAS men's dog tags had been taken from them and buried separately, to hide their identities as much as possible.

As far as Barkworth was concerned, Janzen's testimony was the silver bullet that he'd been searching for. On two occasions now *Sturmbannführer* Ernst had been proved to have disregarded his superior officer's orders, so that he could have his captives stripped naked and shot dead in the forest. In short, *Sturmbannführer* Ernst was responsible for the cold-blooded murder of sixteen of the Op Loyton party, and against all orders.

While Isselhorst may have orchestrated the evil, Barkworth felt certain he would claim that he was only acting on the Führer's instructions – as decreed in his Commando Order. By contrast, *Sturmbannführer* Ernst had disobeyed the orders of a superior so as to pursue some kind of personally motivated vendetta or bloodlust.

On New Year's Eve 1945 Galitzine issued a new wanted list at Barkworth's behest. Top of the table sat 'La Grande Fosse Case – Murder of 8 British PW; Dr Hans Dietr [sic] ERNST. Sturmbannführer i/c SD Kommando . . . took part in Operation Waldfest against 2 SAS in Autumn 44.'

'Description: Dark brown hair, brown eyes, parts hair right side. Strident scar on face. Pale and seared complexion. Wears glasses for reading . . . Exact double of investigator Major E.A. Barkworth . . . Accused of murder La Grande FOSSE and also of 8 British PW at St. DIE in September, 1944.'

Perhaps unsurprisingly, Barkworth demurred when it was suggested that *Sturmbannführer* Ernst was his spitting image, though he clearly kept his dry sense of humour amidst all of the horror. In a 12 January sitrep sent to Eaton Square, Barkworth would comment: 'I enclose photographs of Ganninger, Hardtjenstein's adjutant; Richard Schnurr, involved in the Noailles and Pexonne cases; Dr. Ernst, who I do not think looks like me at all . . .'

Barkworth had by now solved all but two of the cases of the Op Loyton 'missing', and he had a good sense of what had happened to the remaining two. It was time to concentrate fully on the hunt for the killers. But it was just as he chose to do so that the challenges of operating as a 'black' outfit really began to weigh upon the Villa Degler team.

By now Barkworth had worked out his best means to track down those war crimes suspects that he hadn't yet managed to ensnare. Under the heading 'The Tracing of Germans', Barkworth wrote to Galitzine: 'I have got this mapped out in order to try to trace the maximum number of Germans with the least vehicle mileage; and given luck I hope to produce some satisfactory results.'

He went on to outline his main problems. 'Two things have however held us up. The first has been the stoppage of issue of petrol . . . The second is the poor condition of the 4 jeeps . . . I do not think any of them can go on much longer, as they had very high mileage, and two are at the stage of writing-off. I am sure you will appreciate it is no good sending out a party on a long run in bad weather with a vehicle which will probably need a search party to bring it in.'

Beneath the humour, Barkworth's sense of frustration is clear. Now operating completely off the books, he had unlimited freedom. But at the same time he had neither the vehicles nor the fuel to enable his Villa Degler team to fulfil its potential. In truth, as the New Year dawned, Barkworth's operations were somewhat circumscribed.

And, predictably, the problems emanating from the BAOR had far from gone away. 'There are one or two things however which I shall not take lying down, as I am sure you can imagine,' Barkworth's letter to Galitzine continued. 'Assimilation into an existing BAOR unit or any such measure.'

Moreover, owing to the relentless pace of operations and the pressure, Barkworth's health was suffering. For several days he'd been laid up, hospitalized.

'This has been extremely unfortunate and incidentally rather painful,' Barkworth wrote. 'I had a tooth pulled out by a German dentist who must I think have been a werewolf, because I have got my face swelled up; a condition which the Americans call cellulitis.'

But still, Barkworth would prove unstoppable. On 2 January 1946 he was back in action, in spite of his illness.

'Karl HAUG of Gruppe Kieffer in 4 Civil Internee Camp RECKLINGHAUSEN,' he radioed to Galitzine. 'Has given statement on shooting SAS . . . in which he took part. Following also present HSTUF SCHNURR (of PEXONNE case) . . . and driver of truck. HAUG knowledgeable and willing witness . . .'

'Hstuf and KRIM KOMM ALBRECHT ARTHUR now listed in civil prison ROTTERDAM. Consider this is the man from KDO. ERNST. Have arranged to interrogate . . . Will send you following. HAUGS statement. Photos of ERNST . . . Pathologist reports LODGE and DAVIS . . .'

Barkworth sensed now that the quest for *Sturmbannführer* Ernst would take him east. He had secured evidence suggesting that the killer of eighteen of the Op Loyton men had fled into the Russian Zone. He sought Galitzine's help smoothing a way into Stalin's area of occupation, which was never an easy thing to manage.

Galitzine wrote to one of his Berlin-based contacts – Berlin then being divided between the Allies and the Russians, but situated a good way into the Russian Zone.

'Bill Barkworth has suggested I drop you a line . . . He is looking into the fate of 33 SAS personnel murdered in the Vosges during the Autumn of 1944. He has been extraordinarily successful and up to now has got 33 Huns in the bag. His present request is for you to try to get hold of a German believed to be living in the Russian zone . . .'

Galitzine's sense of the numbers seems to have been a little fluid. From missive to missive the numbers of 'Huns' 'bagged' appears to vary. But his lobbying efforts proved tireless and highly effective. They would need to be. An inordinate number of the 'wanted' were thought to be in US Army custody, but getting the Americans to hand them over had proved challenging. Barkworth got Galitzine to use his influence to try to prise apart the doors that needed opening.

In a 5 January 1946 letter addressed to the US Army's War Crimes Section, Galitzine wrote: 'An important British War Crimes Investigation has been proceeding . . . concerning the murder of over 50 British airmen and parachutists . . . There appear to be 136 Germans involved . . .'

The number of murdered men kept rising as Barkworth uncovered more cases. 'It is understood that requests have already been made at various times for the handing over of the Germans in your custody,' Galitzine continued. 'The officers concerned are ready to make immediate arrangements for the taking of these prisoners of war.'

Galitzine attached an outline of the wanted thought to be held by the Americans. It listed twelve names, including Wilhelm Schneider, Isselhorst's right-hand man on Operation Waldfest, plus *Standartenführer* Isselhorst himself. Galitzine had asked for the 'dirty dozen' to be handed over.

The question remained: would the request be granted?

Chapter Twenty-five

One of those amongst the 'dirty dozen' held by the Americans was the very first suspect added to Barkworth's list – Max Kessler. As early as August 1945, letters had been written to the US Army seeking the whereabouts of *Oberscharführer* Kessler.

By January 1946, the suspicion was that Kessler – plus one other wanted man – had been released by the Americans. 'Colonel Haley tells me that he has independent confirmation of the fact that these men cannot be found,' recorded a 22 January note. 'It may be that these PW have been discharged since we made our application.' Either way, 'they cannot be traced'.

They say that the first cut is the deepest. Barkworth, Sykes and Rhodes had never forgotten their first encounter with the horrific evidence of the murders of their SAS comrades. When they had unearthed the three burned bodies at Le Harcholet barn, and learned of *Oberscharführer* Kessler's role, they had their initial inklings of the fate that might have befallen the rest of the Op Loyton missing.

Kessler was hardly the worst of those on the wanted list, but he was the first. Barkworth and his Villa Degler team were determined to get him. When a possible address for some of *Oberscharführer* Kessler's relatives was uncovered, Rhodes set out immediately in one of the battered and barely roadworthy jeeps to investigate.

It was a freezing January and black as pitch when Rhodes rapped on the door, and well past the midnight hour. It took a good while for that door to be opened. Maybe everyone had been in bed asleep, and it had taken time to rouse the household. Or maybe someone was being hidden. Rhodes had learned never to assume anything.

He headed for the kitchen – the heart of any household. A man and a woman were there, with two children 'asleep in their beds'. Rhodes could tell right away that the man seated at the kitchen table wasn't Kessler. He had a photo in his pocket and he had pretty much committed Kessler's features to memory. Rhodes noted food on the table, and he was told that the family had been having a late supper.

'We believe that a Max Kessler is staying with you,' Rhodes announced.

There were blank looks. 'No, he's not with us. We haven't seen Max Kessler for a long time now.'

Rhodes and his team carried out a thorough search of the house. It brought them back to the kitchen once more. Two things struck Rhodes. Firstly, the children had been in bed all right, but in his opinion they had only been feigning sleep. He suspected that someone had woken them up just now and warned them to keep quiet . . . about something.

Secondly, there were three plates of half-eaten soup on the kitchen table.

Two people having supper: three plates of soup.

Max Kessler was in the building somewhere.

Rhodes began to search again, this time a little more thoroughly. In the living room he discovered what he was looking for. Set into the wall in one corner was a small, hidden doorway. It was no more than a metre square and it fitted flush with the wall.

Rhodes levered open the door. By the dim light filtering through from the living room he could see that a set of wooden steps led into a dark void below. He grabbed a flashlight, drew his pistol and prepared to descend. He figured that as soon as he switched on the torch, 'I'd probably get my head blown off', but equally he knew in his bones that Kessler was down there.

He started on the steps. All was brittle quiet. The wooden stepladder led into a cellar. Rhodes flashed his torch around, probing the cobwebbed shadows. There wasn't a great deal of junk. An old box here. A pile of rubbish there. Some rags and sacks lying in one corner. Nothing that was big enough to hide a fully grown male.

Rhodes' flashlight came to rest upon a large silhouette. It was long and low and looked like an old linen basket. As he approached it, he let his foot brush against one side. Sure enough, it didn't budge an inch. For a linen basket it was unnaturally heavy. Rhodes stepped back, raised one leg and booted the thing as hard as he could, slamming it onto its side.

Out tumbled a figure. *Oberscharführer* Max Kessler.

The man who had declared of the SAS captives; 'They are shot as spies and saboteurs . . . They no longer exist', had been captured hiding like a frightened dog in a damp linen basket. The Secret Hunters had tracked down their first ever war crimes suspect. And those at the very top of their wanted list were about to be cornered too.

While *Sturmbannführer* Ernst had the most blood on his hands, *Standartenführer* Dr Erich Isselhorst remained the chief architect of both Operation Waldfest and the wider Vosges horrors. At some stage during the spring of 1946 – the exact date remains unclear – Isselhorst was taken into British (Barkworth's) custody. The means of Isselhorst's capture appears to have been unprecedented, and convoluted and labyrinthine in the extreme.

In early October 1945 a query had gone out from the Eaton Square office, seeking what was apparently a strange piece of clarification. 'The Americans have been asked to say whether they have in custody Dr. Isselhorst of the Gestapo.' As the US 7th Army had held Isselhorst since June of that year, and bearing in mind what a high-profile suspect he was, it seems odd that for five months no one had heard anything of him.

From Galitzine's 5 January 1946 letter, the Secret Hunters clearly suspected the Americans of holding Isselhorst. He was named as one of the 'dirty dozen' for whom the Villa Degler team was 'ready to make immediate arrangements for the taking of these prisoners of war'. There were various responses suggesting that the US War Crimes Branch were preparing to hand him over: 'Not yet cleared; being moved to Camp No. 78, pending clearance.'

But while the US authorities clearly had Isselhorst, there is no evidence that he was actually given up.

* * *

In 2007 the CIA was forced, under the US War Crimes Disclosure Act, to release a mass of files held on former Nazis. Some 50,000 pages of records were declassified, most pertaining to the post-war operational relationship between the CIA and former Nazis. The files include several reports held on *Standartenführer* Dr Erich Isselhorst.

Those CIA records include top secret and confidential memos, telegrams, personality profiles, interrogation reports and more. From them, a scenario can be reconstructed of what happened to the architect of Waldfest immediately after the war, and how Barkworth's Secret Hunters came to get their hands on him.

Isselhorst's US Army interrogation files from late 1945 and early 1946 suggest that he was proving ever more amenable to the US authorities. A confidential memorandum from the 307th Counter Intelligence Corps runs to six closely typed pages concerning Barkworth's most wanted man.

Under the section entitled 'AGENT'S COMMENTS' it recorded: 'Subject is an outspoken and convinced National Socialist [Nazi].' The Agent noted that Isselhorst had been a protégé of SS General Reinhard Heydrich, chief of the Gestapo, one of the key architects of the Holocaust and the overall commander of the *Einsatzgruppen*. Under Heydrich, Isselhorst's 'self-confidence' and 'ambition and ability' had led to rapid advancement and promotion. Striking a markedly positive note, the CIC agent described Isselhorst as having a 'driving and dynamic nature' and being 'too intelligent to be brutal, and he often even warned against unjustified severity'.

Of his experiences on the Eastern Front, Isselhorst complained that the Nazi regime had succeeded largely in turning potential allies into enemies. 'The claimed original enthusiasm [for the Nazi regime] of the Estonian, Latvian, Lithuanian and Ukrainian population was turned into hatred . . . Military Government vainly attempted to lead the destinies of a population whose habits and customs were unknown to the German officer . . . More considerate German officials were considered slackers.'

In another confidential memo on Isselhorst, his Russian experiences were again to the fore: 'Nov 1942–Aug 1943: was attached to the staff of the B.d.S. Riga . . . taking charge of a special commando to counteract the very active Russian Maquis. Here subject earned two decorations, the Tapferkeit's Medaille and the Eisernes Kreuz.' The former appears to be an archaic medal awarded for bravery; the latter was the honour closest to Hitler's heart: the Iron Cross.

Isselhorst's command of 'the fight against the Russian partisans' was clearly of some considerable interest to the 307th Counter Intelligence Corps. But who were the Counter Intelligence Corps, or CIC? By the end of the war the CIC had become the leading intelligence-gathering organization in the American zones of occupation, with over 5,000 people in the field. CIC operators wore either plain clothes or uniform devoid of badges or rank, and identified themselves only as 'Special Agents'.

Facing a new enemy in the coming Cold War, the CIC set up 'ratlines' to spirit informants and defectors out of the Russian zones. Given new identities and employed by the CIC as agents, these included a number of Nazi war criminals. One, former SS officer Klaus Barbie – the infamous mass murderer known as the 'Butcher of Lyons' – worked for the CIC from 1947 through to 1951. In 1988, the US Department of Justice investigated the CIC's murky past, concluding that many suspected Nazi war criminals had been employed as informants.

By the late summer of 1945 the CIC had got their hands on former SS commander and Gestapo chief *Standartenführer* Isselhorst. However, they weren't destined to keep him. Somehow, by late April 1946, the CIC had lost their man. A 26 April confidential note from the CIC amounts to an arrest warrant for Isselhorst. It reads: 'Name (with aliases): ISSELHORST, ERICH DR. REQUEST APPREHENSION OF SUBJECT. REQUEST NOTIFICATION OF SUBJECT'S APPREHENSION.'

By 21 May 1946 the CIC's hunt for Isselhorst appeared to be in full swing. A secret memo from CIC Headquarters states: 'The wife of SUBJECT, who still resides in WALCHEN-SEE . . . stated that on 23 August 1945 she received a visit from an American soldier, named REID, who told her he brought regards from her husband who was, according to REID, in NUREMBERG . . . It is suggested that a complete check of internment camp records may reveal his whereabouts.'

However, in February 1947 the CIC were writing to the British Army's Intelligence Division, seeking Isselhorst's return from British custody. 'Subject SS Standartenführer Erich ISSELHORST . . . is at present held by British War Crimes . . . Subject is urgently required in this Zone as a witness in a non-war crimes trial . . . It would be very much appreciated if subject could be loaned to this Headquarters . . . as soon as he is available.'

So, had Isselhorst been recruited by the CIC in the summer of 1945? And if he had, what had happened to him which led to his sudden spring 1946 disappearance, and subsequent reappearance in British custody?

Others of Isselhorst's Waldfest cronies had been recruited by Allied Intelligence, some even before the end of the war. A confidential report by the Counter Intelligence Corps reveals that Alfonso Uhring – Isselhorst's former foreign intelligence chief, and the brains behind Waldfest – gave himself up to the Americans following their October 1944 seizure of Strasbourg.

Shortly after, Uhring was given 'a mission for the Allied Intelligence Services'. Trained in radio transmissions, Uhring was 'turned' and dispatched, via Switzerland, to Germany. There, he was to work as a double agent during the closing stages of the war, sending intelligence reports on the workings of the Gestapo. Supposedly, Gestapo files captured at Strasbourg had revealed Uhring's role in war crimes, and it was that which had helped 'induce Uhring to accept the Allied mission'.

By the late summer of 1945 had Isselhorst also been turned? Even as Barkworth sought him out, was he secretly working for the CIC? Almost from the very moment he was taken into US custody, Isselhorst had offered his services to the Americans. Repeatedly he had tried to prove his value to those who held him, and they had certainly used him to help track down fellow Gestapo and SS colleagues.

And, for whatever reason, no one seemed inclined to hand Barkworth the man at the top of his wanted list.

It is within this context that Barkworth's most experienced Nazi hunter – Dusty Rhodes – was dispatched on what has to be one of the strangest and most mystery-shrouded missions of the Secret Hunters' entire operation. Speaking several decades after the war (his interview transcripts are held at the Imperial War Museum) Rhodes was only willing to talk about this snatch operation in very veiled terms.

The man Rhodes was after is never named, nor is the exact date of the capture specified. But what is clear is that his target was working for the Americans, and considered one of their 'key personnel'.

Setting out from Villa Degler, Rhodes drove east into the American zone. As was his wont, he headed first for the mystery individual's home address. 'I went to interview him,' Rhodes recalled. 'Went to his home. The lady of the house . . . said he'd be home in five minutes, for he now worked for the American forces in their legal department. So I went outside and sat in the jeep.'

Rhodes waited. He had a photograph of their suspect and he was a patient man. He noticed a figure walking along the street who was apparently unconcerned to see an American-looking jeep parked outside his home. Why would he be concerned? After all, he had wangled himself a nice number working with US forces. Rhodes arrested the man on the spot, bundled him into the jeep and drove him hell-for-leather into the comparative safety of the French zone, and into captivity.

The scale of the upset suffered by the Americans at the shock disappearance of their man can be gauged by their – and Rhodes' – subsequent reactions. Rhodes was forced to disappear for a month. 'The American forces were looking all over for this Warrant Officer Rhodes who had arrested one of their personnel,' Rhodes recalled. 'I was quickly put out of the way for a . . . period of time.'

Was the man Rhodes had seized *Standartenführer* Dr Erich Isselhorst? Isselhorst was by training a lawyer. 'Working for the American forces in their legal department' was a perfect cover, if the CIC had indeed recruited him. The reaction – that one of the Secret Hunters was in turn hunted by the Americans – is unprecedented. No other Villa Degler arrest provoked anything like such a response.

If Isselhorst had been recruited by the CIC, no doubt this was viewed as being 'justified' by the realpolitik of the moment. In the later summer of 1945, the Western powers were just starting to come to grips with a new world order and a new enemy. But it remains deeply reprehensible; Isselhorst had the blood of many thousands on his hands.

He was responsible for the extermination of countless Jews, Russian partisans and other 'enemies' of the Reich on the Eastern Front. He was culpable of the murder of dozens of British and Allied Special Forces soldiers thereafter. He was indictable for war crimes against thousands of French men and women in the Vosges.

But worst of all, as far as concerns the actions of the CIC – then America's foremost intelligence apparatus in the occupied zones – is that Isselhorst was guilty of overseeing the murder of a number of captured US citizens, airmen Curtis E. Hodges and Michael Pipcock amongst them, who were shot in the Erlich Forest.

Not a year before the CIC appeared to have recruited Isselhorst, he had been responsible for hunting down and murdering other American citizens. No matter how 'useful' SS *Standartenführer* Isselhorst might have appeared in the summer of 1945, recruiting him to the cause of the West was not acceptable. Shielding him from justice was even less so.

Predictably, during his interrogation Isselhorst proved to be as slippery as an eel, but in SAS Major Bill Barkworth the SS and Gestapo chief had met his match. Eventually Barkworth managed to corner Isselhorst regarding a group of eight 'British parachutists' that had been brought to his Strasbourg headquarters.

Barkworth: 'Did you give Schneider [Isselhorst's deputy] any particular instructions regarding these men?'

Isselhorst: 'I told him to ascertain if they had been working with terrorists.'

Barkworth: 'What result did he eventually report to you?'

Isselhorst: 'He told me . . . that those soldiers had been dropped by parachute to work with the Maquis, whom they were to train and lead. He therefore decided they were to be treated as terrorists. He put this point to me so strongly . . . and supported it with extracts from the interrogation reports, that I felt unable to disagree with him and decided that these soldiers were in effect in that class referred to by the order which I had received from Berlin.'

Isselhorst was referring to Hitler's Commando Order, of course.

Barkworth: 'Did you give Schneider any specific instruction regarding their disposal?'

Isselhorst: 'I told Schneider that as these soldiers were considered as terrorists they must be treated in accordance with the orders received.'

Barkworth: 'These orders of which you speak – are these relating to the execution of such soldiers?'

Isselhorst: 'Yes.'

Barkworth: 'Did Schneider report to you on the carrying out of this order?'

Isselhorst: 'He told me that it had been carried out. I assume that the method was shooting, but the place I do not know.'

Isselhorst was like a fat fish wriggling on a hook, and unable to break free.

In subsequent exchanges, Barkworth would challenge *Standartenführer* Isselhorst over several other cases of mass killings. It was clear already the kind of defence that Isselhorst – a lawyer by training – would try and construct: *I was only obeying orders*. Yet as Barkworth well knew, that defence was unlikely to stand up in the British war crimes hearings to come.

With Isselhorst in Barkworth's custody and ready to stand trial, the arch manhunter hungered to capture the Gestapo chief's enforcers – the brute killers he had commanded.

Two names were uppermost in his thoughts: *Sturmbannführer* Hans Dietrich Ernst and *Oberwachtmeister* Heinrich 'Stuka' Neuschwanger.

Chapter Twenty-six

Barkworth launched the hunt for Neuschwanger in earnest, and in his own inimitable way. He described the early stages of the chase in a letter to Galitzine.

'On Friday 4th January [1946] Neuschwanger visited his cousin, Ottmar Neuschwanger, in Göppingen. He was wearing a German railway employee's cap and coat; under that a grey coat and Wehrmacht trousers dyed blue . . . This I heard from an inquisitive neighbour of Frau Neuschwanger in Reutlingen . . . I drove to Goppingen and contacted the . . . local police.

'One of the local police said that at about half past four he had seen a man in railway employee's clothing, with a woman. He described both the man and woman so accurately that there is no doubt that these were Neuschwanger and his girlfriend, Margarete Schneider. The house . . . was watched unobtrusively (we had already been careful before entering the town to take off red berets and to hide shoulder flashes) . . .

'I wish you could have seen me,' Barkworth wrote to Galitzine, 'wandering around Goppingen in civilian clothes, with a pair of trousers belonging to the local chief of police, and which were big enough to hold me twice over . . . after dark cousin Ottmar and Neuschwanger's wife were arrested . . . and removed through the back entrance.'

Neuschwanger's cousin and his wife admitted that they were expecting the former *Oberwachtmeister* at any moment. But Stuka Neuschwanger didn't show. Something must have alerted him to the fact that the British had the entire place staked out. Either way, they had missed him by a whisker. Neuschwanger's cousin admitted that the former *Oberwachtmeister* had been 'hiding' in the British zone of occupation, and that he had travelled south to Göppingen to get some fresh civilian clothing.

Neuschwanger and his wife were estranged, and Barkworth figured that the *Oberwachtmeister* had also come here to fetch his girlfriend. 'He is travelling under a false name and has the travel pass given to employees of the German railway,' Barkworth informed Galitzine. 'My own impression is that he came from the British zone in Berlin. I am still hopeful that within a short time we may get some good news concerning him.'

Barkworth concluded: 'Cousin Ottmar knows the false name under which Neuschwanger is travelling, but covers his unwillingness to give it by saying he does not remember, so with our democratic methods I am afraid we shall have to be satisfied. Anyway, he is in arrest, with the promise of release if he tells us, as under existing German law he can be held for six months.'

In the same letter, Barkworth explained to Galitzine how he had managed to nab another suspect – Karl Dinkel, who, like Neuschwanger, was one of the Erlich Forest killers. Recently, and bizarrely, Dinkel had joined a travelling theatre troupe. Perhaps he had thought it a good place to hide. He had been scheduled to perform before the military authorities in Baden-Baden, in the French zone.

'I am afraid he will not be able to keep his appointment,' Barkworth commented drily. 'I was extremely careful to arrest him "bei Nacht und Nebel" and to speak French in front of his landlady. All recognisable pieces of English uniform were left behind in the car, so if any questions are ever asked about Dinkel's disappearance, I found him while he was visiting his wife in Stuttgart.'

From Dinkel – now ensconced in the Villa Degler basement – Barkworth would learn the final vile details of *Oberwachtmeister* Neuschwanger's behaviour on the day of the Erlich Forest murders.

'I noticed that Neuschwanger had been drinking,' Dinkel revealed to Barkworth. 'I had heard that he was brutal and I had been told that when he drank things happened. I had also heard that he had shot a number of people at Schirmek.'

When the mass shooting in the Erlich Forest was done, Neuschwanger – fired up by drink – had returned with a pair of fur-lined boots taken from one of the dead. 'Those were English,' Neuschwanger told Dinkel, as he waved around the purloined boots. 'They will make no more terror attacks on our cities.'

As the kinder, sunnier conditions of March 1946 chased away the winter chills – meaning that the open-topped jeeps could once again be used for long journeys without the risk of the occupants freezing to death, Barkworth began to cast his net further afield. The pace of operations can be gauged by daily sitreps that he was sending back to Eaton Square.

'Programme as follows: 15 March to 3 Army. 21 March finish 70 and 90 camp interrogations. 28 March PARIS interrogations.

3 April BAOR interrogations . . . Loan of DAKOTA to carry jeep this period. Could be based MANNHEIM and would make [the] formidable task contained [in] your signal less difficult. Wish to make clear that transport, lack of drivers etc may make alterations to programme necessary.'

'Loan of Dakota' referred to Barkworth's hope that he would get a DC3 Dakota transport aircraft to help him shift his jeeps from location to location, so as to cope with his punishing schedule. During the war the SAS had used DC3s to fly their vehicles in to front-line airstrips, from where they could sneak behind enemy lines. There was no reason why similar tactics shouldn't work now for the purposes of manhunting.

Further radio skeds reflected how this intense pace of operations was scoring results. 'Following believed involved in NATZWEILER women case. HERBERG, BOSCHER, LEHMAN perhaps also HILKER. All first three located. Add to witnesses NATZWEILER case.'

The 'Natzweiler women case' was the murder by lethal injection and incineration of Vera Atkins' four women SOE agents. The war crimes trial concerning their case was the first of more than a dozen that Barkworth, Galitzine et al. intended to bring, starting in the late spring of that year.

Preparations were hectic. If Barkworth was to secure all the evidence to enable the trials to proceed – not to mention seizing all the suspects – he would have his work cut out. There were also now the legal issues – not least of which was the level of knowledge the accused possessed of Hitler's Commando Order.

'This is a most important item,' Galitzine reported to Barkworth, 'as if it is proposed to charge all who took part in

Operation Waldfest with "conspiracy to murder British PW", it will be essential to prove their knowledge of the Order. It may be the most effective way of charging those who did not actually fire a gun.'

In response to a promise from Galitzine to send a much-needed driver and a typist to beef up his team, Barkworth radioed a typically dry response: 'Thank you very much. At least can look forward to being driven to interrogations and having someone to type for me... Hope to get sufficient evidence against those giving orders for murder... NATZWEILER people if I am not hurried too much.'

With some prisoners, identification proved unusually difficult, because all of the victims who might have testified against them had been murdered. In such instances Barkworth took the accused on an unwelcome journey down memory lane. He drove them back to Moussey, where there were invariably villagers who had played quiet witness to their horrors. The Moussey villagers could be relied upon to find someone who would unmask the SS and Gestapo killers for who they were.

But the mileage accumulated in this way piled pressure upon the Villa Degler's ramshackle vehicles. The pace of the hunt and the dearth of drivers were so acute that Barkworth was forced to press-gang his radio team into taking stints at the wheel: 'Owing shortage drivers am compelled use both signallers on runs. Intend cut skeds forthwith 09.00–10.00 every other day until further notice.'

Yet no amount of such inventiveness could fix the Secret Hunters' make-do-and-mend transport fleet. Being a unit that did not exist certainly had its downsides. 'Reach MUNICH yesterday but had to return for spare parts to replace broken back axle . . . Am leaving for MUNICH again in morning . . . This typical example of impossibility work to programme when we do not get adequate support . . . At present another [vehicle] is having a new engine put in.'

In yet another frantic April 1946 radio report, Barkworth informs Galitzine: 'Am leaving for EAST. Returning here Tuesday. Repeat that dispatch of two drivers to BAOR will hamstring all further movement this end so am taking no action . . . Hope this doesn't sound high handed but you and Hunt keep cracking the whip and therefore I can't stop work here.'

'Hunt' was Major Alastair Hunt, a judge advocate general (JAG) – a military lawyer attached to Galitzine's team to help prepare the war crimes cases for prosecution, and now working out of Eaton Square. Their planned journey 'EAST' appears to have been in search of the elusive *Sturmbannführer* Ernst.

Towards the end of April 1946 Barkworth sent an excited-sounding radio message to Galitzine and Major Hunt: 'Following accused are known with utmost certainty to have been taken prisoner by 3rd US Army: HANS DIETER [sic] ERNST in cage at VOGLAU from 8/6/45 until transferred to officers' camp . . .'

In June 1945 *Sturmbannführer* Ernst had been held in American custody. He'd turned up in a temporary POW camp, at Voglau, dressed in civilian clothes and of course denying that he was ever an SS *Sturmbannführer* or the commander of *Einsatzkommando* Ernst. But if he could be traced to the 'officers' camp' that he was moved to, or if there were leads thereafter following his release, Barkworth might have a trail to follow.

Galitzine's follow-up radio message to the US War Crimes Branch shows how he was hot on that trail. 'Please obtain complete list of names PW held in VOGLAU CAMP in US Zone. Was a Camp containing 1000 PW for 5/6 weeks May/June 45, then closed. Definitely known ERNST was there during that period. If camp list can be obtained SAS WCIT can check false name which ERNST using.'

There followed a description of Ernst. 'Born 3.18.08 [date of birth in US format] . . . 1.75 metres height: dark hair: dark eyes: slim build: wears glasses for reading: prominent scars on left side of face (forehead and mouth): married with 4 children . . .'

The response that came back from the Americans was that following his transfer to the officers' camp, Ernst had slipped beneath the radar. By 9 April 1946 he was classed as 'unlocated', which was as good as 'lost' as far as Barkworth was concerned.

The Villa Degler chief had one last possible lead on the man. Barkworth had secured intelligence that Ernst may have gone eastwards, to cross the border into the Russian zone. The Ernst family kept a log cabin in the forests of eastern Germany as a summer vacation home. There was just a chance that he might be hiding out there.

'We were very close to catching Ernst,' recalled Dusty Rhodes. 'We were on the border and we knew . . . the person we were looking for . . . was hiding away in this small cabin affair, which was about five or six hundred yards into the Russian Zone. We staked him out for about two to three days, and we were then prepared to make the effort and go and fetch him out of there.'

The Secret Hunters had no authority to cross into the Russian zone, and so the snatch would have to be timed to perfection. If they messed up and anyone was captured, it would be a massive diplomatic incident in the making, not to mention spelling disaster for the Villa Degler operation. A clandestine unit made up of individuals from a Regiment that no longer existed would be exposed to the full glare of international publicity. But the prize – SS *Sturmbannführer* Ernst – made the risks worth taking.

Barkworth, Rhodes and their team watched Ernst's place of hiding closely, recording all of his movements in preparation for launching their smash-and-grab raid. They noted down 'timings of when he came out and walked so far and how long it would take him to get back and how long it would take us to get there,' explained Rhodes. 'When we'd done that we decided: "Yes, that's it – that's exactly how we'll do it." Then along came a car and picked him up and took him away, so we lost him again. Somebody was moving him about who shouldn't have been.'

During repeated cross-border stakeouts Rhodes had several run-ins with Ernst's equally objectionable wife and mother-in-law. The two hatchet-faced women remained utterly devoid of remorse regarding all that Ernst had got up to during the war. Rhodes was tempted to 'choke the buggers at times, when you knew they knew where he was and we were so close to catching him, but . . . they wouldn't give in whatever we did to them'.

Rhodes stressed that Ernst's family were never mistreated or harmed in the course of the hunt. 'We didn't ill-treat them in any way. I mean, that's not on. We wouldn't do that. But we'd do all sorts of tricks – baiting one to the other, or taking the kids away from them . . . But that still wouldn't break them, or make them tell us where he was.'

Barkworth and Rhodes decided to play the long game in the hunt for *Sturmbannführer* Ernst. 'It was only a matter of time before we went to pay a visit and he would be at home.'

But, as luck would have it, it was to be *Oberwachtmeister* Stuka Neuschwanger whom the Secret Hunters would first lay their hands upon.

Chapter Twenty-seven

It was a misty May 1946 morning when Barkworth, Rhodes and team led a stiff and reluctant figure into the woods of the Erlich Forest, near the former labour camp of Rotenfels. That figure had shown not a shred of remorse for all that he had done. He'd never once dropped his demeanour of brute arrogance and supposed superiority – he was, after all, one of the so-called *Übermenschen*; the Aryan master race – ever since his capture.

Now, the Secret Hunters were returning a sadist and a mass murderer – a man who had revelled in causing others unspeakable suffering and pain – to the scene of one of his many crimes, to see if that would make him crack. Superficially, there was nothing that seemed to mark out *Oberwachtmeister* Neuschwanger as a brutal killer. With his swept-back, slightly thinning hair, fine features and prominent, almost pointed nose, he resembled a typical junior Nazi officer.

It was only when you looked into the man's dead eyes that you could read the bottomless pits of cruelty that resided deep in his soul. Neuschwanger was led to the lip of the bomb crater in which the bodies of the murdered Special Forces men – Major Reynolds, Captain Whately-Smith, Lieutenant David Dill, Captain Gough, amongst others – had been buried.

Dusty Rhodes had personally known most of the murdered men. But for him, bringing Neuschwanger here was about one thing only: nailing him for his crimes. 'Revenge didn't come into it, as far as we were concerned . . . We had a job to do and that was to bring these people to justice, and once we'd achieved that then we thought we'd done our work. But revenge, no. We didn't seek revenge.'

Barkworth forced *Oberwachtmeister* Neuschwanger to look into the pit into which the bodies had tumbled, one after the other – defenceless men, each of whom had been dispatched with a bullet to the head.

'So, what do you feel now about the murders that took place here?' Barkworth demanded. 'Now that the war is over?'

Neuschwanger shrugged indifferently. He made it clear he felt nothing; no sense of guilt, no regrets. Rhodes found the man's blatant arrogance enraging.

'When he . . . turned and looked at me and I looked at him,' Rhodes recalled, 'and thinking about the people that you knew personally . . . That's when my temper went.'

Rhodes lashed out, launching a punch that knocked Neuschwanger clean off his feet. The *Oberwachtmeister* tumbled down the wall of the crater, coming to rest in some 18 inches of dirty water lying in its bottom.

'He was fortunate, because he was coming out,' remarked Rhodes. 'The people that had gone in there before weren't. We allowed him to come out and took him back to prison . . .'

Barkworth's stalking of Neuschwanger – carefully tracking his movements and unmasking his false identity – had finally paid off. But in his interrogation the man gave a sense of his appalling lack of remorse for all that he had wrought. In the *Oberwachtmeister*'s matter-of-fact recounting of the Erlich Forest killings it was clear that he felt that he had done nothing remotely odious or reprehensible.

'Ostertag asked me how many prisoners we should do at a time. I suggested three, so he gave the order for the first three to jump down . . . I remember as we were marching them down the track one of them took a photograph out of their pocket and looked at it. We turned into the wood for a distance of 20 to 30 metres until we came to the bomb crater . . . We each fired at the prisoner in front of us.'

'My pistol had a stoppage,' Neuschwanger continued. 'The prisoner in front of me ran away through the wood . . . He was stopped by a shot from either Niebel or Korb, and killed as he lay wounded on the ground by another shot through the head. We then took most of the clothes off . . . to make the bodies unrecognizable.'

Neuschwanger and his fellows then returned to the truck for another three. 'We each shot the respective prisoner in front of us through the back of the head . . . Everyone . . . took either some clothing or shoes back with them. I know that Ostertag had a ring and a gold pocket watch. I had a pair of black boots and Dinkel had a leather case with a zip fastener containing travel necessities . . . An identity disk was lying on the ground . . . I took this and threw it away in the woods.'

Those last words were a crucial admission. In getting Neuschwanger to confess to his efforts to conceal the murdered men's identities, Barkworth figured that he had him bang to rights. He might well try to use the defence of 'superior orders' at his trial, but he had clearly known what he was doing was wrong, or else why try to hide the evidence of the identity of the victims?

During his interrogation Neuschwanger also admitted to taking two men – most likely SAS Trooper Gerald Davis and downed US airman Flight Officer Peabody – into the underground cells at Schirmek. One of Neuschwanger's jobs at Schirmek was to move the condemned men from there to Natzweiler, for termination. Davis was subsequently murdered at Natzweiler and his body dumped at Abbé Gassman's church, as a warning. US airman Peabody was very likely also killed at Natzweiler.

Neuschwanger's testimony had his signature appended to it, above the following words: 'SWORN by the said Deponent Heinrich Neuschwanger, voluntarily, at Gaggenau Germany . . . before me, Major E.A. Barkworth . . .'

Finally, the 'SAS' major had got his man.

In Barkworth's definitive Missing Parachutists report – the one that quoted Shakespeare: *But in these cases we still have judgment here* – he listed dozens of war crimes suspects. In one case alone – the Erlich Forest killings – there were sixteen 'Accused and Suspect Accused', including the rogues' gallery of Erich Isselhorst, Wilhelm Schneider, Robert Uhring, Julius Gehrum, Karl Buck and Heinrich Neuschwanger.

By the late spring of 1946, all these men were in custody and scheduled to stand trial. With many, it was the 'domino effect' that had got them – one captive leading to another. As just one example, Isselhorst's deputy, Schneider, had been seized as a result of the evidence Isselhorst had volunteered.

Upon being taken into captivity by the US 7th Army, Isselhorst had given his captors chapter and verse about the command that he had run, enabling them to draw up flow diagrams of the entire Gestapo and SS set-up. Isselhorst also told them about the whereabouts of his key staff. Of Schneider at the end of the war he noted: 'SCHNEIDER was retired and joined his family, living in a small town in northern Baden.' This was enough to lead the Secret Hunters to him.

'Surprisingly . . . prisoners themselves are best able to give information concerning the whereabouts of others, by some mysterious bush telegraph,' wrote Barkworth in his Missing Parachutists report. 'The easiest Germans to find were those who stayed at home . . .' Schneider was one, claiming to have played a supposedly 'innocent' role during the war. 'Schneider had for example described himself to the American prison authorities as a simple "frontier guard"'.

In one of the most celebrated snatch operations – at least within the tiny community who knew about the Secret Hunters – a suspect (it remains unclear who, exactly) had been lured into Barkworth's clutches by means of a black-market ruse. In post-war Germany everything was in extremely short supply, and the black market was thriving. For those wanted on charges of war crimes, and living false lives under false identities, the black market was an obvious way to scratch a living without drawing unwanted attention to oneself.

The suspect black marketeer ultimately fell victim to his blind greed. Barkworth had learned that this man was hiding out in the Russian zone, at Leipzig, a city in east Germany.

Playing on his supposed resemblance to Isselhorst's deputy, Schneider – his spoken German sounded exactly like the former Gestapo chief – Barkworth placed a phone call to the Leipzig address where the man he wanted was hiding out. He explained that he, Schneider, was still at large and had got into black market profiteering in the British and American zones.

'I'm onto a frightfully good thing,' Barkworth enthused. 'If you meet me under the clock in Cologne Railway Station at midnight, I'll cut you in on it and we can share the proceeds together.'

Barkworth suggested a date to meet. His target agreed. Cologne lay across the far side of Germany from Leipzig, straddling the River Rhine. Whatever deal Barkworth had offered his target, it must have been a strong inducement indeed, for he took the bait. Barkworth and his men were waiting beneath the railway station clock at midnight. They nabbed their man, bundled him into a jeep, and from thence to the Villa Degler basement cell.

Barkworth's Missing Parachutists report also listed dozens of witnesses – those who were willing to take the stand and give evidence against the Nazi killers. Foremost amongst them, of course, were the Moussey villagers. But there were also a few good Germans who were keen to testify against their fellow countrymen; those fine upstanding citizens who had never bought into the Nazi lie. Most prominent amongst them was one Werner Helfen.

Major Dennis Reynolds and Captain Victor Gough had been tortured horribly following their capture. Beaten so severely that his bones showed through his skin, Reynolds had had his stomach stamped on repeatedly by Stuka Neuschwanger. But, sometime after their incarceration in Schirmek's *Sicherungslager*, a German prisoner had unexpectedly joined the British captives in their subterranean cell – one who would prove of great help to them all.

Untersturmführer (Second Lieutenant) Werner Helfen had commanded a company of men guarding various strategic buildings. Moved into the Vosges in August 1944, they had been issued with sawn-off shotguns to replace their standard weaponry. With the Americans pressing home their advance, *Untersturmführer* Helfen had ordered his men to throw their weapons into a river. His reasoning was that under the Hague Conventions such guns were banned from being used as weapons of war. If his men were captured with such arms they would forfeit their right to POW status and its protections.

In due course Helfen was arrested and sentenced to death by an SS tribunal, for 'wilful destruction of Government property'. He was sent to Schirmek while his death sentence was being processed. As a German, he was given the job of fetching and serving food to his fellow prisoners, which allowed him some latitude to move around the camp.

Helfen put such freedoms to good use. He managed to get a French doctor to tend to the injured US airman, Pipcock, whose wounds had not been treated, and he smuggled in extra food for the starving Allied prisoners. During his wanderings Helfen noticed a large potato store made of wooden planks. It gave him an idea to build a ladder with which to try to scale the outer fence that ringed the camp.

He shared the idea with his English and American fellow prisoners. Work on the ladder began immediately. The escape committee was led by Helfen, ably assisted by Gough, David Dill and the US airman Lieutenant Jacoby. Collecting pilfered slats at night when there were fewer patrols, they deadened the noise of construction by covering themselves with blankets as they worked. Ladder complete, the escape committee settled on 12 November as the date to make their break for freedom.

But during the day of the 12th the men could hear the crump of Allied shelling and the distant blasts of small-arms fire. Wave after wave of Allied bombers thundered overhead. They figured the front line was no more than 9 miles away. The escape committee tried to weigh up the risks of trying to escape versus the chances of the camp being liberated by the Allies. Lieutenant Helfen attempted to impress upon the men how their SS guards would not give up without a fight; many of the POWs might be killed.

Such agonizing deliberations were overtaken by developments. The camp commandant, Karl Buck, announced that the entire population of the *Sicherungslager* was to prepare to move. They were being trucked east, to a new camp – Rotenfels, at Gaggenau. On their last night together in Schirmek, Gough presented Helfen with his personal SOE-issue silk escape map, as a keepsake.

Gough used to try to brighten his fellow prisoners' days by drawing cartoons of 'camp life'. One showed a prisoner in uniform seated before a dining table, complete with tablecloth, and with a speech bubble coming from his mouth: 'What – no cabbage soup?' Another showed a thickly moustachioed British officer turning around in surprise, as a figure tunnelled through his office floor, pickaxe in hand. 'Captain Jones, reporting from Schirmek, sir!' read the speech bubble.

Bearing in mind how savagely Gough had been beaten, the cartoons bear testimony to the man's incredible resilience of spirit. Following Buck's order to move camp, ten of the prisoners – Gough, Dill, Jacoby and Helfen included – were loaded aboard a German truck. They set off in the early hours and by 06.00 they were moving through the deserted streets of Strasbourg. The two German guards driving the truck slowed, and allowed Helfen to jump down and slip away.

Werner Helfen made his way back to his hometown, where he remained until the Allies overran the area. In due course, Barkworth tracked him down. Helfen proved keen as mustard to stand as a prosecution witness against several of Barkworth's accused. Speaking of one of the priests executed in the Erlich Forest he told Barkworth:

'So it happened that of all people, Abbé Claude, of whom I have the best memories – he was the quietest, most God-loving and selfless person in the prison – would be hunted down by these monsters.'

Barkworth was so touched by Werner Helfen's principled stand, that he penned the German officer a letter of commendation. It read:

During the time he spent in the cells of Schirmek Camp he did the best he could to better the conditions for the English and American prisoners of war . . . although, had he been discovered he would have been severely punished. In smaller matters such as obtaining extra food, and giving these prisoners exercise – both of which were otherwise not allowed to them – and also in the development of an escape plan, he showed his good intentions.

It was from another key witness – a medical doctor, Dr Thomassin – that the true fate of SAS Lieutenant Silly would be eastablished. Dr Thomassin had been called to the ruins of a sawmill in Moyenmoutier village that had been burned to the ground. Human remains had been discovered in the ashes, but they were too badly burned to be identifiable. What the doctor did discover was a pair of steel-rimmed spectacles, with a metal spectacle case from which the leather had been scorched away.

Amongst the blackened ashes there were also the distinctive brass buttons of the type a *garde forestier* (forest ranger) would wear on his uniform. Lieutenant Silly had been held captive along with two such men. Barkworth concluded from the evidence that Silly had met his end here, at the Moyenmoutier sawmill, and that the remains previously identified as his must have been those of SAS Trooper Donald Lewis, one of the few Op Loyton cases that remained unsolved.

By now, the sterling efforts of the Secret Hunters were being recognized by London: 'this has . . . become one of the most important War Crimes operations'. The presence of Colonel Brian Franks' quiet hand at the tiller can be detected from the occasional handwritten missive sent on Hyde Park Hotel headed paper to his manhunters.

To Yurka Galitzine he passed on a letter from Captain Henry Parker, busy investigating war crimes perpetrated against SAS men in Italy. 'The nasty snag at the moment is that JAG [the judge advocate general] here are trying to post me to Austria, but not trying too hard, so I think I can fight a delaying action,' Parker noted to Franks.

Parker was seeking more time to complete his Italian investigations. He signed off his letter: 'Please give my regards to your good lady wife, and also Sgt (bogus, acting and unpaid) Morgan wishes to be remembered to you.' *Bogus, acting and unpaid*: three words that might sum up much of the Secret Hunters' work in the spring of 1946. Colonel Franks – the overall conductor of the Nazi-hunting operations – passed Parker's note to the 'fixer', Prince Yurka Galitzine, at his Eaton Square office.

'Dear Galitzine, I presume the request Parker refers to came from you or Bill B; therefore send the enclosed on to you. Hopefully goes well and Bill uses him in the manner so narrated. I promised to send him some . . . medal ribbon but have failed, but will send to Everitt to pass on. Yours, Brian Franks.'

Barkworth's conclusion to his Missing Parachutists report encapsulated how all-consuming had become the hunt for the Op Loyton disappeared, for the truth and for the killers, and how wide he and his men had been forced to spread their net.

'When this unit began this enquiry in June 1945, it was with no foreknowledge that it would become so protracted or involved.' He characterized Waldfest as being a 'policy of mediaeval brutality', describing those who had designed and implemented it as 'Germans whose courage and exhibition of cruelty was . . . inversely proportionate to the risks they ran . . .'

In other words, they were happy to exhibit cruelty and supposed bravery, as long as they faced no danger in doing so.

But with that most elusive of things – a reckoning – almost within Barkworth's grasp, he appears to have been under an increasing amount of strain. Unless they took the law into their own hands, the Secret Hunters – and with them the Op Loyton victims, the Moussey villagers and the families of all who had been murdered – would get just one shot at justice: the coming trials. How terrible it would be to fall at the final hurdle.

A late spring 1946 radio message to Eaton Square reveals how even Barkworth was close to breaking point, as the frantic work of the trial preparations got underway. Clearly, there was only so far that whisky and Benzedrine could take the Villa Degler operators.

'If trial advanced ten days cannot cope and intend stop now. Your last directive approach bounds impossibility yet considered by day and night work possible to achieve. Alteration date trial makes whole situation impossible and ridiculous. If I worked same hours as War Office this job would take further three months.'

And a few days later: 'Have tried to prepare evidence as thoroughly as possible and am sure you appreciate I do not want to hand in skimped work through wild all haste . . .'

The first of the Op Loyton war crimes trials was only weeks away now. But, frustratingly, as the long-awaited prosecutions loomed, the Secret Hunters were forced to accept that one man – perhaps their foremost target – had eluded them.

As a legal expert's letter to Barkworth made clear, it was of utmost importance to capture all such individuals – those who had served in positions of high command. 'Very essential. He is only member of the HQ that gave the order for the execution. In his absence the lesser fry may attribute all the blame to him and escape themselves.'

But *Sturmbannführer* Hans Dietrich Ernst remained listed as: 'at large with no indication of . . . suspected whereabouts'. Worryingly, Barkworth's most-wanted looked set to escape justice.

Chapter Twenty-eight

On 6 May 1946 – barely a year after Colonel Franks had dispatched Barkworth to Gaggenau to investigate the bodies found in the Erlich Forest – the first of the 'SAS War Crimes Trials' opened. It was held under the authority of a British military court, sitting at the Zoological Gardens, Wuppertal, a city lying just to the north of Cologne, well into the British zone of occupation. With delicious irony, the 'courtroom' was established in the zoo's former banqueting hall.

Galitzine had written to Major Alastair Hunt, the prosecutor, shortly before the trial's start. 'Here are the affidavits that I have collected off Barkworth to date . . . I am having all the accused shifted to near Wuppertal, so that it may be necessary for Bill B to come up and camp there. Anyway, I think it will be better to establish our base there almost immediately after your arrival.'

With the first hearing about to commence, the focus was shifting away from the manhunters and onto the legal experts who would prosecute the cases. But Barkworth, Rhodes and several of his men still had a key role to play. They were billeted in the administration building adjacent to the banqueting-hall-cum-courtroom, while those facing trial were incarcerated in the local jail.

Even now – *particularly now* – the drama was far from over. Barkworth made it clear that he wanted his suspects watched closely at all times, and especially when they were shipped to and from the court. Wherever possible prisoners 'should have no opportunity [of] speaking to' other suspects, to prevent them from better concocting their stories, Barkworth directed.

All prisoners were to be accompanied by 'escorts carrying arms' and none were to be left 'without provision handcuffs or in proper prison trucks'. 'Do not wish to have to look for them again,' Barkworth noted drily.

One prisoner did manage to 'escape' his forthcoming trial. SS officer and war crimes suspect Heinrich Ganninger committed suicide shortly after SAS Major Barkworth had interrogated him.

A 'gagging order' had been placed on the trial hearings; there was to be no media coverage. This was for two reasons: one, so that the relatives of those killed would not be caused further upset by seeing their loves ones' suffering and death splashed over the newspapers. And two, so that those still at large – chiefly *Sturmbannführer* Ernst – would not be alerted to the fact that the quest for justice continued.

This first trial concerned the Erlich Forest killings. The eleven accused – including former Schirmek commandant Karl Buck, Stuka Neuschwanger and Karl Dinkel, the man snatched by Barkworth '*bei Nacht und Nebel*' from his travelling theatre troupe – were appointed German defence lawyers in an effort to ensure 'fair play'. They were charged with the 25 November 1944 murders of fourteen prisoners: six SAS soldiers, four American airmen and four French nationals.

A Frenchman – Air Force Captain Bellet – was included on the six-person prosecution panel, as French nationals had lost their lives in the mass murder. Major Hunt – the military lawyer attached to Galitzine's Eaton Square operation – led the prosecution, and Captain Prince Galitzine himself had been shipped over from London to attach himself to Barkworth's unit for the duration of the hearings.

The argument for the accused's guilt was fairly simple: prisoners of war are protected under the 1929 Geneva Convention and cannot simply be murdered out of hand. If the prosecution could establish that the defendants were guilty of such murders, 'the court would be entitled to convict these accused of a violation of the rules of international law', the judge advocate – the military official presiding over the hearings – explained.

Predictably, the German lawyers for the accused pleaded that they had 'acted under superior orders' – in other words, they were simply doing as they'd been told. They cited Hitler's Commando Order as being 'justification' for their actions. If the defence of superior orders stood, only Hitler would be guilty, and he had reportedly committed suicide in his Berlin bunker in April 1945. The Wuppertal trials would be rendered a farce.

Standartenführer Isselhorst was called as an early defence witness. The former Gestapo and SS commander, himself a highly trained lawyer, argued that the Commando Order bound all German servicemen, including SS and Gestapo personnel, to shoot 'members of so-called Commando detachments who were parachuted . . . behind the German lines to do acts of sabotage or interference'.

Isselhorst claimed to have 'reinterpreted' the Commando Order, such that it would only be applied to those 'parachutists' proved to have worked with the Maquis 'terrorists'. Isselhorst then tried to blame *Sturmbannführer* Ernst – the only senior suspect not in captivity – for the Erlich Forest massacre. Isselhorst argued that it was Ernst who had convinced him that the fourteen men were saboteurs and spies, operating in close collaboration with the Maquis, and that their execution under Hitler's Commando Order was justified.

In other words, under the defence of 'superior orders', only Hitler and *Sturmbannführer* Ernst were guilty, and by their guilt all eleven defendants would be exonerated.

Major Barkworth was called as a prosecution witness in an effort to quash Isselhorst's arguments. He pointed out that it was not in the remit of the Operation Loyton team to organize and support the Maquis; that task lay with 'other units' – a euphemism for the Jedburghs. Members of the SAS did inevitably have contact with the Maquis because 'the operation . . . in the Vosges area was mounted at a time at which the Maquis had risen against the German invaders'.

In other words, there had been no deliberate 'collaboration' with the Maquis, and so Hitler's Commando Order did not apply to the SAS men.

Under cross-examination the eleven accused started to fall upon each other. Karl Buck tried to pin all responsibility on 'orders from Isselhorst'. Those who had taken the victims into the Erlich Forest accused Stuka Neuschwanger of having acted as the enforcer, ensuring that the killings went ahead no matter what. Some claimed to have had no idea that the prisoners faced execution, and to have objected to taking any part in any shootings.

Amidst such mutual recriminations, Neuschwanger tried to strike back against his accusers. His lawyer claimed – rightly, as it happened – that British Sergeant Fred Rhodes had ill-treated him when he was taken back to the site of the Erlich Forest killings. Rhodes had beaten him and thrown him into the crater bottom, the German defence lawyer complained. In light of such behaviour, the British soldiers were little better than the accused.

The judge advocate fixed Rhodes with a gimlet eye. Was there any truth to this accusation, he demanded? Dusty Rhodes fished in his pocket and pulled out a leave pass, 'proving' that he had been in England at the time of the alleged assault, enjoying a rare period of rest time. It was entirely bogus, of course. The document was a forgery, and not the first used by the Secret Hunters. But it was a necessary and justifiable bending of the rules.

That uncomfortable issue dealt with, the judge advocate turned to the letter of the law. The fact that a soldier may have been ordered to do something didn't mean that the act wasn't a war crime; likewise, acting under orders didn't mean that the soldier was immune from punishment for his actions. He also pointed out that the accused must have known that what they were doing was wrong, or else why did they go to such lengths – stripping the victims; burning their clothing; burying their dog tags – to obliterate their identities? Lawful executions did not take place in the midst of the woods, with mass burials in bomb craters and with all identifying marks removed from the victims. In essence, the accused were damned by their own admissions.

The judge advocate moved on to the final debate, whether ignorance of the law offered any defence. 'The Court must ask itself: "What did each of these accused know about the rights of a prisoner of war?" . . . The Court may well think that these men are not lawyers. They may not have heard of the Hague Convention or the Geneva Convention. They may not have seen any book of military law . . .'

The judge advocate paused while his summing up was translated into German. 'But the Court has to consider whether men who are serving as soldiers or in proximity to soldiers know as a matter . . . of military life whether a prisoner of war has certain rights and whether one of those rights is not, when captured, to security for his person.'

All eleven accused barring one – Josef Muth – were found guilty. Five were given prison sentences of up to ten years, and five death sentences were passed down – including for Karl Buck and Stuka Neuschwanger. Even then, their ordeal was far from over. Buck and Neuschwanger were shortly to be passed into French hands, so that the French could try them for war crimes perpetrated against French civilians.

While the trial outcome was largely gratifying, the custodial sentences seemed far too lenient. Two of the accused had only been given two and three years respectively, and with parole for good behaviour they might all be free by the turn of the decade. Barkworth had always hoped that the trials would be seen as 'an example of strict impartial justice and not of revenge'. But the punishment needed to fit the crime.

In the next case – that concerning Lieutenant Dill's rear-guard, who had been captured defending the SAS's final Moussey base – fourteen defendants were charged with the murder of eight SAS men in the forests above La Grande Fosse. The last of the British soldiers had told his executioners the poignant truth: 'We were good men.' Good men who had not deserved to die in such a sordid act of murder – as, hopefully, the trial was about to prove.

All of the accused – Georg Zahringer amongst them, the man who had given Barkworth his game-changing testimony – were former members of *Einsatzkommando* Ernst. Predictably, their defence lawyers argued that they had all been carrying out their commander's orders, and so were not guilty of any crimes. Without Ernst in the dock to testify or to be cross-examined, the prosecution faced an uphill battle.

Amongst countless other crimes, these men were responsible for stripping naked eight SAS captives and marching each to an open grave in the forest – one in which they could see their dead comrades – before shooting them in the head. But sadly, the final sentences handed down for the La Grande Fosse case were close to laughable. Six of the fourteen accused were found not guilty. Of the remaining eight, only one received a ten-year sentence, and two were given just two and three years respectively.

For those who had spent so long hunting down the accused, this was a gross injustice. They had promised the murdered of Op Loyton and their families a reckoning. In this case they, or rather the courts, had failed.

In light of the hopeless leniency of the sentences, Barkworth changed tack. He began offering inducements for key witnesses to turn evidence against their former colleagues. Those who must have known they faced a death sentence were offered the hope that it might be reduced to life imprisonment, if they dished the dirt on their fellows. The Secret Hunters were learning to 'play the legal game', and just in time, for the Natzweiler trial was the next scheduled hearing.

Rightly, there was a public outcry at the pathetic nature of the La Grande Fosse sentences. At least that part of the story – that the killers had escaped proper justice – had made it into the press. The same failures could not be allowed to happen at the forthcoming hearing. The Natzweiler trial would deal with the four female SOE agents injected with poison and burned to death in the camp ovens, but in truth its scope would be far, far wider.

Some 25,000 people had been liquidated at Natzweiler, and the accused were complicit in all of those crimes. When British and American troops had stumbled upon the Nazi concentration camps, they had recoiled instinctively from the horrors they discovered. Such war crimes – such mechanized genocide; the well-ordered liquidation of millions of men, women and children – transgressed all norms of human behaviour.

If the Natzweiler trial ended in a debacle, the resulting outcry would be deafening. Justice absolutely had to be seen to be done.

Prior to the Natzweiler hearings, London mooted a ban on press reporting of the names of the victims. On 24 May 1946 the War Office wrote to the next of kin of Vera Leigh, one of the SOE agents killed, warning that, 'in any publicity concerning the trials mention would be made of her by name . . . In view of the distressing circumstances in which Vera was killed, we are most anxious to spare her relatives any further pain which . . . publicity might entail.'

But, in a 27 May reply, the late Vera Leigh's family made their feelings abundantly clear. 'I have already made known to all members of the family the circumstances in which she met her death and feel that no useful purpose would be gained in suppressing Miss Leigh's name from any reports that may be published . . . it would be preferable that the full story should be published rather than a garbled version should appear in the Press through some indirect source.'

On 28 May the Natzweiler trial opened at Wuppertal and, despite the relatives' wishes, a blanket ban had been imposed on any media reporting of the case. In the dock stood nine accused. They included Werner Rohde, the camp doctor who had administered the supposedly lethal carbolic acid injections. In a war crimes trial such as this, a medical doctor like Rohde was rightly stripped of his respected 'Doctor' title. Standing alongside Rohde were Peter Straub, the camp executioner whose face had been raked by the nails of one of his victims, and Fritz Hartjenstein, the camp commandant.

Amongst the first witnesses to give evidence for the prosecution were SOE spymaster Vera Atkins, plus Brian Stonehouse, the SOE agent whose presence had first been detected at Natzweiler by Captain Galitzine, during his autumn 1944 discovery of the camp. However, from the very start, the German defence lawyers argued persuasively that SOE agents who were not deployed in uniform could enjoy none of the legal protections of soldiers in wartime.

'International law allowed for the execution of irregular combatants,' Dr Groebel, the chief defence attorney, pointed out. He suggested that the court should 'consider this case from the point of view that it was a normal and simple execution of spies'. This was said in defence of a man like Straub, who had by his own boastful admission, 'put four million people up the chimney'. It may have been no exaggeration: prior to his stint at Natzweiler, Straub had worked at Auschwitz.

Major Hunt, the prosecutor, countered this by pointing out that under international law even spies had to be given a trial prior to their execution. 'Killing in such a manner at such a time and in such circumstances raises a presumption that there was no trial . . . If this was a lawful execution, then why such secrecy?'

Groebel countered by stating that, 'for us Germans, our Government in the last years has created an enormous number of special courts . . . courts which everywhere decided the fate of human beings and normally passed sentences of death . . . We Germans have been hermetically sealed off from the rest of the world and I do not know how proceedings are carried out there now'.

In other words, all the defendants were themselves the sorry victims of a totalitarian system of government, over which they had had neither any say, nor any form of control. It was the defence of superior orders by another name and, incredibly, in that May 1946 court in Wuppertal it seemed to be working.

In an effort to sink such arguments, Hunt called Barkworth's evidence. The SAS major had secured a statement from Georg Kaenemund, a political prisoner and internee at Natzweiler. Kaenemund had overheard the interrogation of one of the four women prisoners. She had made it clear that she was 'a Lieutenant in the British Army', and she had 'demanded to be brought before a proper Court Martial', saying, 'that as a member of the armed forces she should not be in prison'.

The trouble was, several witnesses for the defence – Brian Stonehouse included – had made it clear that the four agents had turned up at Natzweiler dressed in civilian clothes. It was hard – approaching impossible – to claim the legal defences due a soldier, when these four women prisoners had been masquerading as civilians.

In his summing up the judge advocate suggested that the four women had been executed without trial because, in the autumn of 1944, the Germans would have had 'considerable apprehension as to the final results of the war'. They knew they were losing and they wanted to hide the evidence of their war crimes. If the lack of a trial could be made to stick, the accused should be found guilty.

That was the hope as the 'jury' – in reality, this being a military court, the panel of military officials – retired to consider their verdict. Forty minutes later they were ready. Natzweiler 'doctor' Werner Rohde would face the death penalty. But SS *Obersturmbannführer* (Lieutenant Colonel) Fritz Hartjenstein, the camp commandant who had presided over the liquidation of tens of thousands at Natzweiler, received only a life sentence.

Far worse for Barkworth, Rhodes and team, Peter Straub – the man who had shoved a living British woman into the camp oven – received only a prison sentence, and even that was of just *thirteen years*. Of the six other accused, all received light custodial sentences or were acquitted.

The Natzweiler trial had proved a travesty.

The Villa Degler team had scoured Europe searching tirelessly for the guilty. They had worked a crazy schedule and broken every rule imaginable in an effort to ensnare them, and when the SAS itself had been disbanded, they had risked 'going dark' to continue the good fight, come what may. Against all odds they had succeeded in the seemingly impossible – in tracking down the killers.

And now this: the courts – an arena in which they could exert little control or influence – were failing them. And that failure would force the Secret Hunters to some of their most extreme actions yet.

Barkworth, Galitzine, Rhodes et al. called a council of war. At Natzweiler four defenceless women agents had been injected with deadly carbolic acid and one at least had been burned alive. Yet the language of the trial had been so sanitized, civilized and almost . . . mundane in its treatment of the case. Nothing had captured the horror.

No one had got to the heart of the matter, conveying the depths of the inhumanity and the sheer terror inflicted on the victims. And owing to the ban on any media reporting, the great British public wasn't even aware of what had transpired, or that those responsible had largely got away with it.

As far as Galitzine was concerned, Natzweiler was the 'Belsen of France', and yet for a second time now its very existence had been covered up and buried. So it was that Galitzine – himself a former journalist – decided to break the silence. He penned an article for the *Sunday Express*. Published on 2 June 1946 – the day following the trial's conclusion – the headline screamed: 'Four British girls burned alive – one German to die. Girl fought at oven door.'

Galitzine's article blew the story wide open. It began with a description of the court scene. 'The Germans, pale and trembling, stood to hear the verdict. The man who is to hang, Werner Rohde, the camp doctor, cracked a joke with one of his fellows as sentence was pronounced. The three who were acquitted sank to their seats with sobs of relief. So ended the trial of a group . . . who were guilty of "sheer brutality unparalleled in the history of mankind" at the Struthof-Natzweiler concentration camp in the Vosges mountains . . .'

The story included vivid eyewitness testimony of how the SOE agents were killed, and went on to recount the grim history of Natzweiler, from its earliest beginnings: 'Shaven-headed prisoners in striped clothes arrived to hew granite from the mountain. The hotel became a gas chamber. A crematorium was built. A concentration camp was born.'

Wisely under the circumstances, Galitzine had penned his article anonymously. The fact that he was the author is revealed only from his private papers, which are fortuitously filed at the Imperial War Museum. On his copy of the article, Captain Prince Galitzine had scribbled in his own hand: 'Written by Yurka.' Attached to this is his – far longer – original, handwritten draft of the news report. That draft concludes that at Natzweiler, the Germans had devised a process of 'death so inhuman that even savages would hesitate before turning to such methods'.

No doubt Galitzine had filed his papers at the Imperial War Museum – including his original and seminal Natzweiler investigation report; the one he had been forced to 'bury' – so that this vital piece of history, and his role within it, might be preserved for posterity. And, as the Secret Hunters had doubtless intended, publication of that *Sunday Express* article provoked a veritable storm.

The powers that be were apoplectic. London went as far as suggesting a court of inquiry be formed to investigate how 'matters not brought before the court or proved in evidence appeared in press as statement of fact'. There were fears the leak had originated in Germany, and that 'there may well be representations that press protests have influenced court . . . No need to stress most regrettable effect of this on members of future courts.'

The 'future court' mentioned was the next major hearing, in which the big guns – most notably Isselhorst – were to stand trial.

Chapter Twenty-nine

The trial of Isselhorst and five others – including his deputies, Wilhelm Schneider and Julius Gehrum – opened on 17 June 1946. It would take twenty-two days to complete, largely due to Isselhorst's wily prevarication and the convoluted legal shenanigans he employed.

All six were charged with: 'committing a war crime in that they in FRANCE and in particular in the VOSGES ... in violation of the laws and usages of war were concerned in the killing of a number of airborne troops and personnel of aircrews'. They were specifically accused of running a 'system of extermination of 32 members of the SAS Regiment ... who took part in operations to disrupt enemy communications in the VOSGES mountains ...'

From the outset Isselhorst quoted Hitler's Commando Order, as if it was his get-out-of-jail-free card. The order provided for the following, he told the court: ' "All members of so called Commandos whether in uniform or not, whether armed or not, whether landed by water or air, or parachutists are to be shot if caught." The order also provided for punishment of those who did not carry it out or failed to pass it on.'

Unbelievably, Isselhorst claimed to have had no knowledge of the torture and ill-treatment meted out to the captives held under his command. 'I never had any knowledge of such happening, and . . . if it had come to my knowledge I would have taken severe measures against it.' He also denied all responsibility for – and almost all knowledge of – Natzweiler. 'I have never seen or entered the camp. I had nothing to do with it . . . and I had no reasons whatsoever to go there.'

Of his fellow accused and former deputies, Isselhorst spoke warmly, describing kindly 'uncle-like' figures. 'Schneider was a considerably older comrade whom I respected for his age. I always knew him as a proper fellow worker, although on account of his age and sickness he was a bit of a muddle-head. He was liked by all on account of his comradeship.'

But Isselhorst's opinion of Schneider was as nothing compared to his view of *Sturmbannführer* Ernst. 'Dr Ernst was a hard-working man, intelligent and conscientious, and he was always personally very deeply interested in all matters concerning his group, and he was described to me as one of the best officials in France.'

Even under cross-examination by the prosecutor, Major Hunt, Isselhorst's carefully crafted cover showed little signs of cracking.

'Did you know that international law requires captors to safeguard the lives of prisoners of war?' Hunt demanded.

'Generally, yes,' Isselhorst answered.

'In spite of that you agree . . . that you did transmit orders which resulted in the death of a considerable number of prisoners of war?'

'Not in this form, because these captives did not represent prisoners of war in our view . . .'

'Did you know that when these orders were carried out many helpless men were led up to bomb craters, stripped naked, shot and buried?'

'I said when this question was put to me by my own defence counsel: no.'

'How did you think your orders were carried out?'

'As a quiet, normal shooting, just in the way as was ordered by me . . .'

Hunt appeared increasingly exasperated at Isselhorst's answers. 'What I want you to explain is how is it, if all these men were shot in this irregular manner, that you did not know about it?'

'I cannot answer this question.'

'Why not? It seems a simple question.'

'Because I do not know.'

Even more frustratingly, as the trial dragged on Isselhorst tried to deflect responsibility for any killings onto the usual suspect: *Sturmbannführer* Ernst.

'We have heard from the witness Buck that . . . 125 Maquisards were sent to Natzweiler. Do you know who gave orders concerning that?' Hunt demanded.

'I believe it was Commandant Ernst.'

'And what did you know regarding the 125 men?'

'Nothing more than that it was reported to me later on.'

In other words, Isselhorst had had nothing whatsoever to do with the mass murder of the Maquis. Only *Sturmbannführer* Ernst was to blame. Isselhorst seemed happy to stand in the dock at Wuppertal arguing that black was white, with barefaced and haughty insouciance.

All Isselhorst would admit to was directing that the Maquis be used as forced labour. 'The Maquis . . . should be sent to places of work in Germany itself . . . All Maquisards were sent [through] Schirmek camp to the Mercedes-Benz works in Gaggenau.'

For Barkworth, Galitzine and Rhodes this must have been agonizing to watch. Isselhorst the skilled, professional lawyer seemed to be parrying every thrust attempted by the court. It was approaching two years since the men of Op Loyton had been murdered, and a thousand villagers deported from the valleys of the Vosges to the Nazi concentration camps. Was the architect of all that going to get off scot-free?

Galitzine felt the courts were being 'far too soft'. Far too few life sentences and death sentences were being handed down. The accused had committed 'the most terrible crimes, and we couldn't understand why they were given a year, four years, six years imprisonment'.

Hunt's questioning returned to Hitler's Commando Order. 'Knowing the provisions of international law, how could you reconcile a printed order to kill as being right?'

'As I said before, in the National Socialist regime the will of the head of Government was law, and therefore in consequence this order was law.'

When challenged over why the Op Loyton men had received no kind of trial, Isselhorst craftily argued: 'The reason is the Führer Order, which excludes any sort of trial.'

Isselhorst's stubborn, boorish circularity of argument – I cannot bear any responsibility because of Hitler's Commando Order – grated on the court mightily. Doubly so, in fact, because Barkworth's original interrogation of Isselhorst had nailed him on that point – one that he now tried to deny, claiming forget-fulness as the reason for any inconsistencies.

'You now say that your previous statement is inaccurate, is that it?' Hunt challenged.

'Not quite . . .' Isselhorst replied. 'Not because I wanted to state something wrong at the time, but that I have remembered in the meantime the real sequence of events.'

Finally, the judge advocate himself seemed to crack. 'I cannot believe you are so stupid as you make out,' he snapped. 'The Court are getting very tired of this constant going back on what you said on oath in your affidavit, with the result it is always exonerating somebody who is in the dock.' And a little later: 'I suggest that Isselhorst is not a fool and that he could not get so mixed up.'

Fortunately, at least two witnesses had been persuaded by Barkworth's 'incentives' to turn evidence against Isselhorst. One was Karl Buck, the former Schirmek commandant. He testified to Isselhorst's culpability in sending hundreds of maquisards to their deaths at Natzweiler – something that Isselhorst of course denied. The other witness against Isselhorst was his former deputy in Waldfest, Julius Gehrum.

The trial turned to Gehrum's evidence. 'You consider your-self to be a very humane man, do you not?' the judge advocate challenged Isselhorst.

'Yes.'

'Gehrum thinks you are a man with very cruel ideas, apparently.'

'I believe there have been two witnesses who have said that is nonsense and a lie.'

'It is a matter for the Court . . . to decide as to who is lying in this case; but you heard Gehrum say it in his affidavit, did you not?'

'Yes.'

The judge advocate cited Isselhorst's 'career' on the Eastern Front as typifying his cruelty, outlining how he had commanded one of Hitler's death squads and hunted down Russian partisans. Gehrum's testimony – that Isselhorst was a man 'with very cruel ideas' – could hardly be denied in light of that.

'Some pretty cruel things were done in Russia, were they not?' the judge advocate demanded. 'Except for a Jew I suppose a Russian was the least important person in the eyes of a German?'

'No . . . I had no opportunity there to commit any acts of cruelty . . . My duties there, with the Einsatzkommando were only of a military nature. There were no partisans or guerrillas or anything of that kind in that area, as it was only a front area.'

In spite of Isselhorst denials – which were, of course, barefaced lies – the judge advocate had scored a point: he'd painted Isselhorst as a man with a long history of involvement in Nazi atrocities.

He turned next to the fact that the Op Loyton men had all been in uniform when captured. Isselhorst tried to argue that he was ignorant of this fact, or that it wasn't a relevant factor in deciding whether to execute the men. Again, the judge advocate's anger boiled over.

'But what is the matter with everybody in the German service?' he demanded. 'Do you not realise it would be complete madness to send British soldiers to Germany dressed as civilians?'

'I was of the opinion . . . that those British personnel were only put into British uniform so as to camouflage their unlawful actions – unlawful against international law . . . The Führer Order speaks quite clearly about these people whether in uniform or not.'

The judge advocate produced a copy of the Commando Order. 'The main order has at the bottom "signature illegible" but do we gather it was Hitler who issued this order?' he asked of Isselhorst.

'Yes.'

'And he ends with the blood-curdling threat: "I will summon before the tribunal of war all leaders and officers who fail to carry out these instructions – either by failure to inform their men or by their disobedience of this order in action?"'

'Yes.'

The judge advocate was building an argument that Isselhorst had engaged in illegal acts – murder – owing to his fear of the Führer's retribution should he not do so. In other words, he had knowingly committed war crimes out of fear for his own person. Another key point had been scored.

After twenty-two days in session, the hearing wound up with the judge advocate clarifying of which crimes Isselhorst and his cohorts stood accused. None of them had taken part in the direct killings. Rather, they had issued the orders while commanding Operation Waldfest. The shootings were carried out by 'thugs' who took men into the woods, shot them in the back of the head, threw them into bomb craters, buried them, and removed all traces of the killings.

On 11 July the court pronounced its verdicts: while there were custodial sentences for two of the accused, Isselhorst and

Schneider were both condemned to 'death by hanging'. One other, Oberg – a senior ranking SS and Gestapo officer serving in France at the time of the Vosges campaign – was also sentenced to death by hanging.

Julius Gehrum was acquitted. Towards the end of the trial his lawyer, Dr Kohrs, had painted a chilling picture of life in the final days of the Reich.

'In the course of this trial you have already heard of the Führer Order . . . that was posted in every company's office, in every staff quarters and in every officer's mess. According to this, no soldier, nor officer either, was permitted to receive knowledge of things that did not have to be made known to him for official reasons.

'This duty to keep secret even unimportant matters was one of the reasons why National Socialism was so successful in suppressing the majority of people for such a long time. It was dangerous to know too much. It was more dangerous to ask too much. It was still more dangerous to say too much.'

In Hitler's Germany, knowing, asking or saying too much could prove a life or death issue. But in the summer of 1946 it was Isselhorst's knowledge that would serve to postpone his execution for the time being. The hearing done, Isselhorst was returned to the custody of his nemesis: Barkworth. He was wanted as a trial witness in three further British cases. And the French were also after him, to stand trial in France for widespread crimes against humanity in the Vosges.

Similarly, Gehrum's apparent acquittal was only to provide a momentary respite. On 4 August 1946 Barkworth handed him over to the French so they could try him for war crimes. In due course Gehrum would find himself condemned by his own words during Barkworth's interrogation, in which he'd admitted to 'the liquidation of certain prisoners' when in charge of a special execution commando.

He would be sentenced to death by the French in May 1947.

A month or so after the trial of Isselhorst and his cohorts, Bill Barkworth and Dusty Rhodes travelled to Hamelin, a small town in central Germany famous for the children's tale of the Pied Piper who pipes a plague of rats out of the town. It was late September 1946 and the two Secret Hunters were going to Hamelin prison to witness a hanging.

Barkworth and Rhodes were led along a series of bare, echoing corridors towards the execution room. They took their places amongst the various officials present. A figure was brought out by the hangman and led to the place of his final few minutes of life on this earth.

Oberwachtmeister Heinrich 'Stuka' Neuschwanger kept his head erect as the hangman slipped the noose around his neck. Even now, at the moment of his death, he betrayed not the slightest sign of regret at anything that he had done. 'Right up to the moment he was hung I don't think it worried him one little bit,' remarked Rhodes. 'I don't think he had any sorrow or remorse at all in him, that man. He was cruel.'

At least Neuschwanger was afforded the luxury of a quick and clean death. The drop was sufficient to break his neck. That was more than any of his Natzweiler victims had ever been given.

Having seen *Oberwachtmeister* Neuschwanger hang, Barkworth and Rhodes returned to their jeep feeling strangely downcast and silent. There had been no real joy – no sense of catharsis – in witnessing his hanging, in spite of the fact that he had been one of the Nazi war criminals that they had sought most exhaustively. Neither man would ever attend another execution.

'It was something that one doesn't want to do more than once,' recalled Rhodes. 'When we came out of that prison we were both pleased we'd come out. I believe we were both of the opinion that it's not nice to see somebody die.'

For the Secret Hunters their mission had never been one of brute revenge. It was always about ensuring that justice was done. By the autumn of 1946 they had a sense that some of the justice that they had so hungered for had been delivered. Neuschwanger was dead. Isselhorst and Schneider were scheduled to hang, as was Werner Rohde, and Karl Buck would face 'death by shooting'.

Gehrum would eventually follow them to his death, as would Peter Straub, the Natzweiler executioner, after he too faced a further trial. The architects of Waldfest had been hunted down, tried before a court of law and were facing the death penalty.

All except one: *Sturmbannführer* Ernst remained at large.

Chapter Thirty

After the trials, Barkworth and his team might have been forgiven for easing off a little, but not a bit of it. Their Villa Degler operation continued full steam ahead.

By December of 1946 Barkworth had expanded the scope of his work to cover a plethora of new investigations: Kolbshein – war crimes against US servicemen; Natzweiler IV – a Stalag Luft killing of RAF officers; Captain Gunston and 7 ORs (other ranks) – the SAS in Italy; Bennett and Claridge – again, the SAS in Italy; plus a dozen or so more cases.

The focus was no longer Operation Loyton. Colonel Franks' determination to trace the thirty-two SAS who had gone missing in the Vosges had spawned an investigative phenomenon all of its own. In a 26 December letter to the War Office, summing up the Villa Degler team's successes and ongoing priorities, Barkworth was clear about the need to expand his force, and of the need to recruit independently.

'This is considered to have the advantage that men can be hand-picked, a course which is essential in so small a unit where no passengers can be carried.' He summarized the gargantuan efforts that had produced the results so far achieved at trial. 'Since 1st January 1946 the vehicles of this team have covered 245,238 miles . . . During the past year 105 persons involved as accused or witnesses were located in camps, and 44 arrested by members of this team.'

Barkworth also wrote of the ongoing challenges in tracking down suspects, and especially the one man that he sought above all others. 'The difficulties encountered in finding wanted persons have not decreased. It is known, for example, that Ernst of the St. Dié and Saales cases, was released by the Americans . . . He subsequently visited his wife in December 1945 and is now thought to be . . . in the British zone, since he has appeared there twice . . . It is hoped to bring this search to a successful conclusion in the near future.'

By early 1947, London was clear in its acknowledgement of Barkworth's unrivalled expertise and experience in war crimes matters. In spite of the 'peculiar nature of the SAS investigations' – and not to mention the team's ill-defined status – 'Major Barkworth's knowledge of the broad picture of the crimes . . . is so extensive and his appreciation of the characters of the various suspects so detailed', that it should be relied upon wherever possible, stated a letter from the judge advocate general's office.

Tracking down the Nazi war criminals remained essential for many families seeking closure, those whose sons and daughters were still listed as missing. Some at least of the bereaved were keen to witness in person that justice had been done.

In the spring of 1947, the father of SAS and Op Loyton man Donald Lewis – killed at Le Harcholet – wrote of his son's death and pending trial: 'I should be very grateful if you could, in any way at all, assist in my application for permission to be allowed to attend the trial of those who were responsible for his and his comrades' death.'

For Barkworth and his Villa Degler team the burden of responsibility was far from being lifted. This was especially so in light of the new cases that they were taking on.

In June 1944 a squadron from 1 SAS had been dropped into western France, near the city of Poitiers. Establishing their base of operations in a forest to the south-east of Poitiers, their mission was to harass and disrupt German forces speeding northwards to repel the D-Day landings. Code-named Operation Bulbasket, it ended in disaster as thirty-one men were captured. At the end of the war, they – like those of Op Loyton – were listed simply as 'missing'.

With the Op Loyton cases largely concluded, Colonel Franks, Galitzine and Barkworth turned their attention to doing a similar job for the Op Bulbasket missing. Barkworth wrote to Franks regarding the killings: 'Unit responsible for executions . . . identified as Recce. Squadron of the 158th Division, 80th Corps, German Army.'

There followed a list of eight names – the key commanders suspected of wiping out the Bulbasket thirty-one. By February 1947 Barkworth had three of them in custody, and interrogations were under way. In April 1947 the main culprits were tracked down and brought to trial at Wuppertal. Two men – including the general in command of the 80th Corps – were sentenced to death by hanging.

Barkworth would go on to investigate a whole plethora of Commando Order cases. They included the murder of Captain Bill Blyth, a Special Boat Service (SBS) operator who had served with the legendary Anders Lassen. While carrying out shipborne raids against German forces, Blyth had been taken captive on the eastern Mediterranean island of Alimnia, along with several of his crew. All had been swallowed up into the *Nacht und Nebel*.

Barkworth also turned his attention to the so-called Cockleshell Heroes, more formally known as Operation Frankton – a 1942 mission by a group of commandos using canoes to raid the German-occupied port of Bordeaux. And he would investigate the aftermath of Operation Source, the 1943 raid in which British commandos piloting X-Craft mini submarines attacked the heavy German battleships *Tirpitz* which was lying at anchor in a Norwegian fjord.

But while the Operation Loyton accused – and those of Op Bulbasket – had been dragged before the courts, many of Barkworth's later manhunts would be terminated prematurely. It would be political expediency and cant that would sink these investigations.

On 29 April 1948, the French sent a copy of Isselhorst's execution certificate to the British war crimes authorities. Following his British trial Isselhorst had been tried in France and condemned to death two further times. The certificate recorded that a firing squad had assembled at Strasbourg to shoot Isselhorst, as opposed to his being hanged. But dead was still dead.

Isselhorst had been pronounced dead by 'Médecin-Colonel BOUCHARD', and his crime recorded as 'COMPLICITE D'ASSASSINATS' – complicity in murder. The British recorded the verdict somewhat more prosaically: 'Erich Isselhorst was executed in STRASBOURG on 23 Feb 48 following confirmation of the Court of Cessation of the sentence of death passed upon him by a French Military Tribunal.'

Sadly, Isselhorst would be one of the last to face the justice of the Wuppertal courts. In the autumn of 1948 the British government signalled a halt to all British war crimes trials. Incredibly, this was halfway through the Stalag Luft trials – those covering the spring 1944 murder of the seventy escapees from the Stalag Luft POW camp.

The first Stalag Luft trial had been held as early as July 1947, with eighteen defendants facing charges of murder. The second Stalag Luft trial was held in October 1948, but in the midst of it the then Foreign Secretary, Ernest Bevin, announced a British government decision not to prosecute any further Nazi war criminals.

While the second Stalag Luft trial was allowed to reach its verdict, the British quest for justice was officially over. It had lasted a little longer than three years. This was a politically motivated decision at a time when the West was gearing up for the Cold War. West Germany was seen as the new ally and the crucial bulwark against the Russian threat and Communism. In the eyes of many in power hunting down Nazi war criminals had become counterproductive, and something that Britain could ill afford.

The sensitivity of this decision, and of the SAS war crimes trials already completed, was reflected by the British government's determination to close what few official files did survive on the subject for seventy-five years. Indeed, if that time frame had been adhered to, the files would be closed to this day. For Barkworth, of course, it signalled not only the end of an era – the Villa Degler dark operation was being brought to an end – but it spelled the cruellest cut of all. Even after he had dedicated more than three years of his life to the search, Hans Dietrich Ernst had still not been run to ground.

While everyone wanted a slice of the notorious *Sturmbannführer* – the Americans and the French were also seeking him on war crimes charges – no one seemed able to get a trace on the man.

But for Colonel Brian Franks, Captain Prince Yurka Galitzine and Major Barkworth, the Secret Hunters had achieved one of their most cherished aims. Through their very existence, and their wearing of the winged-dagger beret on operations, they had kept the spirit of the SAS alive long enough for it to rise, phoenix-like, from the ashes.

In July 1947 the esteemed Artists Rifles regiment – a volunteer light infantry unit formed in 1859 – had merged with the 'defunct' SAS to form the 21 Special Air Service Regiment (Artists) (Reserves). This was a reservist Territorial Army unit, but it represented the much longed-for – if partial – resurrection of the SAS. Fittingly, the new regiment's first commanding officer was Lieutenant Colonel Brian Franks DSO, MC – the man who had done so much to keep the SAS alive since its 1945 official demise.

Yet even at the very end, the sense of sniffy antagonism that Barkworth and his men had attracted endured. An August 1948 letter from a brigadier in the judge advocate general's London office is typical: 'I think when this officer has completed his task . . . and has had an opportunity of tidying up every SAS case . . . what must be obtained from him are all documents he has . . . If it is necessary to do so, he should be given an order to hand over these papers. They are not his private property but are the property of the military authorities.'

Had officialdom been allowed to hold sway, the dead of Op Loyton, the SOE agents who perished at Natzweiler, the villagers of Moussey and the wider Rabodeau Valley, and the victims of numerous related war crimes would doubtless have remained listed as 'missing in action'. The most high-profile Nazi war criminals would have been prosecuted, but not those responsible for the crimes that the Villa Degler team doggedly pursued.

Had the SAS not mounted its own increasingly secretive investigations, the mass killers – Isselhorst included – would have very likely got away with their crimes. As it was, each of the Secret Hunters was hugely affected by this work, which left scars that would take an age to heal. Immersing oneself so deeply in such cases of unspeakable human degradation was psychologically damaging. And even the outcomes – the trials and the verdicts, such as they were – left many dissatisfied and hungering for more.

The Nazi atrocities were an unforgivable crime against humanity, argued Galitzine. He was shocked by the leniency that was being shown. He put the failings of the trials down to 'the natural reaction against killing and against all the horrors of war'. The court's view seemed to be that these men had been caught, tried and branded as war criminals, and that once released they would be marked men – which was enough of a punishment. Galitzine believed otherwise. He felt these men needed to be made examples of, to deter any future war criminals.

However, he didn't let his anger at the trial outcomes colour his sense of all that the Secret Hunters had accomplished. Summarizing their work in the twilight of the unit's days, he wrote: 'Bill found that his missing comrades had been killed after being taken prisoner of war. He found nearly all their bodies and went on to seek out their murderers . . . They have traced or arrested in Germany, France, Italy and Austria over 100 Germans involved . . . and at last brought the . . . criminals to justice.'

Chiefly through Galitzine's own efforts, the Villa Degler team had achieved one other crucial milestone in the war crimes investigations: they had ensured that the silence was broken over Natzweiler, and over the wider issue of such war criminals getting away with murder. That in and of itself was a seminal achievement, and it could only have been carried out by men such as the Secret Hunters.

Barkworth and his cohorts' energy, personal motivation and sheer drive lent a dedication to their task which none could match. Their willingness to break all the rules meant that very rarely did they fail to get their man. No other unit could have achieved this. The fact that they did so working in the deepest secrecy, with scant resources, and more often than not fighting against a 'Blimpish' military bureaucracy, is further testament to their unique role.

To all intents and purposes the work of the Secret Hunters was wound up in early 1949. Barkworth and his men had completed the mission they were given at the beginning: they had sought and delivered a full reckoning for Op Loyton. Indeed, they had achieved so much more. And as one band of hunters passed away, so another was fully resurrected – the Secret Hunters helping give birth to the modern-day SAS.

On balance, Colonel Franks, Galitzine, Barkworth and Rhodes would have had every right to feel a certain sense of satisfaction had it not been for one thing: their failure to get *Sturmbannführer* Hans Dietrich Ernst. But, as it happened, the story of the hunt for Ernst was far from over, though the drama would play out in another theatre entirely.

Those who served on the Villa Degler unit would get little recognition for what they had achieved. So secretive was the unit's existence that even the SAS's official war diary for the years 1941–1945 contains just a brief, four-line entry concerning their crucial work. Even that is contained in a limited edition released in 2011, and not available to the general public.

It reads: 'In October 1945, the SAS was disbanded. Franks came to an unofficial arrangement with one individual from the War Office and the [war crimes] unit continued. It operated totally openly, as if it was official. The unit ended its hunt in 1948, three years after the SAS was disbanded.'

The final words, perhaps, should fall to Captain Prince Yurka Galitzine, without whom the Secret Hunters may never have had their success. He for one would never forget what had happened in the Vosges, at Natzweiler and elsewhere. He believed that the subsequent hunt for the Nazi war criminals and their bringing to jutice was of vital importance, lest we forget. It was crucial that 'young people of this generation and the next . . . know what happened. Because it could happen again.'

There is perhaps no more fitting epitaph for the Secret Hunters.

Afterword

A great degree of controversy and subterfuge surrounds the fate of two of the accused that Barkworth and his men spent so much of their energy hunting down after the war. The first, predictably, is *Sturmbannführer* Hans Dietrich Ernst. The second, somewhat less predictably perhaps, is *Standartenführer* Erich Isselhorst.

On 13 June 1962 the CIA chief of base in Frankfurt dispatched a secret memo to colleagues, regarding a 'Hans Dieter Ernst'. As the man in question was, by the document's own admission, 'sought on a charge of having murdered six Americans, thirty-three British soldiers and four British women', it seems inconceivable that this was not *Sturmbannführer* Hans Dietrich Ernst. Indeed, in later CIA documents he is referred to as Hans *Dietrich* Ernst, and it records his year of birth as 1908, the correct year for Barkworth's most-wanted man.

The 13 June 1962 memo, which appears to be a review of available intelligence on Ernst, states: 'We found that CARETINA listed Hans Dieter ERNST as a fellow inmate of the camp at Vorkuta in the USSR and that as of 1957 CARETINA reported that Ernst was in the Leer/Ostfriesland . . .'

Ostfriesland is a coastal area of north-west Germany, bordering Holland. This means that Ernst was incarcerated in a Soviet prison camp – the Vorkuta Gulag was a major Soviet-era labour camp – before somehow making his way to Leer, a region of Ostfriesland, in (West) Germany, by 1957 – eight years after Barkworth et al were forced to drop their hunt for him. CARETINA is the CIA cryptonym for their agent, whose identity is not revealed.

Crucially, the memo continues: 'CARETINA categorized his fellow inmates of camps in the USSR under a) suspected as cooperating with the Soviets; b) possibly suspicious; c) "positive", i.e. above suspicion. ERNST fell into the "positive" category which is understandable if he was a member of the SS and SD, thus having a background somewhat similar to CARETINA, a former Amt IV, RSHA officer.'

'Amt IV' was the Gestapo, and the 'RSHA' was the Reich Security Main Office – the Nazi intelligence services and secret police, known more commonly as the *Sicherheitsdienst* (SD). Of course, *Standartenführer* Isselhorst would fit the bill for being CARETINA, as he was both an Amt IV and RSHA officer, and we know from his trial how positively he viewed his former deputy Ernst: 'A hard-working man, intelligent and conscientious . . . one of the best officials in France.'

But surely CARETINA could not possibly be Isselhorst, because Isselhorst was executed by the French in 1947? Whoever CARETINA was, his 'positive' opinion regarding Ernst rests purely upon Ernst's opposition to the Soviet regime. On the premise that the enemy of my enemy is my friend, any enemy of the Soviets was presumably a friend to the CIA and the West, especially in 1962, approaching the height of the Cold

War. Unsurprisingly, Ernst's alleged war crimes get a very minor billing in the memo.

Moreover, Hans Dietrich Ernst was also allocated a CIA '201 File', more commonly known as a 'Name File'. The 1962 memo was released under the US Nazi War Crimes Disclosure Act. The CIA has released few documents concerning Ernst's 201 File; the pages run to three or four at most. The 13 June 1962 memo makes up the bulk of the material cleared for release. But there is a handwritten note on the front cover of the memo regarding Ernst: 'Please reclassify to above subject's 201.'

The CIA itself describes the opening of a 201 File as a means to 'provide a method for identifying a person of specific interest to the Operations Directorate, and for controlling . . . all pertinent information about that person . . . Only a small number of personalities are of sufficient interest to justify opening a 201 dossier. These are normally subjects of extensive reporting and CI investigation, prospective agents and sources, member of groups and organisations of continuing target interest . . .'

In other words, a 201 Name File is only ever created for what the Agency considers to be a significant intelligence asset, informer or agent, or other individual of major interest.

So, in the summer of 1962 it seems that Hans Dietrich Ernst was alive and well, resident in West Germany and of remarkably significant interest to the CIA. Lest we forget, this was a man who had been condemned to death in absentia four times by the French courts for war crimes committed in the Vosges and elsewhere.

This is where things start to get even more bizarre.

On 22 November 1957 the CIA also raised a 201 'Personality File Request' – a Name File – on Erich George Heinrich Isselhorst. The 201 File gave his 'Country of Residence' as France. How is that possible? *In 1957?* How could the CIA raise a 201 File on a man supposedly dead for ten years and record him as living in France, the country that had supposedly executed him a decade earlier for war crimes?

On 28 March 1974 – some twenty-five years after Isselhorst's supposed execution – the CIA Name File received a fat dossier of new information, from the Central Records Facility of the US Army Intelligence Centre. The key document contained therein is a 3 July 1957 report entitled: 'CONSOLIDATION OF ISSELHORST, Erich (Dr.)'

Funny that, 'consolidating' someone who was supposedly executed ten years previously. The reports opens: 'DESCR: BORN 5 Feb 1906, Height 5'0", strong build, dark blond hair, grey-blue eyes, fresh complexion, round fresh face, large nose.' What an odd description for someone who was supposedly executed over a decade previously. Surely it should read: 'Shot dead by the French. Buried six foot under at Strasbourg.' Or so one would have thought.

Under the subheading 'CAREER' it lists Isselhorst's wartime exploits – eschewing any mention of his war crimes – and then his immediate fortunes after the war.

'Alleged to have been sentenced to death by Allied authorities, but released by the movement called the VECHTA group. Belongs to an organisation which is headed by Martin BORMANN, the aim of the movement was alleged to be anti-Russian, but possible . . . Soviet Connections have been observed.'

(For now, forget the 'Martin BORMANN' reference. Bormann was a senior figure in the Nazi regime, one rumoured to have escaped all efforts to find him after the war. Investigating any alleged Isselhorst–Bormann links lies outside of the scope of this book, certainly.)

Unpacking that paragraph a little, according to the US Army's Intelligence Centre, Isselhorst was not executed by the French. Whatever the VECHTA group may be – and I can find no trace of it – they seem to have had the power to 'release' Isselhorst from Allied custody and to save him from both 'death by shooting' and 'death by hanging' – respectively the French and British sentences handed down on him.

So certain of this is the US Army's Intelligence Centre that they repeat that 1957 assertion: 'Alleged to have been sentenced to death by Allied authorities, but released by the movement.' From studying the CIA 201 File on Isselhorst, there is no suggestion that what the US Army's Intelligence Centre states isn't true.

So, what is one to make of all of this?

If the CIA and the US Army's Intelligence Centre are to be believed, Isselhorst was never executed – not by the French, not by anyone. Instead, he was rescued by some shadowy group (VECHTA), after which the CIA raised a 201 Name File on him. Which would suggest in turn that Isselhorst – resident in 1957 in France, according to the CIA – was an ongoing intelligence asset of some value to the Agency, and long after he was supposedly executed for war crimes.

If this is true, then maybe Isselhorst *was* CARETINA, the agent referred to in the 1962 memo about former *Sturmbannführer* Ernst. But put that to one side. Is there any corroborating evidence to suggest that any of this may be true; that Isselhorst, and even Ernst, were somehow recruited into the CIA?

Well, as it happens, there is.

On 10 May 1945 the US Joint Chiefs of Staff issued a directive to General Dwight Eisenhower, commander of US forces in Europe, to arrest and hold all Nazi war criminals. However that directive was tempered with the following guidance: 'in your discretion you may make such exceptions as you deem advisable for intelligence and other military reasons.'

In June 1945, Brigadier General Reinhard Gehlen – the former head of Hitler's Fremde Heere Ost (FHO, or Foreign Armies East), the *Wehrmacht*'s intelligence organization for the Eastern Front – made the American military a juicy offer. He would hand over intact all files gathered by his organization, including those on current undercover agents operating across Stalin's Russia, if the Americans let him work for them.

Gehlen's name was rapidly removed from any captured POW lists, and he became the US spy chief in Germany for the following two decades. Under what was code-named Operation Rusty, but became known as the Gehlen Organization, Gehlen reassembled his staff and files and got to work. Unsurprisingly, they made great use of former Gestapo and SS officers with experience serving on the Eastern Front. Gehlen reactivated his former agent network across Russia, only now it was to serve a new master.

Naturally, the newly formed Gehlen Organization worked closely with the obvious partner within American intelligence circles – the US Counter Intelligence Corps (CIC). In 1947, under the National Security Act, the Central Intelligence Agency came into being. Reinhard Gehlen and Allen Dulles, the director of the new organization, hit if off immediately.

In July 1949 the CIA took full control of the Gehlen Organization, and CIA officer Colonel James H. Critchfield officially ran it for the next six years, although Gehlen himself remained the real man in control. After the war, CROWCASS – the Central Registry of War Crimes and Security Suspects – was the repository of records on wanted Nazi war criminals. At the same time as the CIA took control of the Gehlen Organization, the CROWCASS records were turned over to Reinhard Gehlen and his clandestine intelligence outfit.

The lunatics had truly been placed in charge of the asylum.

In March 1950 the US decided to formally appoint Reinhard Gehlen as the head of the West German Intelligence Service. The Soviet Union objected vociferously; unsurprisingly, as Gehlen was wanted by the Soviets on charges of war crimes. In 1955, when West Germany was given back her sovereignty, the Gehlen Organization became the German foreign intelligence service, the BND.

Under the US War Crimes Disclosure Act, the CIA was forced to release an assessment of its links to former Nazis, marked 'secret' and entitled: 'America's Seeing-Eye Dog on a Long Leash'. The opening paragraph stated: 'In 1949 . . . The CIA assumed responsibility for the nascent West German

Intelligence Service. More than any single project, this action linked the Central Intelligence Agency with veterans of Nazi Germany's intelligence services, some with notorious wartime reputations.'

The CIA report continues: 'The Gehlen Organization has long been accused of acting as a shelter for Nazis and those who committed crimes during the Third Reich. Because of their sponsorship of the German intelligence service, the US Army and the CIA are implicated in this criticism. From the earliest days . . . CIA recognized this as a problem and, in fact, warned the Army about supporting Gehlen. After 1949, CIA inherited these same concerns and, while it curbed Gehlen's viewpoint on the American war crimes program, the Agency could never get the Germans to "clean house".'

In 1972 Reinhard Gehlen published his memoirs, denoting the level of 'respectability' and status he had achieved in civilized society. Entitled *The Service*, the book proclaims: '*The Service* is the memoir of General Reinhard Gehlen, legendary spymaster-in-chief, Hitler's head of military espionage in Russia who, as the war ended, transferred his mammoth files and network of spies to the United States, ultimately to become chief of the unofficial West German intelligence agency.'

In 2006, a limited number of Gehlen Organization files were released under the US War Crimes Disclosure Act. From the study of those, the highly respected Federation of American Scientists (FAS) Project on Government Secrecy listed the names of the top Nazi war criminals employed by the Gehlen Organization, and thus also by the CIA.

These included: former SS *Oberführer* Willi Krichbaum, responsible for the deportation of Hungarian Jews, of whom some 300,000 lost their lives; SS *Standartenführer* Walter Rauff, who personally designed and supervised the mobile extermination vans used to gas Jews; SS *Oberführer* Dr Franz Six, who in 1941 commanded an *Einsatzgruppe* that exterminated the Jews of the Russian city of Smolensk; SS *Sturmbannführer* Alois Brunner, a Gestapo official who worked directly under Adolf Eichmann, and who 'purged' Paris of its Jews.

And lest one concludes that this was purely an American phenomenon, the British proved equally adept at recruiting suspected Nazi war criminals either to spy on the Russians, or because they were privy to Nazi Germany's much-sought-after technological and military secrets. If there were an equivalent British act to the US Nazi War Crimes Act – which sadly there isn't currently – files would doubtless emerge that would prove equally disconcerting.

The FAS list of the top Nazi war criminals employed by the Gehlen Organization and the CIA goes on and on. It includes SS commanders who served at Auschwitz, Treblinka, Buchenwald, Dachau and other Nazi concentration camps.

It also includes the following entry:

SS Obersturmbannführer Dr. Erich Isselhorst, SS No. 267313. Born February 5, 1906. Subject was Commander of the Police and SD at Strasbourg and also Inspector of the SD, Stuttgart. He was also Commanding Officer of Einsatzkommando 8 of Einsatzgruppe A.

Isselhorst had attained the rank of *Standartenführer* by the end of the war.

The question has to be asked, therefore: was Isselhorst ever executed, as the French claimed? Or, as the CIA and related papers appear to suggest, was his 'execution' some kind of a cover, under which former *Standartenführer* Erich Isselhorst survived, to work for the Gehlen Organization and the CIA?

A copy of the French record of Isselhorst's execution is held in the National Archives, together with the various items of correspondence from the British authorities, asking for proof that the death sentence passed down by both French and British courts had indeed been carried out. Yet the various CIA documents lodged in the US National Archives suggest that Isselhorst went on to have a long and useful career with the Gehlen Organization and the Agency.

Ultimately, whom does one believe?

Certainly, the Federation of American Scientists Project on Government Secrecy has few doubts: Isselhorst is listed as one of a few dozen top Nazi war criminals who worked for both the Gehlen Organisation and the CIA.

Either way, it is perhaps fortunate that the possibility that Isselhorst escaped justice and went on to work for Western intelligence did not come to the notice of the Secret Hunters. It would have been the cruellest of blows to learn that Isselhorst may have escaped the justice that they believed had been rightly served.

Finally, we must return to *Sturmbannführer* Hans Dietrich Ernst. On 9 March 1977 a German newspaper carried the following short article:

A former SS officer accused of participating in the deportation and murder of numerous French Jews has been deprived by a court in Oldenburg, north Germany, of his right to practise as a lawyer. The action against Hans Dietrich Ernst, wartime regional commander of the German Security Service and Security Police in France followed representations by the French anti-Nazi lawyer, Serge Klarsfeld.

Ernst was sentenced to death four times by French courts, in absentia. The sentences were not recognized by West Germany, although the Cologne State Prosecutor is currently investigating Ernst's wartime activity.

Incredibly, for three decades after the Secret Hunters were forced to abandon their search for him, Hans Dietrich Ernst led a quiet life in his native Germany, working as a lawyer and, very probably, as a Gehlen/CIA/BND agent. In the early 1980s the German authorities apparently got their act together to finally indict Ernst on war crimes charges.

He died of old age before he could face trial.

In the forties, fifties and sixties, as the West geared up for the Cold War, there appears to have been a triumph of amoral pragmatism over what was just and what was right. Was this – is this – ever justified or, indeed, sensible? Laying aside the moral issue, the simple fact of the matter is that the hiring of former Nazi war criminals to run our intelligence apparatus was a flawed policy, purely in terms of the results secured.

Those 'former' Nazis had a bankrupt moral code, were permanently damaged by the war crimes and unspeakable horrors they had perpetrated, and were loyal to no one – certainly not to the Western powers, who had vanquished the Nazi dream and, once again, left Germany in abject defeat. They owed their allegiances only to themselves and to their own kind. They proved at best questionable allies, and their intelligence of highly questionable value.

But even had they proved world-beating spies, was hiring those 'former' Nazis justifiable morally? The simple answer is no. If there had been a poll at the end of the war asking the people of the Allied nations if they backed such a policy, the answer would have been overwhelmingly negative. There are certain lines that should never be crossed. Hiring former mass murderers, rapists, child-killers and racist war criminals to people our intelligence apparatus was wrong, and it denied the victims of so much suffering that most crucial of things: justice.

When we speak of the Nazi war crimes, we – rightly – stress that such atrocities should never be allowed to occur again (although in the Balkans, Rwanda and Darfur we have, largely, failed). But we should also guard against those who have committed terrible crimes against humanity being allowed to escape unpunished, simply because it is hoped they might furnish some advantage to our cause. That is equally unacceptable. Shielding Gehlen, Barbie, Rauff – and possibly Isselhorst and Ernst – from justice was reprehensible in the extreme.

Our democratic institutions – including our military and intelligence apparatus – should never put themselves above the law.

Epilogue

During the war Lieutenant Colonel Brian Morton Foster Franks had been awarded the Military Cross (MC) in 1943, and the Distinguished Service Order (DSO) in 1944, following Operation Loyton. After the war he was awarded the French Légion d'honneur and the Croix de guerre. He achieved the rank of honorary colonel in command of 21 SAS, the Territorial regiment which he commanded until 1950, and which would form the basis for refounding the SAS Regiment proper, in the early 1950s.

From 1959 to 1972 he was the managing director of the Hyde Park Hotel in London, and he also worked for the Trust Houses Forte group. Having been made honorary colonel of 21 SAS, he went on to become colonel commandant of the reformed SAS Regiment. Some decades after the war Franks returned to Moussey, on one of the many SAS memorial visits to the area, and was given something of a hero's welcome by the locals, despite all that they had suffered at the hands of the Nazis. He married and had two children, and passed away in 1982, in Suffolk.

Bill Barkworth left the Army in February 1949. He subsequently married a German woman who had lived and worked in England before the war, and had served with him on his war crimes investigations work, in Gaggenau. He emigrated to

Australia in 1951 where she joined him in 1952, and they started a family. He never lost his sense of justice or fair treatment of others. He became a Director of the Queensland Good Neighbour Council, a Government-funded body helping migrants settle well in Australia, where his language skills – by then he spoke seven languages – were of great help to many newcomers. He died of a heart attack in July 1985.

After his time working out of Eaton Square, Captain Prince Yurka Galitzine set up a London public relations company in Mayfair. It took him a very long time to forgive the German people as a whole for Natzweiler, and the many other horrors he had witnessed. 'I didn't recognize the difference between Germans,' he remarked. 'To me all Germans were cruel, and as a result I was very vengeful . . . Time is the great mellower.'

Galitzine was married four times, had two sons and three daughters, and became a successful international businessman. He retired to the East Midlands county of Rutland – England's smallest county – where he became the chairman and then president of the Rutland Society. He remained proud of his Russian heritage, and was pleased to return to the country of his forefathers following the collapse of the Soviet Union. Some of his private papers are filed in 'The Prince Yuri Galitzine Room' at the Rutland County Museum. He died in November 2002 after a short illness.

Captain and then Major Henry Carey Druce was awarded the Distinguished Service Order and the Croix de Guerre with Palm for his work during Op Loyton, his DSO citation praising his skill, daring and complete disregard for his own safety. In the Vosges Druce had won 'the admiration of not only all British troops with whom he came into contact, but also of the local French people amongst whom his name became a byword'.

Having crossed over the lines to rejoin Colonel Franks' Op Loyton force, and failing to find them, he then crossed back over the lines for a third time and made it safely to the American forces, although they – temporarily – arrested him as a suspected 'German spy'. He then went on to serve with distinction with the SAS in Arnhem, where he commanded a fleet of ten jeeps that pushed behind enemy lines, ambushing German columns and seizing an airfield.

Post-war he joined MI6 – the British Secret Intelligence Service – serving in Holland and Indonesia. He was honoured again by the French in 1951, when he was invited to rekindle the flame at the Arc de Triomphe. That year he left MI6, moved to Canada with his wife and three children and launched a marine shipping business. He died in 2007 at the age of eighty-five.

Throughout his active life after the war, Druce was a regular visitor to Moussey. On one occasion he visited the bar from which he had been forced to escape from the Germans by stealing and riding off on a child's bicycle. The barman remembered him, and reminded him of the episode. Druce subsequently sent him a model of a child's bicycle, which to this day the bar owner keeps proudly above his bar.

SAS Captain and then Major Peter Lancelot John Le Poer Power survived the war, earning a Mention in Dispatches and a Military Cross (MC). He worked as a tea planter in civilian life, and died in February 1998, aged eighty-six.

Captain John Hislop – fine amateur jockey and Op Loyton Phantom – survived the war and went on to become a successful sports journalist, writer and racehorse breeder, as well as winning 102 races on the flat, and being champion amateur jockey for thirteen consecutive seasons. Hislop was racing correspondent for the *Observer* for sixteen years and he authored numerous books on racing, including his excellent mixed horse-racing and wartime memoir, *Anything but a Soldier*. He married and had two sons, and died in February 1994, in Suffolk.

Captain Chris Sykes, the Op Loyton Intelligence Officer, was awarded a Mention in Dispatches and a Croix de guerre. He survived the war and went on to become a novelist and biographer in civilian life, being invested as a Fellow of the Royal Society of Literature. He authored more than a dozen books, including *Four Studies in Loyalty*, the final part of which deals – somewhat tangentially – with his experiences of Operation Loyton.

He counted the author Evelyn Waugh and, prior to the war, Robert Byron, amongst his close friends. He reported for BBC radio extensively, and also wrote for British and American magazines, including the *New Republic*, the *Spectator* and others. He was married twice and had one son. He died in December 1986.

Ralph 'Karl' Marx – the Op Loyton raider extraordinaire – was awarded an MC for his part in Op Loyton. The effects of the Vosges missions on his health resulted in him being given a 100 per cent disability benefit at the end of the war. After that Marx went to Cambridge to read engineering, and won a Blue for boxing; he insisted on handing back his disability pension. He went on to forge a successful career as an engineer. He married, had a son and two daughters, and died in December 2000, aged seventy-eight.

Lou Fiddick, downed Canadian airman and honorary Op Loyton SAS operative, survived the war and returned to his native Canada, from where he kept in regular touch with his one-time SAS comrades, Captain Druce first and foremost, who became a fellow Canadian resident.

French guide and honorary SAS man Roger Souchal survived the war and became a successful lawyer in the French city of Nancy.

Sergeant Fred 'Dusty' Rhodes returned to his native Barnsley after his stint with the Secret Hunters, taking up again his job with the local council in the parks department. In 1985 he returned to Moussey and laid wreaths in the graveyard on behalf of his comrades and to honour those buried there. He returned to La Grande Fosse and left a plain black cross bearing the inscription: 'At this place, eight members of the 2nd SAS Regiment were murdered on 15 October 1944.'

Rhodes was one of those who refused to remain silent about the work of the Secret Hunters. After the war he gave various interviews, some of which are lodged with the Imperial War Museum. In one Rhodes made clear his feelings on the official files regarding the SAS war crimes work being closed for seventy-five years:

'What constituted the records of Loyton . . . why they put a seventy-five year restriction on that I really don't know. I wonder if that seventy-five years applies to any other [files]?'

Rhodes granted the interviews that he did in an effort to help break that silence.

Today Moussey, Operation Loyton and its aftermath forms part of the legend of the SAS Regiment. To those who know of it, Op Loyton is often referred to as 'the SAS's Arnhem'. The manhunting operations of the Secret Hunters are still studied by the Regiment today, as a model for modern-day war crimes snatch operations like those pursued by the SAS following the conflict in the Balkans.

Members of the Regiment still return regularly to that small village in the Vosges to honour the fallen; both their own SAS comrades and those hundreds of French civilians who perished alongside them. On the last Sunday in September every year, the village of Moussey remembers. Following a service in the church – in which hangs an official SAS Regimental pennant – wreaths are laid on the graves of the SAS men buried in the churchyard, and on the memorial to those villagers who were deported, never to return.

One of the dwindling band of survivors reads out the long list of those who disappeared, and after each name another veteran pronounces the words: '*Mort pour la patrie*.'

End Note

Several decades after the war ended, a man called Peter Mason published a book called *Official Assassin*. In it he claimed to be a former SAS soldier who worked for a beyond-dark arm of the SAS, killing off those war criminals who, for whatever reason, could not be brought to justice. Mason's supposed exploits received some coverage in the newspapers at the time: 'British Hit Squad "executed" Nazis' ran a December 1977 headline in the *Sunday Times*.

Mason claimed he worked from a converted stable block near Stuttgart, and that his activities were covertly supported by the War Office. He claimed to have executed sixteen Nazis who would otherwise have escaped 'justice'. Mason related how they would collect the wanted man from a POW camp, execute him covertly, and then claim that he had either committed suicide or was shot trying to escape.

There is no documentation in any of the archives that would directly support such claims. This doesn't mean that they are untrue. There was a Parachutist P. Mason listed as one of the SAS men on Operation Loyton. He was one of the fourteen-man stick that dropped into the Vosges on the night of 21–22 September 1944. P. Mason was also the 'fitter' on Colonel Franks' jeep that tore about the Vosges, shooting up German targets.

Of course that does not mean that the P. Mason of Op Loyton and the Peter Mason who authored *Official Assassin* are one and the same person. But one of Peter Mason's claimed assassinations is of Fritz Opelt. A Fritz Opelt served under *Sturmbannführer* Hans Dietrich Ernst in the Vosges. Opelt was one of those who made up the team of killers who shot dead the eight men of Op Loyton in the forests above La Grande Fosse.

In 1946 Opelt was listed as wanted by the British for 'the murder of 16 British parachutists' – sixteen of the Op Loyton missing. There does not appear to be any evidence that the Fritz Opelt wanted for war crimes was ever brought to trial.

Bibliography

Asher, Michael, *The Regiment*, Viking, 2007

Bloxham, Donald, *Genocide on Trial*, Oxford University Press, 2001

Bonn, Keith E., *When the Odds Were Even*, Presidio Press, 1994

Breitman, Richard, Norman J.W. Goda, Timothy Naftali and Robert Wolfe, *US Intelligence and the Nazis*, Cambridge University Press, 2005

Brun Lie, Arne, with Robby Robinson, *Night and Fog*, W.W. Norton, 1990

Burbidge, Colin, *Preserving the Flame*, YouWriteOn.com, 2008

Clutton-Brock, Oliver, and Raymond Crompton, *The Long Road*, Grub Street, 2013

Cookridge, E.H., *Gehlen, Spy of the Century*, Corgi Books, 1972

Cowburn, Benjamin, *No Cloak, No Dagger*, Pen & Sword, 2009

Farran, Roy, *Winged Dagger*, Cassell, 1948

Fiennes, Ranulph, *The Secret Hunters*, Little, Brown, 2001

Ford, Roger, *Fire from the Forest*, Cassell, 2003

Ford, Roger, *Steel from the Sky*, Cassell, 2004

Gehlen, Reinhard (David Irving – English translation), *The Service*, World Publishing, 1972

Grehan, John, and Martin Mace, *Unearthing Churchill's Secret Army*, Pen & Sword, 2012

Hislop, John, *Anything but a Soldier*, Michael Joseph, 1965

Hunt, Linda, *Secret Agenda*, St Martin's Press, 1991

Jones, Benjamin F., *Freeing France: The Allies, the Résistance and the JEDBURGHS*, University of Nebraska-Lincoln, 1999

Jones, Tim, *SAS: The First Secret Wars*, I.B. Tauris, 2005

Kemp, Anthony, *The SAS at War 1941–1945*, Penguin Books, 1991

Kemp, Anthony, *The Secret Hunters*, Michael O'Mara Books, 1986

McCue, Paul, *SAS Operation Bulbasket*, Leo Cooper, 1996

Millar, George, *Maquis*, Cassell, 1945

Mortimer, Gavin, *Stirling's Men*, Cassell, 2004

O'Connell, Brian, *John Hunt*, O'Brien Press, 2013

Russell, Lord, of Liverpool, *The Scourge of the Swastika*, Cassell, 1954

Scholey, Pete, *Who Dares Wins*, Osprey Publishing, 2008

Seel, Pierre, *I, Pierre Seel, Deported Homosexual*, Perseus Books, 2011

Stevenson, William, *Spymistress*, Arcade Publishing, 2007

Sykes, Christopher, *Four Studies in Loyalty*, William Collins, 1946

Walker, Jonathan, *Operation Unthinkable*, History Press, 2013

West, Nigel, *Secret War*, Coronet Books, 1992

Index

24